DISCARD

In the Name of Heaven

In the Name of Heaven

MARY JANE ENGH

3,000 YEARS OF RELIGIOUS PERSECUTION

 **Prometheus Books**

59 John Glenn Drive
Amherst, New York 14228-2197

Published 2007 by Prometheus Books

Inquiries should be addressed to
Prometheus Books
59 John Glenn Drive
Amherst, New York 14228–2197
VOICE: 716–691–0133, ext. 207
FAX: 716–564–2711
WWW.PROMETHEUSBOOKS.COM

11 10 09 08 07   5 4 3 2 1

Library of Congress Cataloging-in-Publication Data

Engh, M. J.
   In the name of heaven : 3000 years of religious persecution / by Mary Jane
Engh.
        p. cm.
   Includes bibliographical references and index.
   ISBN-13: 978–1–59102–454–5 (hardcover : alk. paper)
   ISBN-10: 1–59102–454–4 (hardcover : alk. paper)
   1. Persecution—History. I. Title.

BL65.P47E54 2006
200.9—dc22

2006022923

Printed in the United States of America on acid-free paper

Contents

5

Introduction

I am in the right, and you are in the wrong. When you are the stronger, you ought to tolerate me; for it is your duty to tolerate truth. But when I am the stronger, I shall persecute you; for it is my duty to persecute error.
—Thomas Babington Macaulay,
Critical and Historical Essays, 1870

Macaulay put the rationale for persecution in a nutshell; but real life is more complicated. Every instance of religious persecution has its own particular causes, justifications, and consequences—usually unexpected. No wonder there is no general history of religious persecution available for the curious reader. The subject is really a hundred different subjects, too vast and too varied to squeeze into a single volume.

In spite of that, it is well worth the effort to attempt an overview of persecution history. A long view that covers three thousand years and six continents can only be superficial and incomplete, but it is the best way to get the subject into perspective. We will find that

Macaulay's dictum does not describe all the situations that lead to religious persecution. We will see that not all religions are equal in their potential to persecute or be persecuted. We may even glimpse ways of preventing further persecution.

To fit this project into one volume, I have had to draw some arbitrary boundaries. I stop my survey with the year 1900. The twentieth century, sadly, is too rich in persecution; it cannot be compressed into one or two chapters.

The structure of the book is both geographical and chronological. Each chapter deals with a single area and time period, some of them very broad. For readers who want to learn more about subjects I can only skim over, I have made a few suggestions for further reading at the end of each chapter, as well as indicating the sources on which our information is based.

I have tried to keep within a fairly narrow definition of religious persecution, including only repressive actions initiated or condoned by authorities against their own people on religious grounds. That leaves out "wars of religion" as such, though it will cover many of their effects, as when each side abuses some of its own citizens or subjects for sharing "the enemy's" religion, or imposes its own religion in conquered territory. I have also tried to avoid private individual terrorism, mob violence, and reciprocal massacres between competing religious groups. These topics do insist on creeping in, however, when one side or another is supported by government authorities.

In the same way, religious persecution is sometimes part of a larger package. When one nation extends its power over others, it may try to extend its religion as well. To suppress a "barbarous" religion in the name of civilizing, modernizing, or pacifying an inferior people has been a recurring theme of imperialism ever since the Romans confronted the druids.

Finally, although my coverage is worldwide, it is frankly unequal. My own ignorance of non-European languages has prevented me from giving Asian, African, and Middle Eastern sources the attention they deserve. I am deeply grateful to the generations of scholars who have made a general survey like this one possible.

We begin with history's first persecutor.

Chapter 1

Egypt

Fourteenth Century BCE

The divine powers had never smiled more gloriously on Egypt. King Amenhotep III, true son of the great god Amun, was preparing to celebrate his third jubilee, commemorating some thirty-eight years of prosperous rule and internal peace.

Wealth flowed into Egypt like the nourishing Nile flood, and brought forth new and splendid monuments. Egyptian armies and Egyptian diplomacy had forged an empire that stretched from the northeastern satellite states of Syria (including what would one day be Palestine, Israel, Lebanon, Jordan, and much of Iraq) south to the conquered territory of Lower Kush, in what would later be northern Sudan. Egyptian farmers' harvests were so rich that centuries after Amenhotep's death he would be worshipped as a god of agricultural fertility. Up and down the Nile, literally thousands of gods and goddesses received a grateful people's thanks.

Twenty years later, a young king lamented his country's desolation: "The temples of gods and goddesses from Elephantine as far as the Delta marshes had fallen into ruin, and their shrines become dilapidated. They had turned into mounds overgrown with weeds. . . . This land had been struck by catastrophe: the gods had turned their backs upon it. If the army was sent to Syria to extend the borders of Egypt, they had no success. If anyone prayed to a god, the god would never answer; if anyone asked a goddess for help, she would not hear. Hearts were weakened in bodies, whatever had been made was destroyed."

What had gone wrong?

When Amenhotep III died,* probably in 1353 BCE, his son was crowned as Amenhotep IV. The new king was young, devoted to his wife Nefertiti, and full of strange ideas. Like his father, he worshipped the sun god's most blazing aspect—the Aten, or "disc"—but he worshipped it in a distinctly different way.

For most Egyptians, the Aten was only one face of the great god Amun-Ra. And Amun-Ra, for all his magnificence, was only one of the thousands of deities whose combined efforts kept the Egyptian universe running. Amenhotep III had encouraged worship of the Aten, but he had supported all the gods and goddesses—chief among them Amun, the ancestral god of the city of Thebes.

The new king's first actions as pharaoh gave warning of what was to come. He changed his name from Amenhotep ("Amun is satisfied") to Akhenaten ("glory of the Aten"), and began to build a very peculiar temple.

A normal Egyptian temple was a series of rooms, each one smaller and darker than the one before. In the innermost "holy of holies" lived the god or goddess—a statue that priests and other attendants "woke," bathed, dressed, "fed," and sang to every day. No one else, except the king, was ever allowed to enter the temple. On festival days, the statue was carried out in a boat-shaped shrine—travel in Egypt almost always meant a boat—and paraded down a route lined with cheering people.

But Akhenaten's new temple was not even a building. It was a huge unroofed courtyard surrounded on all four sides by a tall colonnade. There was no inner room, no statue to be fed and wor-

---

*Or possibly before. Some Egyptologists think that Amenhotep IV/ Akhenaten was co-regent with his father for some time.

shipped and carried out for people to see. Akhenaten saw his god in the open sky above—the Aten, the visible disk of the sun, pouring heat and light on the earth. This strange structure, built in the sacred city of Thebes, was only the first of a series of Aten temples scattered through Egypt. And there was more to come. If Akhenaten's first moves had been disturbing, his next was devastating.

Major temples in Egypt had long been tax supported, with certain taxes earmarked for their use. They drew additional revenues from the land they owned and from donations and offerings, mostly at the times of their many festivals. At one stroke, Akhenaten ended the temple subsidies—or rather diverted them to the Aten's temples alone—and abolished the festivals. That must have caused consternation all over Egypt. Religious festivals were not just holidays. They were the only times when ordinary Egyptians could see and approach their gods and goddesses. At the great temple of Amun in Thebes, a dozen priests lifted the god's sacred boat, shouldered its carrying poles, and brought him out into the sunlight—a living god for all to see. Officials and dignitaries of all sorts followed closely, enjoying the spectators' cheers. Musicians and dancers brightened the procession.The priests put down their burden at shrines along the processional route, and here the crowding people could bring their prayers and their questions to the god, and sometimes receive oracular answers. Huge amounts of food and drink were prepared for major festivals, lesser amounts for lesser holidays. Whatever the priests and other temple personnel could not eat themselves was presumably distributed to the spectators. These were not rare occasions. Over the course of a year, they averaged out to more than one holiday a week in Thebes.

Suddenly, all this was finished. There were to be no more festival processions. Unlike Amun and every other god and goddess in the Egyptian pantheon, the Aten could not be paraded through the streets—there was nothing for the priests to carry. There could be no statues of the Aten.

The abrupt stoppage of temple subsidies must have thrown much of Egypt's economy into confusion. That economy was based on goods, not money. (Coins would be invented some nine centuries later, in Asia Minor.) Taxes were collected in the form of grain, livestock, cloth, lumber, and other staples. Wages were paid in bread, meat, vegetables, and beer. Farmers were often sharecroppers, paying their rent with a specified percentage of their harvests. There was a lively trade up and down the Nile, and even beyond the borders of Egypt, all conducted by barter. And a large proportion of goods from all sources circulated through temples.

Major temples hired their own professional traders, who might travel far to strike bargains for their particular deity. All temples received tax subsidies in the form of food and other goods. They also collected offerings from pious citizens, grew crops and raised livestock on their own lands, and owned bakeries, breweries, butcher shops, and other processing facilities.

All this bread, beer, meat, and produce went first of all to feed the priests and other temple staff, which could number hundreds of people, as well as their families. Some of it was distributed to needier temples, some was handed out to worshippers at festivals, a good deal of it was stored, and no doubt some of it was sold. Wealthy temples had a host of everyday jobs to fill—farmworkers, bakers, brewers, cooks, cleaners, weavers, carpenters, sailors, traders, unskilled laborers, and the ever-present scribes. When temples were put out of business, people were put out of work.

Akhenaten had effectively established Aten-worship as the state religion. The government of Egypt no longer recognized the existence of any other deities. This was a staggering change. In the past, every official act and every royal portrait had been surrounded by divine images. The king himself was the earthly manifestation of the royal falcon god Horus. Isis, the great healing and mothering goddess, protected his throne and nourished him with her milk. The vulture goddess Nekhbet and the cobra goddess Wadjet, guardians of southern and northern Egypt respectively, looked out on their domains from his royal headdress.

The king was the country's chief priest, charged with performing vital rituals. And for generations, every king's right to the throne was validated by the claim that the great god Amun was quite literally his biological father, who had impregnated his mother in a night of divine passion.

Akhenaten, however, recognized only the Aten as his supernatural father. Worse, he began an active campaign against Amun. The ancient god's temples were defaced. His name and image were chiseled out of inscriptions all over Egypt. Not even a goose could be pictured, since the goose was sacred to Amun.

At the same time, Akhenaten withdrew from the divinity-infested cities of Egypt. He announced that the Aten had selected a site for a new city, sacred to the Aten alone. Here, on barren ground, he built his new capital—Akhetaten, "Horizon of the Aten"—a city that would rise and fall within a single generation. Here some of the unemployed workers from the old temples probably found jobs, building the strange, roofless temples of the Aten, as well as palaces and houses for the king's family and the royal court.

The king may have hoped that Egyptians would forget their old deities, but evidence from the Aten's own city shows that they did not. In the ruins of house after house, archaeologists have found statuettes and carvings of Taweret (the hippopotamus goddess who presided over birth), Isis, and other ancient powers. Even the king could not dictate what people felt.

Akhenaten has often been called "the first monotheist." He could well be called the first recorded religious persecutor, although by later standards his persecution was mild. Only those who shared his religious views—or claimed to share them—could hope for a place in his court or a high government position. But the records are too incomplete to show if he killed, tortured, or imprisoned people who did not subscribe to the new creed.

Many people must have subscribed to it. The Aten, after all, was not a new god. Indeed, his official name was "The living Ra-Horus of the horizon who rejoices in the horizon in his identity of light which is in the Aten," later changed to "The living Ra, ruler of the horizon, who rejoices in the horizon in his identity of Ra the Father who has returned as the Aten." (The reference to Horus smacked too much of polytheism, while "Ra" could be accepted as a synonym for "sun god.") Akhenaten's father, the revered Amenhotep III, had already emphasized the sun disc as Ra's greatest manifestation.

Nevertheless, the new religion had a traumatic effect. Ancient Egyptian religious tradition was one of inclusion and balance. Every part of the world was infused with divinity. The sky goddess Nut, her gown embroidered with stars, arched over her reclining consort, the earth god Geb. Ra, that overpowering deity of sun-drenched Egypt, sailed masterfully across the sky each day, adored in his changing manifestations—Khephre at the eastern horizon, Aten in his full glory, Atum in the west.

The night, too, was sacred, and no less important than the day. Darkness revealed the divine stars, among the oldest powers of Egyptian religion. Meanwhile, Ra underwent his own dangerous ordeal, sailing beneath the earth in his "night boat," continually attacked by monsters. Osiris, lord of the dead, revivified the weary sun god each night, so that he could be reborn from Nut at dawn. Other deities defended the boat—notably the fierce warrior Set (also spelled Seth), whose spear fended off the devouring serpent Apep (Apophis).

Set, the god of disorder, master of the desert that surrounded the fertile Nile valley and master of unpredictable storms that sent flash floods down dry streambeds, would later be equated with the Christian devil; but such an idea was alien to ancient Egyptian thought. Set's tumultuous power was necessary to defend, support, and balance the orderly cosmos that the Egyptians cherished—just as the cooling, restful, star-revealing night was necessary to balance the blazing, life-giving, merciless sun.

Keeping the universe running was a cooperative project. No deity could do without help. Ra had a crew of gods and goddesses to sail and steer his boat, to tow and moor it, and to get it past the dangerous sandbank of noon (when, as anyone who has been outdoors in Egypt at midday can testify, the sun seems to be stuck at its zenith). During the night, Ra traveled through the world of the dead, restoring life and light to the grateful souls in the darkness.

Neither could the gods do without human help. On earth, the king performed daily rituals that kept the sun boats moving and on course. Throughout Egypt, priests' hourly rites and the prayers of ordinary people helped assure that the sun would rise for another day.

Akhenaten's religion overturned this inclusive, self-balancing system. If the sun disc was the only deity, darkness was worthless at best, possibly evil. In Akhenaten's cosmos there was no nighttime sun. At night the Aten, the only god, was simply absent, and there was no one else to pray to—except the king, the Aten's son and chosen agent on earth. Akhenaten's theology put himself in a position of supreme importance, only slightly subordinate to his god.

Throughout most of human history, people accepted that every nation and ethnic group had its own religious tradition, worshipping its own divinities in its own way. Believing that "my" religion was true did not mean believing that "yours" was false. Your gods might be distorted perceptions of mine, or they might be separate and independent beings. Either way, I had no reason to doubt their existence. I might look down on your revolting style of sacrifice or your silly methods of divination, and in time of war I might pray earnestly that my deities could beat your deities; but afterward I might think it prudent to worship some of yours along with mine.

Monotheism radically changed all that. If I believe that there is only one god, then all other deities are either demons or delusions. If my religion is true, all others must be false. With one divisive stroke, Akhenaten had created religious intolerance.

Akhenaten died after seventeen years of rule, his new city still unfinished. An ephemeral king named Smenkhkare either succeeded him for a short time or simply served as co-regent during his last years. Akhenaten's "Great Royal Wife" Nefertiti had borne six daughters but no sons. Smenkhkare may have been the son of a secondary wife, or—a more intriguing possibility—Smenkhkare may have been Nefertiti herself. It was not quite unheard-of for an Egyptian queen to rule as "king."

In any case, Smenkhkare's reign was brief. The next king crowned was a boy named Tutankhaten, no more than eight or nine years old—probably a son, nephew, or cousin of Akhenaten. Obviously he could only be the puppet for someone behind the throne.

The two most powerful individuals in Egypt were now the high official Ay and the army commander Horemheb. Both had served Akhenaten faithfully, but both must have found his policies harder and harder to swallow. And Egypt was ready to boil over. While the country struggled to cope with economic and social disruption, its empire was crumbling. Horemheb was forced to lead or send troops both north and south, to Syria and Kush. The expanding Hittite Empire threatened Egyptian dominance. Worst of all, a plague had broken out in Syria and spread to Egypt. It was clear to many people that the gods had abandoned Egypt. And why not, since the king had rejected them?

With no more than a few months' hesitation, the new boy-king's handlers began undoing what Akhenaten had done. They did not deny the Aten, but they restored the worship of the old deities. From now on, as in the good old days before Akhenaten, the Aten would be only one among an innumerable host of gods and goddesses. The temple subsidies that Akhenaten had abolished were reinstated and increased. New priests were appointed. The old festivals were celebrated again. Within a few years, the young king changed his name from Tutankhaten to Tutankhamen, substituting Amun for the Aten, and the royal court returned to Memphis, the ancient capital. Akhenaten's short-lived city was abandoned.

The new king's restoration work provides clues to the destruction Akhenaten had wreaked. Tutankhamen had new and larger statues made of Amun, the creator god Ptah, and other deities, which may imply that the former statues had been destroyed. He rebuilt quays along the river—perhaps the quays at which Amun embarked and landed on his Nile journeys, or the quays where produce and supplies were unloaded at the great temples. And Tutankhamen appointed many new priests, who may have been needed to replace priests killed or exiled by Akhenaten.

The young king reigned for some nine years. When he died unexpectedly, Ay—now a very old man by ancient standards—took the throne. Ay survived another four years. At his death, Horemheb had himself crowned king as quickly as possible.

Now it was payback time. Horemheb's decision was drastic: to erase—quite literally—Akhenaten and his family from Egyptian history. Henceforth the records would read that King Horemheb had succeeded Amenhotep III directly. There was to be no sign that Akhenaten, Smenkhkare, Tutankhamen, or Ay had ever existed. Nefertiti and her six daughters must also disappear. Not only their names but their images must be destroyed.

Horemheb embarked on a major program of construction and deconstruction. His workers methodically demolished every structure that Akhenaten or his successors had built, and used the debris as fill for the walls of new buildings erected at Horemheb's instructions. The entire city that Akhenaten had built for the glory of the Aten was destroyed, and records of it wiped out.

Akhenaten's name and very existence were forgotten. But the

anguish of those years was remembered, with strange results. Within two or three generations, the memory of Akhenaten's dictatorial monotheism had been connected with another historical trauma—the rule of the Hyksos. These foreign kings, descendants of immigrants from the Syria-Palestine region, had been driven out of Egypt after a bitter war two centuries earlier.

According to an anti-Hyksos story written after Akhenaten's death and obliteration, "King Apophis [a fictional Hyksos king] chose for his lord the god Set. He did not worship any other deity in the whole land except Set." This was certainly not true of the historical Hyksos, who worshipped Set but also accepted the other Egyptian gods. It sounds like a displaced recollection of Akhenaten's exclusive Aten-worship. But it had the odd effect of bringing Set into bad repute, thus paving the way for a dualistic view of the world as a battleground between good and evil gods, quite unlike the balanced, orderly, and benign universe of traditional Egyptian religion.

There was another unintended result of Akhenaten's religious experiment and Horemheb's vengeance, which still haunts the world today. Once the idea of intolerant monotheism was linked to the Hyksos—Semitic aliens in Egypt—it was easily transferred to the Jews who settled there later. An Egyptian "Exodus" story circulated in many versions, with the Jews appearing as lepers, rebels, and/or criminals, who were expelled from Egypt because their wickedness and disease polluted the country. This story was picked up by the Roman historian Tacitus and entered Western tradition, where it contributed to the growth of anti-Semitism and many persecutions to come. However lofty his motives may have been, Akhenaten left a very troubled legacy.

SOURCES AND FURTHER READING

A few important documents are available in English translation. The *Amarna Letters*, edited and translated by William L. Moran (Baltimore: Johns Hopkins University Press, 1992) is an archive of diplomatic correspondence with foreign rulers, mostly from Akhenaten's reign. Tutankhamen's Restoration Decree, parts of which are quoted in this chapter, can be found in several books on Tutankhamen,

Akhenaten, or the period in general. A famous hymn to the Aten, known as the "Great Hymn" and thought to have been written by Akhenaten himself, is included in many works on Akhenaten and analyzed in detail in Jan Assmann's *Moses the Egyptian: The Memory of Egypt in Western Monotheism* (Cambridge, MA: Harvard University Press, 1997). Otherwise, the sources for Akhenaten's life are almost entirely archaeological, and readers who are not Egyptologists must rely on scholars' interpretations. Much of his story has been pieced together from fragments of carvings, paintings, and inscriptions found in the debris of his destroyed buildings.

Donald B. Redford's *Akhenaten: The Heretic King* (Princeton, NJ: Princeton University Press, 1984) is a good general account. The theological aspects of his reign are well covered by Erik Hornung's *Akhenaten and the Religion of Light*, translated by David Lorton (Ithaca, NY: Cornell University Press, 1999). The second edition of Barry J. Kemp's *Ancient Egypt: Anatomy of a Civilization* (London: Routledge, 2006) is not a history but an analysis of the basic elements of Egyptian civilization and their major developments—good reading for anyone who wants to understand anything about ancient Egypt. It includes a section on Akhenaten.

Chapter 2

Judah and Israel
Seventh Century BCE

King Josiah was thunderstruck. Hilkiah, high priest of Yahweh, had just presented him with a book found during a cleanup of the great temple in Jerusalem. This document gave detailed instructions on how to worship Yahweh. (Yahweh's name, also spelled "Jehovah," is usually translated as "the LORD" in English versions of the Bible, but it is actually the god's personal name.) The people of the kingdom of Judah (roughly the southern half of the modern state of Israel) had long worshipped Yahweh as their patron god—but according to the newly discovered book, they had been doing it all wrong.

The young king called a great public meeting. There he read the book to the assembled people, swore to abide by its instructions, and accepted their oath to do the same. Josiah had no intention of establishing a new religion. On the contrary, he only wanted to reestablish the ancient contract between Yahweh and the god's chosen people. The terms of that contract were strict, but the promised rewards were substantial: for individuals, long life, prosperity, and many descendants; for nations, unfailing victory in war.

Josiah set about purging Judah of everything that violated the contract's terms. First, he stripped the Jerusalem temple of much of its equipment and personnel—the altars and priests of Baal and Asherah; the sacred utensils used in the worship of sun, moon, and stars; the hangings woven by pious women for the goddess Asherah. Yahweh must not only be worshipped—he must be worshipped alone.

Next, Josiah's soldiers took the purge throughout the country, and even across the northern border into what had been the kingdom of Israel and was now an Assyrian province. Everywhere, Josiah's troops smashed and burned altars, images, and holy places, not only of Baal, Asherah, Chemosh, Moloch, and Milcom but altars and holy places of Yahweh too—for Yahweh's worship henceforth was to be highly centralized. Only the hereditary priests of the Jerusalem temple were authorized to offer sacrifices, and only at the Jerusalem temple itself.

This was certainly an innovation. The holy heroes of Jewish tradition, from Abraham through David, had set up altars wherever they went. In Josiah's modernized state, such free-and-easy worship was no longer acceptable. At one sanctuary after another, troops slaughtered priests and burned human bones on their altars before breaking those altars to bits.

This is the account given in the Bible (2 Kings 22–23 and, with embellishments, 2 Chronicles 34–35). Scholars generally agree that the mysterious book found in the temple was an early version of the book of Deuteronomy ("Second Law"). It repeated, summarized, and expanded the religious and social regulations found in Exodus and Leviticus, with a new emphasis on centralized worship and the authority of written revelation—in other words, holy scriptures.

As the biblical accounts show, Yahweh was only one of several deities worshipped in Iron Age Palestine. The devout Yahwists who produced the book of Deuteronomy had an explanation for that fact. Yahweh had chosen the Israelites ("children of Israel") for a special relationship with him at the very beginning of their history. He had brought them out of slavery in Egypt, led them to the land of Canaan—what would later be Israel and Judah—and promised

them unending prosperity. All they had to do in return was to anni-
hilate the native Canaanites and to keep his commandments, of
which the first and most basic was to worship only him.

According to this version of history, Yahweh had kept his word,
but the Israelites had not kept theirs. They had failed to kill all the
Canaanites. Even worse, they had repeatedly allowed the pure worship
of Yahweh to be contaminated with the worship of other deities, all
borrowed from Canaanites and other aliens. Whatever prosperity
Yahweh's chosen people had enjoyed had come in the rare intervals
when their leaders had held them strictly to Yahweh's regulations.
Whenever they were allowed to lapse, defeat and misery followed.

Grim as this view of the cosmos might seem, for believers it was
reassuring and empowering. Far from being a chaotic hodgepodge
of unconnected happenings, the world made sense. There were com-
prehensible reasons for whatever happened, and many of those reasons were human actions. That meant that the people of Judah and
Israel could control their own destiny—up to a point. If they and
their rulers submitted themselves to Yahweh's will, they were virtually guaranteed the rewards of victory, peace, and prosperity. But
since an entire population might be punished for the sins of one
ruler, it was very important to get the right rulers.

Josiah was not the first king of Judah who tried to reform the
national religion. His great-grandfather Hezekiah, in the late eighth
century BCE, had also outlawed worship at the rural "high places"
and attempted to concentrate religious authority in Jerusalem. He
was said to have destroyed many idols, including the bronze serpent
that Moses had set up as instructed by Yahweh himself to act as a
cure for snakebite (Numbers 21:4–9, 2 Kings 18:4).

Even before Hezekiah's time, the neighboring kingdom of Israel
(roughly the northern half of the modern state of Israel) had faced
a religious crisis when two forms of worship clashed violently in the
mid-ninth century BCE. Unlike the chronically poor kingdom of
Judah, Israel was prosperous. Under its most successful kings, Omri
and his son Ahab, Israel had established itself as a significant power
in the region. Like Judah, Israel worshipped Yahweh as its patron
god, but not to the exclusion of other deities.

Ahab extended the borders of Israel, fostered trade with neighboring kingdoms, built a new capital city named Samaria, and married the Phoenician princess Jezebel. Jezebel brought a whole new emphasis on the worship of Baal, to whom Ahab built a grand temple in his new capital city. "Baal" was actually a title, meaning "master" or "lord," applied to several different gods in the ancient Near East. The Baal who was Yahweh's chief competitor was probably Baal Hadad, or Adad, whose statues show him as a young man wielding a thunderbolt.

According to 1 Kings 18:19, Jezebel supported four hundred and fifty prophets of Baal and four hundred prophets of Asherah. Prophets of Yahweh had always been royal advisors, and they must have objected to sharing their high status with Jezebel's protegés. At some point, the queen crossed the line from advocacy into persecution. As told in 1 Kings 18:4, she condemned all prophets of Yahweh to death. Many were executed, and others went into hiding.

Yahweh's prophet Elijah fought back dramatically. He challenged the prophets of Baal to a miracle contest. In a public display on Mount Carmel, Elijah and Baal's prophets built altars to their respective gods, killed sacrificial animals, laid the ritually correct portions on the altars, and stood back, praying for miraculous fire to strike. Baal did not oblige his worshippers, and their altar stayed cold; but fire rose up on Yahweh's altar, consuming the sacrifice. The spectators burst into applause. Urged on by Elijah, they massacred the prophets of Baal.

If this account is based on fact and Jezebel did order a sweeping execution of Yahweh's prophets, it was probably not because they preached the worship of Yahweh. More likely, Yahweh's prophets led the opposition to Queen Jezebel and the Phoenician alliance. She may also have suspected them of conspiring with the kingdom of Judah against Israel. That would be treason, which would explain the mass executions.

The city of Samaria fell to Assyrian troops in 722 BCE, and Israel was incorporated into the Assyrian Empire as the province of Samaria. Judah survived as a satellite state, and occasional attempts at rebellion failed to free it from Assyrian dominance. During the reigns of Hezekiah's son and grandson, the rising kingdom of Babylonia defeated Assyria and took over its empire.

Caught between Assyria, Babylonia, and Egypt, Judah tried to preserve some degree of autonomy by playing them off against each other. But the odds were too great. In 598 the Babylonian king Nebuchadrezzar deposed Josiah's grandson Jehoiakim and installed a puppet king. The kingdom of Judah came to a violent end in 586, when a last revolt was crushed. The great temple in Jerusalem—the only place, according to Josiah's reforms, where Yahweh could be properly worshipped—was reduced to a heap of ruins.

Following usual Babylonian practice, the conquerors deported thousands of people to Babylon and its vicinity. Others fled to Egypt. Between battle, deportation, flight, and pillage, the cities and countryside were severely depopulated. For the next half century, the lands that had been Israel and Judah remained part of Babylonian territory, and it took decades longer for the local economy to recover.

To many of the defeated, the Babylonian conquest was an overwhelming trauma. Everything they believed in had been violated. Their religious faith had been tightly linked with a sense of place and a sense of kinship. Yahweh's earthly dwelling was in Jerusalem and could not be elsewhere. Their ancestors had received the land as a personal gift from Yahweh, to be their inheritance forever. They had been promised prosperity, many children, and success in war. Now heathen foreigners had wrecked the temple, routed their armies, taken over their property, depopulated their country, and uprooted them from their Promised Land. Was their god powerless to protect his own house and his own people?

Most biblical experts have concluded that much of the Old Testament as we know it is the work of Jewish scholars during and soon after the "Babylonian captivity." They perfected an explanation that could account for the disaster and give their people hope. To this end, they edited and reworked ancient traditions, written and oral, and added new material, weaving it all into a pattern that shaped history as the unfolding of God's purposes, illustrated throughout by human crime and punishment.

The message they drew was heartening. Yahweh, their special god, was not merely powerful, he was all-powerful—so much so that he could be referred to simply as "God," the only god worth mentioning. Furthermore, God had always looked out for the original

Hebrews and their descendants. All he asked was complete and wholehearted obedience.

Most important, the message also assured believers that the whole territory of what had once been Canaan belonged to them. Regardless of inhabitants who were there before the Israelites, regardless of conquests by Egyptians, Assyrians, Babylonians, or whoever might come after, the Children of Israel were entitled to a sovereign state on that land, and no one else had any legitimate claim to it.

The brutal business of international relations did not stand still while Jewish scholars worked out their theological problems. Without warning, a new power erupted from the East. The Persians, an Iranian people with no famous history behind them, suddenly emerged with a king and an army bent on conquest. Within a decade, Cyrus of Persia had built the most extensive empire that Central Asia had ever known. The former empires of Assyria and Babylonia were now part of his domain.

In an age before rapid transportation and communication, Cyrus administered his sprawling territory through deputies. He made a point of respecting the multitudinous cultures and nations now subject to Persia. One of his techniques was to support local religious beliefs and practices. In Babylon, Cyrus portrayed himself as the champion of the high god Marduk, and returned to their home cities the various captive deities that Babylonian kings had carried off.

For the benefit of the Jews, Cyrus ordered the rebuilding of the ruined temple at Jerusalem, and decreed that Jewish exiles who wanted to help could either return there to work or contribute money toward the reconstruction. Grateful Jews hailed Cyrus as Yahweh's anointed, or "messiah"—a word that had not yet attained the full religious significance that would later be attached to it.

Most of the exiles who returned to Jerusalem were puritanical Yahwists. When "the people of the land"—the Judeans who had not been exiled—offered to help rebuild the temple, the returned exiles rejected their help indignantly. To the exiles, people who had stayed behind were little better than collaborators with the foreign conquerors. They had continued to worship Yahweh, but apparently in the more relaxed style of worship popular before Josiah's reforms— the very style that had brought down Yahweh's wrath upon Judah.

These tensions soon came to a head. The scribe Ezra, one of the returned exiles, was deeply disturbed to learn that many Jews had intermarried with "foreigners"—a term that included all the other ethnic and religious groups with which the Israelites shared their Promised Land. Armed with letters from the Persian king that gave him authority to rule on Jewish religious matters, Ezra assembled "all the men of Judah and Benjamin" and pronounced his decision: any man who had married a foreign wife must renounce both her and their children.

As the book of Ezra tells it, the Jewish leaders all agreed, and proceeded to systematically annul all such marriages. It is not clear whether the children were labeled illegitimate. Whether or not this marriage purge was actually carried out, the story shows how determined the strict Yahwists were to purify their nation, and how disruptive such a purification could be. For devout believers, it was worth it.

One of the most cherished strands of Jewish tradition was that Yahweh had led the ancestors of the Jews out of Egyptian slavery to the Promised Land. According to the book of Joshua, Yahweh had carefully supervised the Israelite conquest of Canaan. Obeying his commands, Israelites massacred the whole population of every city they conquered—men, women, and children, down to nursing babies, and sometimes all the livestock as well.

If the biblical accounts were historically accurate, it would be the earliest recorded genocide. But in recent decades, many archaeologists have concluded that there is little or no evidence of a conquest by Israelite tribes escaping from Egypt. One thing is clear: whether the events described in the book of Joshua actually happened or not, at least some influential people in Israelite society wanted to believe that they did.

But why invent the gruesome story of the conquest, featuring their revered ancestors in the role of brutal murderers? Most scholars agree that the legends are a blurred reflection of ancient quarrels among the native tribes of the Palestine area. After the Babylonian conquest of Judah, these tales were collected and written down in the form we know them.

The "Egyptian connection" may go back to the sixteenth century

BCE, when the Egyptians expelled the Semitic Hyksos, some of whom may have settled in Canaan. It is certainly a very old tradition—and a grim one. The book of Exodus relates that between the time they left Egypt and the time they arrived in Canaan, Yahweh personally killed more than forty-nine thousand Israelites, for sins ranging from worshipping other gods to complaining about their diet.

For people who believed that these stories were the literal word of God, they offered divine backing for some very harsh principles of justice. People who disobeyed God—or disobeyed human authorities constituted by God—deserved to die. People who complained about God's rule deserved punishment. Whole populations were held responsible for what their leaders or their ancestors had done. Religious freedom was flatly forbidden.

When Moses climbed Mount Sinai to confer with God, he stayed there for forty days, and the people left behind at the foot of the mountain grew understandably restless. For all they knew, Moses had abandoned them, or perhaps died on the mountain. They decided to go on without him, and asked Aaron, Moses' brother, to make a divine image that could lead them onward.

Aaron obliged by constructing a "golden calf," which may have symbolized Yahweh himself, and told the people, "These are your gods, O Israel, that brought you up from Egypt." Emphasizing his own and the Israelites' loyalty, Aaron also made an altar and declared a feast day in honor of Yahweh, which the whole people duly celebrated.

But Yahweh did not like images. In the confused account that follows, Yahweh first told Moses what Aaron and the Israelites had done, declaring that in his anger he would immediately wipe out the Israelites and produce a new Chosen People from Moses' offspring. Moses pleaded for mercy, and Yahweh agreed to spare the Israelites. Moses then came down the mountainside, carrying two stone tablets on which Yahweh had personally handwritten his law and commandments (apparently much more than the famous Ten Commandments). He arrived at the Israelite camp in the evening, while the people were winding up their daylong celebration of Yahweh with singing and dancing.

Oddly enough, Moses now acted as if he were surprised, although a little earlier he had persuaded God to spare the Israelites for this very behavior. He threw down the tablets so violently that they shattered, then smashed the golden calf, burned it, mixed the ashes with water, and ordered the Israelites to drink it.

Still not satisfied, Moses stationed himself at the entrance to the camp and issued a startling call, "Who is on Yahweh's side? Come here to me!" The priestly tribe of Levites rallied to him, and Moses, speaking in Yahweh's name ("This is what Yahweh, the God of Israel, says . . ."), ordered them to draw their swords and go through the camp, killing their friends and relatives. They did, slaughtering about three thousand people. Moses praised the Levites for proving themselves worthy of their God, and went back up the mountain to get another copy of the commandments. Aaron, who had actually made the golden calf and instituted the festival, escaped with a scolding.

There is no doubt that the stories told in the Hebrew Bible have had a profound effect on the lives of millions of people ever since. We may never know to what extent the authorities in ancient Judah and Israel actually persecuted religious dissidents. Clearly, however, the Judean tradition that became dominant and was enshrined in the Bible promoted persecution as the will of God. It was a tradition that in later centuries would be used against the Jews themselves.

SOURCES AND FURTHER READING

The only contemporary sources for the kingdoms of Israel and Judah in this period are inscriptions from that area and from neighboring countries. English translations of some of these texts can be found in several collections, including: William W. Hallo and K. L. Younger, eds., *The Context of Scripture* (Leiden: Brill, 2003); Bill T. Arnold and Bryan E. Beyer, eds., *Readings from the Ancient Near East: Primary Sources for Old Testament Study* (Grand Rapids, MI: Baker Academic, 2002); and James Bennett Pritchard, ed., *Ancient Near Eastern Texts Relating to the Old Testament*, third edition (Princeton, NJ: Princeton University Press, 1969). The relevant books of the Bible include 2 Kings, Isaiah, Jeremiah, and 2 Chronicles (which, though written centuries later, may reflect early traditions), all easily available in a variety of English translations. Be warned, however, that most English translations follow the medieval Jewish practice of replacing the sacred name YHWH (Yahweh) with the euphemism "the LORD."

There is a vast modern literature about early Israel and its people, much of it historically worthless. A good introduction is *The Bible Unearthed: Archaeology's New Vision of Ancient Israel and the Origin of Its Sacred Texts*, by Israel Finkelstein and Neil Asher Silberman (New York: Free Press, 2001). J. Maxwell Miller and John H. Hayes's *A History of Ancient Israel and Judah*, second edition (Louisville, KY: Westminster John Knox Press, 2006) is an excellent introduction to the time, place, and peoples, and a gallant attempt to extract history from Old Testament stories. John Rogerson's *Chronicle of the Old Testament Kings: A Reign-by-Reign Record of the Rulers of Ancient Israel* (London: Thames and Hudson, 1999) is a quick, readable survey of ancient Israel and the problems involved in studying it. Much broader than its title indicates, the brief text covers leaders and heroes from Abraham to the final destruction of the temple in 70 CE.

Chapter 3

Greece

Fifth and Fourth Centuries BCE

Tension ran high in the streets of Athens. The year was 415 BCE. The unstable peace between Athens and Sparta was crumbling. A fleet of Athenian warships was ready to set sail against Sparta's allies in Sicily. But today Athens was shaken by an unheard-of crime: sometime in the night, some party or parties unknown had defaced almost all the *herms*—holy images of the god Hermes that stood guard throughout Athens, protecting homes and public spaces.

Rumor spread quickly that this sacrilege was the work of reckless young aristocrats, led by the notorious Alcibiades, a brilliant soldier and politician with a rare talent for shocking his elders. He was one of three commanders who had been elected to lead the Sicilian expedition. In fact, the expedition was his idea, and he had pushed hard to get it approved. It was outrageous to think that he would endanger it at the last moment by an act of sacrilege—but Alcibiades had done outrageous things before.

The city magistrates quickly issued an appeal to the public, calling for anyone with information about this or other sacrilegious acts to come forward. One man volunteered that he had seen a gathering of people in the middle of the night in question, and recognized several of them. He named names—none of them Alcibiades—and the suspects were promptly arrested.

Meanwhile, other people had come forward with another disturbing story. On several occasions, they claimed, Alcibiades and a few of his friends had parodied the Eleusinian Mysteries in their own homes. The Mysteries were one of the most sacred rituals of Greek religion. It was deeply shocking that anyone, let alone a prominent Athenian, could make fun of them, turning them into a drunken parlor game. Alcibiades might not have anything to do with the mutilation of the herms, but profaning the Mysteries was at least as bad. The Sicilian expedition was put on hold. The war could wait while Athens dealt with its citizens' impiety.

The mutilation of the herms was a relatively easy case. One of the imprisoned suspects struck a deal with the prosecutors. In return for personal immunity, he testified against a number of other men, who were all convicted and either executed or exiled. Apparently, the vandalization was a last-minute attempt to derail the Sicilian expedition—in which it almost succeeded.

Alcibiades demanded a speedy trial so that he could get on with the expedition. He pointed out that delay gave their enemies more time to prepare. The Athenian government accepted that argument but drew a different conclusion. Yes, the expedition should go forward immediately, and Alcibiades should go with it. He could return later to be tried for impiety. With this unsatisfactory compromise, the expedition set sail. Most of the other men accused of profaning the Mysteries quietly left the city.

Before any battles had been fought in Sicily, Alcibiades was recalled to Athens to stand trial. On the way, he escaped from his government escort and defected to Sparta. That defection killed any chances he might have had with an Athenian jury. He was condemned to death in absentia. So were the other suspects who had fled Athens. One man who had stayed put was convicted and executed.

The Sicilian expedition ended in disaster. The war fleet that Athens had been so proud of was shattered, and Spartan allies took control of the sea. Athenian popular opinion blamed Alcibiades. By

404 BCE the Peloponnesian War was over, and Athens had lost. Stripped of fleet and empire and forced to endure a tyrannical government imposed by Sparta, Athens was at the low point of its long history. Though the city regained its freedom and something of its fame as a cultural center, it never fully recovered—and it never forgave Alcibiades.

Sixteen years after the night of the herm mutilation, a former friend and teacher of Alcibiades went on trial for his life. He was a veteran who had served honorably in the war, and a familiar figure around the Athenian agora, where he spent much of his time talking to friends and passersby. His name was Socrates.

The Athenian justice system depended on private individuals taking the initiative to prosecute suspected offenders. In Socrates' case, a man named Meletus charged him with impiety. The indictment had three counts. First, Socrates did not recognize the deities of Athens. Second, he invented new divine entities. Third, he corrupted young people. Scholars have debated for centuries exactly what the charges meant and whether Socrates could be considered guilty of any of them.

The first puzzle is the charge that Socrates did not recognize the city's gods. This is contradicted by Plato and Xenophon, both of whom knew him well. Plato's dialogues show Socrates referring respectfully to well-known deities of Athens. Xenophon goes further, insisting that Socrates "was often seen sacrificing at home, and often at the common altars of the city."

Yet if Plato's dialogues reflect Socrates' own philosophy to any great extent, that philosophy may have been more subversive than Socrates himself realized. In the dialogue *Euthyphro*, Socrates spells out his ideas about divinity. The gods must be perfectly wise, therefore they must be perfectly just and good. Since they were all perfectly wise, just, and good, they must all agree about everything, must need nothing, and must know what is best for everyone. This lofty view of the divine really destroys the basis of polytheism and of normal Greek religious practice. Prayers and sacrifice are quite unnecessary—and since the gods and goddesses all agree perfectly about everything, there might as well be only a single deity.

This part of the prosecution's charge—that he did not recognize the gods of Athens—seems to have been based purely on Socrates' ideas, not his actions. From a conservative Athenian viewpoint, those ideas would be harmless as long as he kept them to himself. But Socrates was above all a communicator, a teacher. If he spread his ideas to very many Athenians, Athens was in danger of offending Athena and the other deities who watched over the city.

The second part of the charge—that he introduced new divine entities—was supported by considerable evidence. Socrates often talked of his *daimonion*, his personal divinity. It seems to have functioned like a conscience, warning him to stop whenever he was about to do something unwise. At the trial, he apparently replied to this part of the charge by explaining that his daimonion was not a new deity but simply the voice of "the gods."

At first sight, the final part of the prosecution's charge seems out of place. No doubt "corrupting the young" was a bad thing, but what did it have to do with impiety against the gods?

In fact, this may have been the most important part of the prosecution's case. No member of an Athenian jury would forget that one of Socrates' pupils and friends had been Alcibiades. So had other prominent men who had abused the public trust in one way or another. Where had they learned their wicked ways, if not from Socrates?

Socrates' supporters replied indignantly that he was not responsible for the misdeeds of former students, and that he had labored hard to make them better men than they would otherwise have been. Socrates himself complained that certain inaccurate caricatures had prejudiced Athenian public opinion against him. Most famously, the comic dramatist Aristophanes had written a play, *The Clouds*, that lampooned him most unjustly.

The play has survived, and is still funny. The Socrates of *The Clouds* is a complete materialist who explains rain and thunder as natural meteorological phenomena—instead of the great god Zeus pissing and farting—and who teaches his students to argue as persuasively for falsehood as for truth. Aristophanes was making fun of two kinds of teachers who had revolutionized Greek thought during the course of the past century: the natural philosophers who laid the foundations of physical science, and the sophists who taught their students to understand both sides of every question and (like modern lawyers) to be prepared to give each side the best presentation possible.

The real Socrates had a right to complain. He prided himself on *not* investigating clouds, stars, and the rest of the physical cosmos. For someone as interested in human morality as Socrates was, studying the physical world looked like a waste of time. And he strongly disapproved of the sophists' relativistic methods. His aim was to find universal and everlasting truths to live by, not to win court cases or persuade voters.

Ironically, the majority of Athenians might well have agreed with him on both points. They too distrusted both sophists and natural philosophers. But Socrates had been tarred with the same brush, and in 399 BCE Athenians were not in a charitable mood. They had been hurt too badly by the Peloponnesian War and its aftermath. Socrates was found guilty of impiety and condemned to death.

By Socrates' time, Athens already had a long history of impiety trials. "Impiety" was as vague a legal term as "disturbing the peace"—though its consequences could be much more serious. In practice, it meant anything that an Athenian jury thought endangered the city's good relations with the gods. For example, in the early fifth century BCE the priestess Ninos was charged with impiety, apparently for introducing worship of the foreign god Sabazios to Athens and for organizing groups of his worshippers. She was also charged with distributing magical potions, and is said to have been condemned to death.

So far, impiety had meant impious acts. But around 432 BCE the Athenians issued a decree (the decree of Diopeithes) that made it a crime to express disbelief in the city's gods—or to teach doctrines about the heavenly bodies. That decree opened the door to true religious persecution, at the same time closing the door to progress in astronomy. Henceforth, a person could be sentenced to death for a religious opinion—or a scientific one.

The law's first victim was one of the founders of natural science, the philosopher Anaxagoras. He was charged with saying that the sun was an incandescent stone—a shockingly atheistical statement. As Plutarch later explained in his *Life of Nicias*, "Public opinion was instinctively hostile toward natural philosophers and visionaries, as they were called, since it was generally believed that they belittled the power of the gods by explaining it away as nothing more than the operation of irrational causes and blind forces acting by necessity."

The modern idea that religion is primarily spiritual would have baffled most Athenians of that time. With few exceptions, classical Greek religious outlook was completely practical, and largely physical. The gods might withdraw to another plane of existence, but they dealt with humans in a very down-to-earth way. They sometimes directly possessed a person, speaking through that person's mouth. More often, they appeared in human or other form.

What the gods did for humans, or to humans, was palpable—disease and recovery, lightning strokes, sudden attacks of mass panic, victory in war, answers to specific questions in the form of omens and oracles. Furthermore, some deities were always visible, even to skeptics. The mysterious stars, changeless yet always in motion, tantalizingly arranged in patterns, were clearly divine. And the sun, life-giving and all-seeing, was an obvious god.

When Anaxagoras demoted the divine sun to the status of a glowing lump of rock, he probably did not mean to attack traditional Greek religion. He was simply a scholar trying to explain phenomena in naturalistic terms. But that approach inevitably threatened the religious worldview of most Athenians.

As usual in Athens, there were political factors as well. Anaxagoras was a foreigner, from the city of Clazomenae in Ionia (the west coast of what is now Turkey). He was also a friend of Pericles, the leading statesman in Athens. Pericles' policies were helping to make Athens both a cultural and a military power in the Greek world—and leading her into the disastrous Peloponnesian War. Anaxagoras was known as a teacher and advisor of Pericles, and the Athenian political opposition may have brought charges against him as an indirect way of attacking Pericles. But there is no reason to doubt that the jury, composed of more than two hundred Athenian citizens, considered the case a religious one.

There are conflicting reports about the result of the trial, ranging from execution to acquittal, but the likeliest seems to be that Anaxagoras was fined and exiled. He apparently returned to Ionia and died some time later at the city of Lampsacus, which honored him with a commemorative statue.

Some fifteen years later, another intellectual faced another

Athenian jury on a charge of impiety. Protagoras was the most notable of the sophists, famous for teaching his pupils to see both sides of every question. Socrates was a younger contemporary of Protagoras, and Plato's fictionalized dialogue *Protagoras* showed Socrates making fun of the great sophist's inability to establish any certain truth.

Protagoras's great mistake was writing a book that began, "Concerning the gods, I cannot know whether they exist or do not exist." Not surprisingly, an indignant citizen charged Protagoras with impiety. Again, there are differing reports as to the outcome, but the consensus of modern scholars is that he was either exiled or forced to flee for his life.

Perhaps the most thoroughly religious case of impiety was that of Diagoras of Melos. He was a lyric poet who was notorious for his atheism and his mockery of ordinary Greek piety. When a priest tried to convince him that the gods answered prayers, showing him the many testimonies of people who had been saved from shipwreck, Diagoras retorted, "Yes, but we don't have the testimonies of the ones who were drowned!" In the late fifth century BCE, he was convicted of impiety at Athens and sentenced to death, but escaped before the sentence could be carried out.

With this historical background, the trial of Socrates in 399 BCE no longer seems anomalous. It was part of a long-lasting pattern. Decades after Socrates' execution, the famous courtesan known as Phryne was prosecuted at Athens for impiety. A well-known beauty, Phryne is reported to have been the model for some of the most noted works of the painter Apelles and the sculptor Praxiteles. It seems that Phryne, like Ninos, was charged with introducing a new god—in this case, the obscure deity Isodaites—and with forming unauthorized groups of worshippers, both men and women, as well as leading a procession through the Lyceion, an area sacred to Apollo. The story goes that at her trial the orator defending her uncovered her breasts at a critical point in his argument. The jury was dazzled, and she was acquitted.

Philosophers were particularly vulnerable to impiety charges. After the death of Alexander the Great in 323 BCE, his former tutor Aristotle—one of the greatest philosophers of all time—was forced out of Athens. According to one story, he withdrew from the city when he was threatened with a charge of impiety. With Socrates' fate in mind, Aristotle declared that he left to save Athens from committing a second crime against philosophy.

Aristotle's pupil Theophrastus succeeded him as head of his philosophical school. Theophrastus was a wide-ranging practical scholar, best known today for his surviving works on botany and a collection of "characters" describing different human types. But like his teacher, he is said to have been charged with impiety. The exact content of the charge is unknown (assuming that there actually was a charge), but in any case Theophrastus was not convicted, and he continued to teach at Athens.

Stilpon of Megara was another Ionian philosopher who taught at Athens and achieved his greatest fame there. In the late fourth century BCE he taught moral philosophy in the tradition of Socrates, and his pupils included Zeno of Citium, the founder of Stoicism. Apparently he was considered disrespectful of the gods. According to one story, he was tried for impiety, but defended himself successfully.

By this time the great days of Athens had passed. There were other centers of philosophical inquiry, including Cyrene in North Africa. Here the Cyreniac school developed ideas that would later become the basis of Epicureanism. One of the most notable thinkers of Cyrene was Theodorus, who acquired a reputation for ungodliness. He taught that the philosopher's goal was to avoid pain, and that much mental pain could be avoided by ascribing no importance to such things as poverty and wealth, slavery and freedom, even life and death. He wrote a book on the gods, which apparently attacked the traditional Greek view of divinity.

Driven from his home city by a political crisis, Theodorus settled in Athens. Here he is said to have been charged with impiety, but saved by one of the Hellenistic kings who wanted him as a court philosopher. If the story is true, Theodorus seems to have been the last ancient philosopher to be prosecuted for impiety.

With the notable exceptions of Socrates' case and the scandals of the herms and the Mysteries, the evidence for all these prosecutions is scant and fragmentary. For most of them, we cannot be sure whether they actually happened. Yet these stories demonstrate that strong feelings about impiety were rife in ancient Athens. Analytical thinking, skepticism, a material universe governed by natural laws—these were dangerous and unholy concepts, and many people thought they should be stamped out. It is just possible that Socrates was the only philosopher or teacher actually tried and convicted on a charge of impiety at Athens, but it seems clear that he was not the only one coerced or threatened by religious intolerance.

Ancient Athens was by no means a utopia of free speech and religious toleration. Pressure to conform religiously could be very strong, but it was more the pressure of a conservative community than of an oppressive government. As we have seen, most impiety trials were about actions, not ideas. Ninos and Phryne were convicted not for worshipping Sabazios and Isodaites, but for worshipping these gods in the wrong places. This is more like a charge of trespassing than a case of religious persecution. Yet the effects were to restrict certain religious activities, and to punish certain religious functionaries for doing their jobs.

Greek religion had no dogmas, creeds, or sacred scriptures—but that did not mean there was perfect religious freedom. Every city had its patron deities and its official rites, and everyone in the city had to respect them. People could worship as they chose in private, but not necessarily in public. The gods of the city did not tolerate competition. Thus religious conservatism could stifle both free inquiry and spiritual development. Ninos's religious leadership, Anaxagoras's scientific speculations, Protagoras's educational innovations, Socrates' moral philosophy, all were decried as attacks on traditional values. The threat of death hung over priestess, scholar, teacher, and philosopher.

SOURCES AND FURTHER READING

The best-known sources for Socrates' trial are Plato's *Apology* and *Crito*, which give a fictionalized and philosophized version. Xenophon's *Memorabilia* and *Apology* give a different contemporary view. *Lives of the Philosophers*, by Diogenes Laertius, includes traditional accounts of the trials of philosophers. Other fragments of information and rumor are found in the works of Demosthenes, Josephus, and Strabo. The only complete study of the Athenian impiety trials is still Eudore Derenne's *Les Procès d'impiété intentés aux philosophes à Athènes au Vme et au IVme siècles avant J.-C.* (Paris: Champion, 1930). Among the best recent works on the trial and death of Socrates, *The Trial and Execution of Socrates: Sources and Controversies*, edited by Thomas C. Brickhouse and Nicholas D. Smith (New York: Oxford University Press, 2002) includes new translations of all the ancient sources, plus a sampling of recent scholarship.

Chapter 4

Rome

Second and First Centuries BCE

Faecenia Hispala was a lucky woman. Like many other slaves, she had learned a trade—prostitution—as a young girl. Unlike most, she had been freed when she was still attractive enough to make an excellent living for herself. She had a comfortable home in a good neighborhood, and even supported her lover, an impecunious young man of honorable birth.

But Hispala was worried. She had received an invitation she could not dream of refusing—from Sulpicia, an awesomely respectable lady who happened to be the mother-in-law of one of the consuls for 186 BCE. The two consuls, Rome's highest magistrates, had broad executive and military powers, and it was unsettling for a mere freedwoman to be summoned by a family member of one of them.

When she arrived at Sulpicia's house, her worst fears were confirmed. The consul himself greeted her when she entered. He led her to the inner room where Sulpicia received guests, and there Hispala's ordeal began.

The consul wanted her to talk about the Bacchanalia—secret ceremonies held in honor of the god Bacchus, also known as Dionysus. That Greek deity had long been worshipped by the Greek settlers of southern Italy and by their neighbors. The Romans identified him with their ancient agricultural god Liber Pater, and in recent years his rites had become popular in and around Rome. More and more people—young people, especially—were being initiated into his cult. What did Hispala know about it?

It was no use for her to protest that she knew nothing; Sulpicia had already heard from her friend Aebutia, whose nephew Aebutius was Hispala's lover. She knew how Hispala had warned Aebutius not to let himself be initiated into the cult of Bacchus, as his mother wanted—warned him of crimes and atrocities that he would have to share in, either as victim or as perpetrator.

Trembling, Hispala admitted that she had warned Aebutius to stay away from the Bacchanalia. But she insisted the only reason was that he would have had to leave her for ten days before his initiation, as part of a purifying ritual. She had made up stories to frighten him, because she knew that otherwise he would have obeyed his mother and gone through with the initiation. When she was a young slave girl, she had been initiated into Bacchic worship along with her mistress—but that was years ago, and she knew nothing of any crimes.

The consul was furious. He gave Hispala a choice: she could tell him about the felonies and obscenities committed at the Bacchanalia, in which case he and Sulpicia would protect her from any retaliation—or she could stick to her story, in which case he could guarantee nothing.

In the hours that followed, the terrified Hispala gradually produced an amazing account of gratuitous evil. As the consul presented it to the Senate a few days later, she had revealed an enormous conspiracy against Roman values and the Roman state. Young men were initiated by sodomy—voluntary or otherwise—and those who objected were tortured and sacrificed to the god. All initiates were bound by oaths to commit crimes of many sorts, ranging from fraud and forgery to rape and murder. The Bacchanalia were orgies of the worst sort, with drunken raving, sexual promiscuity, and indecent dances. There were thousands of members, more than anyone had suspected, and it was only a matter of time before the government itself was threatened. The rot must be cut out before it spread further!

In this crisis, the Senate immediately passed a decree banning Bacchanalia, calling for the arrest of all Bacchic priests and priestesses, and charging the consuls to conduct a thorough investigation. The consuls called a general meeting of the Roman people, where they explained the urgent threat. They warned citizens of terrible consequences if they allowed their sons or daughters to be initiated. Corrupted and perverted, such boys and girls were likely to become a generation of effeminate men and debauched women—if they were not murdered first.

The consuls took pains to emphasize that there was nothing inherently evil in worshipping Bacchus. In his old Roman form as Liber Pater, he was a benign and familiar deity. As the Greek Dionysus, he was recognized as one of the great gods, and had been worshipped for centuries in southern Italy. What was new, evil, and dangerous was the spread of foreign rites among the Roman people. And no one should worry that prosecuting people for Bacchanalian activity would offend the gods. On the contrary, the gods were indignant at the crimes committed under the cloak of religion, and would welcome the prosecutions.

Citizens were invited to report any Bacchanalian activity to the authorities. In case civic duty was not incentive enough, the consuls offered a monetary reward for anyone bringing them the names of initiates. Those named were required to appear and defend themselves, or be condemned in absentia. In the days and weeks that followed, some seven thousand individuals were accused. Many fled from the city of Rome, but the supposed ringleaders were among those arrested. The consuls' investigators searched outlying towns and villages for fugitives.

Initiates who could convince the consuls they had simply gone through the initiation ceremony and had committed no crimes were relatively lucky—they were merely imprisoned. All those who had been involved in "debauchery" or any sort of criminal activity were considered guilty of a capital crime. The men convicted were executed, the women turned over to their families for punishment. That was longstanding Roman practice, and fathers had a legal right to kill their delinquent daughters. If a convicted woman had no family, the state would execute her. According to the historian Livy, "More people were killed than imprisoned."

The next step was to wipe out the dangerous cult in all of Roman Italy. This was tricky. Rome was not yet an empire; it was only the leading city-state in a central Italian federation. And Bacchus was a well-established god. The Senate's compromise was that ancient Bacchic shrines were legitimate sites of worship, but all others must be destroyed. No more Bacchanalia could be held. Sacrifices were permitted only with a special permit from the Senate, and even then no more than five people could participate. The whole Bacchic priesthood was abolished. Henceforth, only private citizens, alone or in very small groups, would be allowed to worship Bacchus.

Such an extensive and rigorous suppression was virtually impossible to enforce. Rome was the leader and dominant member of a federation of nominally independent Italian states, whose boundaries must be formally respected. The Roman Senate took advantage of the Bacchanalia alarm to extend its legal jurisdiction into allied territory, apparently on the grounds that such a widespread conspiracy was a threat to all the allies. Two years later, Roman magistrates were still arresting suspects in southern Italy, and Livy refers mysteriously to "large conspiracies of shepherds" in that area.

Meanwhile Hispala had been moved, for her own protection, to an apartment in Sulpicia's house. Once the first thousands of Bacchus worshippers had been executed, the Senate rewarded her lavishly. She received a cash payment so large that it put her into the highest grade of Roman citizenship, like the senators themselves. She was exempted from all the legal disabilities of a freedwoman, and awarded privileges that even some freeborn women did not have. The Senate guaranteed her lifetime protection. Her lover—perhaps now former lover—received the same monetary grant plus exemption from military service.

We do not know how long the Bacchanalian scare lasted. Three centuries later, the decrees suppressing and limiting Bacchic worship had evidently lapsed. A surviving inscription in southern Italy lists the cult personnel of a group of some five hundred men and women organized for the worship of Dionysus, and led by an upper-class Roman woman. Bacchanalia had become respectable.

Why did the Roman government suppress the Bacchanalia so vehemently in 186 BCE? Certainly there was a tradition of distrusting foreign cults. It was perfectly legal to worship such deities—as long as the worship was private. But temples of foreign deities could not be built within the city limits of Rome without special authorization.

The Roman Senate took religion seriously. When the nation was in danger or distress, they consulted the Sibylline books, a collection of oracles entrusted to a group of religious officials. More than once, the Sibylline books had advised that a particular foreign deity should be imported to aid Rome. Thus the Greek god of healing, Asklepius, was officially brought to Rome about 290 BCE under the Latin name of Aesculapius, though he had been worshipped there much earlier.

Less than twenty years before the Bacchanalian persecution, in 204 BCE, there had been such a crisis. The Second Punic War (218–201 BCE) between Rome and Carthage was at its height. The great Carthaginian general Hannibal controlled much of Italy. His army had repeatedly defeated the Romans. It was time to consult the Sibylline books.

What the officials in charge of the books reported was surprising. According to the oracle, the Romans should import an obscure Phrygian goddess, worshipped in her own country in the form of a black stone. The Senate immediately opened negotiations with the priest-king of Pessinus, in what is now central Turkey. He agreed to let the goddess Cybele travel to Rome.

The new goddess seemed to turn the tide of war. Within three years, the Romans had rallied, defeated Hannibal's army, and conquered Carthage. For the first time, Rome controlled the Mediterranean Sea. Yet there was a downside. Cybele came with a package of decidedly un-Roman customs. Her cult personnel included eunuch priests, their hair, robes, and gestures shockingly effeminate by Roman standards. The Senate, embarrassed, decreed that Roman citizens could not join this priesthood.

In the centuries to follow, Cybele, the Great Mother of the Gods, would become a very popular deity throughout Roman territory. But in 186 BCE she was still a disturbing newcomer. Her advent may actually have hardened conservative Roman distaste for foreign deities.

Rome at that time was unquestionably the dominant power in Italy, but not the only one. A patchwork of city-states and tribal territories shared the peninsula. Most were members of the federation led by Rome. During the seventeen-year Second Punic War, many of them had suffered badly. Hannibal's invasion had taken a toll. Rome had called on them again and again to provide troops.

When the Second Punic War ended, Italy looked forward to a period of peace and recovery. Instead, within a few years Rome was calling on the allies for new musters of troops for wars in Greece and elsewhere. People who had migrated from allied cities to Rome in hopes of finding better jobs and possibly attaining Roman citizenship were expelled. Returning to their native towns, they were subject to military service to help fight Rome's foreign wars. In many of the allied states, there was growing resentment. Rome seemed to demand their service without the rewards that Roman citizens enjoyed.

A century later, that developing resentment would erupt in the Social War, when the allied states fought Rome to gain the benefits of Roman citizenship, and won. But in 186 BCE the allies were not yet ready to attack their leader. Popular challenges to Rome's sovereignty had to take other, more subversive, forms.

Starting from Greek-speaking southern Italy, the worship of Bacchus had spread throughout most of the Italian peninsula and to Rome itself. Along the way, it had changed. Bacchus worship had long been known as a women's religion. Conservative Roman men may have been suspicious about the wild outdoor dances with which women worshippers celebrated Bacchic holidays, but custom sanctified those celebrations.

Then Paculla Ania, a priestess in southern Italy, dramatically reorganized Bacchic worship. She began to initiate young men, starting with her own sons. She moved the celebration of Bacchanalian rites to the hours of darkness rather than daylight, and multiplied their frequency. By the time that Hispala made her terrified confession to the consul and his mother-in-law in 186 BCE, the Bacchanalia had all the trappings of a dangerous secret society. Crowds of men and women met by night in the woods, where they performed hidden ceremonies and flamboyant dances. Outsiders were not allowed to see what went on, but they sometimes heard the exotic music and wild cries of the worshippers. Most disturbing, young men of military age were flocking to be initiated into these mysteries.

The consuls' investigation of the Bacchanalia began with horrendous allegations of multiple rapes and murders, as well as promiscuous sexual orgies. One of the consuls asserted that all the crime of recent years originated with the Bacchic organization. Yet, so far as we know, none of the seven thousand men and women arrested were charged with crimes such as burglary, vandalism, assault, extortion, or disturbing the peace.

Instead, the specific charges listed by Livy were "false testimony, forged seals, substitution of wills or other frauds." These are crimes that might have helped young men to avoid military service, or might have helped people from allied states to become Roman citizens—fraudulent solutions for the grievances of the allies. One of the rumors about the Bacchanalia was the allegation that men who refused to participate in crime were carried off to secret caves where they were tortured and murdered. Yet their bodies were never found. Perhaps the disappearing young men were simply draft dodgers.

The panic produced by the consuls' announcement at the public meeting can be glimpsed through Livy's account. That very night many Romans were arrested at the city gates, where they were trying to escape. Others succeeded, at least for a time. So many suspects and witnesses disappeared that legal proceedings in Rome had to be suspended for thirty days while the magistrates rounded up fugitives.

The suddenness of the blow must have been devastating. One night, Bacchic worshippers had been celebrating their god with all the fervor of a camp-meeting revival. The next day, they were subject to arrest, their priests and priestesses were dragged off to execution, and their religious practices were declared illegal, subversive, and immoral. Those who were bold enough to plead that the worship of Bacchus was an ancient and honorable variety of religion might—or might not—be granted a permit to practice it in a pitifully truncated form.

Even if Livy's estimate of seven thousand victims is exaggerated, the purge changed the religious landscape of Italy, and must have added a new element of fear to the already tense atmosphere. In many ways, the suppression of the Bacchanalia seems like a radical break with Roman tradition, which absorbed so many cults and religious ideas over the course of centuries. Yet that suppression also had its roots in Roman custom. There would be worse suppressions in centuries to come.

SOURCES AND FURTHER READING

The one contemporary source for the suppression of the Bacchanalia is a lengthy Latin inscription recording the Senate's decree. The historian Livy's detailed account, in book 39 of his *History of Rome* (*Ab Urbe Condita*), was written almost 180 years later but apparently based on sources written close to the events. It is available in several English translations, including those of B. O. Foster and J. C. Yardley. The political background is explored in an article by A. H. McDonald, "Rome and the Italian Confederation (200–186 BC)," *Journal of Roman Studies* 34 (1944): 11–33.

Chapter 5

Judea

Second Century BCE

A scandal was brewing in Jerusalem. Two qualified candidates for the high priesthood had squared off, each presenting his case to the one man who could choose between them.

Things had changed since Ezra's time. The Persian Empire had collapsed under the onslaught of a youthful conqueror from Macedon, Alexander the Great. Alexander's empire had briefly set a new record for size, stretching from Greece to the border of what is now Pakistan, with Egypt added for good measure. But Alexander's premature death had left his conquests at the mercy of his bickering generals, and his empire had shattered into three main pieces— Egypt, Syria, and Macedonia, with smaller principalities between and around them. These new states, large and small, were the Hellenistic kingdoms—heirs to classical Greek culture but part of a more cosmopolitan world to which societies of western and central Asia added their potent legacies.

As usual, Judea (more or less what had been the kingdom of

Judah) found itself part of a disputed area. It had fallen to the Seleucid dynasty of Syria, but Syria and Egypt were almost constantly at war and Judea lay directly between their core territories. That was dangerous, but it also put Judean leaders in a position to strike deals with the rival kings.

The office of high priest was not a purely religious position. Under Seleucid rule, the high priest functioned virtually as governor of Judea. He also controlled the Jerusalem temple's treasury, which served as a savings bank for local depositors as well as a storehouse for the temple's own wealth. And he represented the people of Judea to foreign powers.

In theory, the high priest was the supreme arbiter of all religious questions for Jews—but only in theory. Jews had a long tradition of thinking for themselves. In Judea and elsewhere there were Jewish groups who disputed the high priest's decisions, and sometimes his right to leadership. Not all worshippers of Yahweh agreed on what writings made up the Torah. Not all practiced circumcision, or recognized the authority of the Jerusalem temple. In what had been the kingdom of Israel, north of Judah, the former Israelites, now called Samaritans, built their own temple on the sacred Mount Gerizim.

Politics complicated the priesthood's role. In Jerusalem and the surrounding countryside, Judeans were split into opposing factions. Some favored Hellenization, some resisted it. Some insisted on keeping up good relations with Syria, the ruling power; others wanted a secret alliance with the king of Egypt. And when members of rival families competed for the same important position, their relatives and dependents prepared for a fight.

As one of his first official acts, each new king of Syria either appointed a new high priest for Jerusalem or confirmed the one currently in office. The high priesthood was restricted to certain priestly families, but it was a position well worth campaigning for, and there were almost always competing candidates. In 174 BCE the competing candidates were Menelaus and Jason—like many other Judean Jews of the time, both had Greek names—and the new Seleucid king was Antiochus IV, known as Epiphanes.

The new king's hold on the royal diadem was not perfectly secure. There were other contenders for the throne of Syria. In addition, he had an ongoing war against Egypt to manage. He wanted a high priest who would keep Judea loyal and increase Syria's revenues. Both candidates tried to convince him they could do just that, but Jason was the more persuasive. He struck a deal with Antiochus, promising to increase Judea's tribute in return for two things: the high priesthood and permission to build a gymnasium in Jerusalem.

That concession, which sounds harmless to modern ears, raised a storm of protest. In Greek tradition, the gymnasium was the training ground for male citizens, where they developed not only bodily strength and agility, but also the civic virtues of cooperation, discipline, and competitive excellence. The gymnasium and the youth association that went with it constituted the heart of any Greek city. Compounding the innovation, Antiochus even authorized Jason to enroll Jews as "Antiochenes in Jerusalem"—perhaps meaning honorary citizens of Antioch, the Seleucid capital, or perhaps citizens of a new "Antioch in Jerusalem," a Greek-style city within the ancient holy city of Judea.

Some pious Jews were shocked. In their eyes, a gymnasium was not merely frivolous; it was immoral. Greek exercise was usually done in the nude, and nudity was taboo in Jewish tradition. Besides, a gymnasium was a foreign institution. Teachings like those of Ezra had convinced many Jews that the only way to preserve their special connection with the God of Israel was to isolate themselves culturally from the rest of the world.

Not everyone agreed. In the four centuries since the Babylonian conquest of Judah, Jews had spread far. Since the time of Alexander the Great, Jews in the Hellenistic kingdoms had learned Greek and adapted to their surroundings. Jewish scholars in Egypt had translated their scriptures into Greek (the Septuagint version), and many had studied the classics of Greek philosophy. Jews were involved in businesses, skilled trades, military service, and local civil service that brought them into close daily contact with Hellenistic culture. Educated Jews were absorbing and developing radical ideas, such as the resurrection of the dead and the Greek concept of immortal souls. Many saw no contradiction between the Jewish religion and the sophisticated life of Hellenistic society.

Jason clearly expected to make money on his gymnasium and its accompanying organization. That was how he could afford to offer Antiochus an increased tribute. Many up-and-coming young men were eager to join the gymnasium, nudity and all. Some of them even had plastic surgery to disguise their circumcisions. Priests and their families were among the members. Enterprising businessmen and politicians no doubt found it useful to be enrolled as "Antiochenes."

Jason's rival Menelaus had not given up his ambition. In about 172 BCE he presented Antiochus IV with a new offer, almost doubling Jason's tribute rate. Antiochus promptly deposed Jason and appointed Menelaus high priest in his place. But the increased revenues were not forthcoming. Judea was not a wealthy province, and Menelaus's attempts to raise money alienated many people. In desperation, he started selling some of the gold and silver vessels from the temple's treasure.

That was too much. Riots broke out in Jerusalem, and his enemies charged Menelaus with theft. King Antiochus, busy with his war against Egypt, dismissed the charges and left Menelaus in his position as high priest. When a rumor reached Judea that Antiochus had been killed in battle, the deposed priest Jason collected a small army of his followers and stormed Jerusalem. He managed to capture the city briefly, but his opponents rallied and drove him out. Judea was in the throes of civil war.

Antiochus was not dead, but he was very angry. Returning from Egypt with an army, he inflicted a brutal punishment on Jerusalem's population. His troops killed thousands, and in the aftermath Antiochus enslaved thousands more, confiscated treasures from the temple, and once again confirmed the hated Menelaus as high priest.

It is clear that at this time Antiochus had no intention of interfering in his Judean subjects' religion. Aside from confiscating sacred vessels and equipment, he did no physical damage to the temple. He supported the priestly hierarchy, and he raised no objection to any part of Jewish worship.

He was, however, oblivious to Jewish sensitivities. He entered the sacred precincts of the temple itself, which to strict Yahwists was a sacrilegious act for a foreigner to commit. Yet according to 2 Maccabees 5:15 he was escorted into the sanctuary by Menelaus, the high priest. This might be a slanderous report invented by Menelaus's enemies—or it could be an indication of how varied second-century BCE Judaism was, with what would later be considered unorthodox practices at the highest levels.

Antiochus returned to Egypt to pursue his war. He had other troubles as well. In the past forty years, the expanding power of Rome had reached into the Near East. Rome considered Egypt its own satellite, and now, in 168 BCE, Rome wanted Antiochus to leave Egypt alone. Reluctantly, he withdrew from Egypt and turned his attention again to Judea.

That turbulent province seemed to be in full revolt. Jason had fled from Judea, but there were more riots in Jerusalem and elsewhere. All too obviously, Menelaus could not control his people. Exasperated, Antiochus cracked down hard. He sent a military commander with twenty thousand troops to restore order and set up a permanent garrison in Jerusalem's citadel—a serious blow to local autonomy.

Since most of the trouble stemmed from rivalries over the high priesthood, Antiochus apparently decided to make that position less attractive. He revoked the authority that had made the high priest virtually governor of Judea. No longer would Jewish religious commandments—the law of the Torah—be recognized as the official law of the province. Presumably it was replaced by the laws of the Seleucid kingdom. Traditional daily sacrifices at the Jerusalem temple were abolished, and monthly celebrations in honor of King Antiochus were instituted.

Antiochus may have thought that he was establishing law and order and promoting loyalty to himself. To some Judeans, his actions looked quite different. This is the story told in 1 Maccabees 1:20–64:

> The king wrote to all his kingdom, for all to become one people and for each to abandon his own customs. All the gentiles agreed to the terms of the king's proclamation. Many Israelites, too, accepted his religion and sacrificed to idols and violated the Sabbath.
>
> The king sent letters by messengers to Jerusalem and the towns of Judah containing orders to follow customs foreign to the land, to put a stop to burnt offerings and meal offering and libation in the temple, to violate Sabbaths and festivals, to defile temple and holy things, to build illicit altars and illicit temples and idolatrous shrines, to sacrifice swine and ritually unfit animals, to leave their sons uncircumcised, and to draw abomination upon themselves by means of all kinds of uncleanness and profanation, so as to

forget the Torah and violate all the commandments. Whoever disobeyed the word of the king was to be put to death. Letters to the
same effect he wrote to all his kingdom, and he appointed officers
to watch over all the people and sent orders to the towns of Judah
to offer sacrifices in every town. Many from among the people
gathered around the officers, every forsaker of the Torah, and they
committed wicked acts in the land and drove Israel into hiding
places in all their places of refuge.

On the fifteenth day of Kislev in the year 145 [i.e., 167 BCE] the
king had an abomination of desolation built upon the altar, and in
the outlying towns of Judah they built illicit altars, and at the doors
of the houses and in the squares they offered illicit sacrifices. Whatever scrolls of the Torah they found, they tore up and burned; and
whoever was found with a scroll of the Covenant in his possession
or showed his love for the Torah, the king's decree put him to death.
Through their strength they acted against the Israelites who were
found in the towns each month, as on the twenty-fifth day of the
month they would offer sacrifices on the illicit altar which was
upon the temple altar. The women who had had their sons circumcised they put to death according to the decree, hanging the babes
from their mother's necks and executing also their husbands and
the men who had performed the circumcisions. Many Israelites
strongly and steadfastly refused to eat forbidden food. They chose
death in order to escape defilement by foods and in order to keep
from violating the Holy Covenant, and they were put to death.
Indeed, very great wrath had struck Israel.

From the standpoint of a modern reader, accustomed to the centuries of persecution that culminated in the Nazi Holocaust, this
account seems horrific but not surprising. But to scholars of ancient
history, it is baffling. So far as we can tell, no other ancient ruler ever
tried to force religious unity on ethnically diverse subjects. If 1 Maccabees is correct, Antiochus IV's policy and actions were unprece-
dented, and bizarrely out of character for a Hellenistic monarch.

Historians have resorted to explanations that sometimes border
on the bizarre themselves—Antiochus was insane (at least eccentric
and mentally imbalanced), or he was a fanatical worshipper of Zeus,
or he was an ignorant brute, or he was a scholarly antiquarian trying
to restore a more ancient form of Yahwism, or he was imposing the
native cult of his Syrian soldiers, or he was setting himself up as a

god, or he was trying to establish a utopian form of Greek culture. What facts could underlie so many wildly varying interpretations?

Clearly, the authors of 1 and 2 Maccabees believed that Antiochus had tried to outlaw Judaism, with the death penalty ruthlessly applied for all the basic Jewish practices and beliefs. More recently, scholars have come to realize that these books, dating from between fifty and a hundred years after the events, were written for propagandistic purposes and should not always be taken at face value. Most significantly, their authors had no insight into the king's motives and very little knowledge of Hellenistic practice outside Judea.

Nevertheless, whatever the reasons and whatever the details, the crackdown by Antiochus triggered a revolt that gave birth to an independent Judean kingdom and one of the major sacred holidays of Jewish culture, Hanukkah. If we cannot know exactly what happened in the years around 167 BCE, we can make plausible guesses.

Were Jewish parents executed for having their baby boys circumcised? The book of 2 Maccabees, apparently written before 1 Maccabees, includes the circumcision story on a much smaller scale: "Two women were brought to trial for having their children circumcised. Their babies were hanged from their breasts, and the women were paraded publicly through the city and hurled down from the walls" (2 Maccabees 6:10). This seems to have been a single incident, which the author of 1 Maccabees generalized into a policy.

But if the women's only offense was circumcising their babies, why were there only two of them? And why were the fathers and the ritual specialists who actually performed the operations not condemned as well? Perhaps the women were condemned for some more blatant form of rebellious activity, and nothing but the military judge's brutality brought circumcision into the case. In fact, not all Jews practiced circumcision, and not all circumcised Near Easterners were Jews. The practice was common in Syria and Egypt. Later in the course of the Maccabean revolt, we are told that rebels forcibly circumcised people in some of the villages that opposed them. This was not resistance against a foreign oppressor, but an internal Jewish quarrel about what it meant to be a Jew.

Were Jews executed for keeping the Sabbath? Not likely. Much more probably, Syrian troops massacred Jewish rebels—or Jews who they thought were rebels—on the Sabbath. The authors of 1 and 2

Maccabees could have interpreted such acts as "punishment for keeping the Sabbath."

Were Jews forced to sacrifice "unclean" animals such as pigs at altars throughout Judea, and even forced to eat the meat of such sacrifices? Yes and no. The decree instituting Seleucid law in Judea no doubt required every Judean town to celebrate the king's birthday—not just once a year, but every month. This was common practice in Hellenistic kingdoms. The main feature of that celebration would be a sacrifice for the king's welfare.

It has often been assumed that such a sacrifice must have been to "pagan idols," that is, Greek or Syrian deities. The "abomination of desolation" built on Yahweh's altar in the Jerusalem temple is usually interpreted as a pagan altar or image, perhaps even a statue of Antiochus himself. The main support for this view is that the Seleucid soldiers stationed in Jerusalem would have needed altars and other religious facilities for their own worship. That does not mean, however, that Jewish worship must have been suppressed.

In fact, Jews had been performing sacrifices to Yahweh on behalf of their foreign rulers at least since Ezra's time. Centuries later, they would still be sacrificing to Yahweh for the welfare of Roman emperors. From the Jewish point of view, what was unusual—and to some Jews outrageous—about the new demand by Antiochus was that the sacrifice had to be made so often and in so many different places. According to the priesthood of Jerusalem, sacrifice to Yahweh could only be performed in the Jerusalem temple.

This had long been a point of contention. Besides the Samaritan temple on Mount Gerizim, Jews had built at least two temples in Egypt. Furthermore, from earliest times there had been shrines and altars to Yahweh scattered throughout the countryside of Judea. Hezekiah, Josiah, and Ezra had done their best to stamp out the use of local altars, but some of them may have survived to Hellenistic times. If so, local people would no doubt have used them for the required sacrifices on behalf of Antiochus. Where the altars themselves had been destroyed, the tradition may have survived, and villagers may have rebuilt the sacred sites as soon as they were authorized to do so.

That would not account, however, for altars in every village, and certainly not for the sacrifice of "unclean" animals. So it seems probable that some people—Seleucid troops, local inhabitants, or both—also set up altars dedicated to other deities. Pigs were normal sacrificial animals in Greek tradition, and eating the meat of sacrifices was a major part of religious celebrations. Some Jews may have had no objection to eating such meat, while to others it was an abomination. It is easy to picture confused and impatient soldiers and officers enforcing their king's birthday celebrations in the crudest and most violent way. Once the altars were in place, protesting Jews may well have been coerced into sacrificing there.

According to 1 Maccabees 2:15–26, that was a major mistake:

> The king's officials in charge of enforcing apostasy came to the town of Modein to make them sacrifice. Many Israelites came up to meet them, and Mattathias and his sons were brought into the gathering. The king's officials addressed Mattathias as follows, "You are a respected and distinguished leader in this town, supported by sons and kinsmen. Now be the first to come forward and obey the command of the king as all the gentiles have done, as well as the people of Judah and those who have been allowed to remain in Jerusalem. In return, you and your sons will be raised to the rank of the Friends of the King, and honored by grants of silver and gold and many gifts."
>
> Mattathias replied in a loud voice, "If all the gentiles under the king's rule listen to his order to depart from the religion of their fathers and choose to obey his commands, nevertheless, I and my sons and my kinsmen shall follow the covenant of our fathers. Far be it from us to desert the Torah and the laws. We shall not listen to the words of the king, that we should transgress against our religion to the right or to the left."
>
> When he had finished uttering these words, a Jewish man came forward in the sight of all to offer sacrifice upon the altar in Modein in accordance with the king's decree. When Mattathias saw this, he was filled with zeal and trembled with rage and let his anger rise, as was fitting; he ran and slew him upon the altar. At the same time he also killed the king's official in charge of enforcing sacrifices, and he destroyed the altar. He acted zealously for the sake of the Torah, as Phineas acted against Zimri the son of Salom.

This was the beginning of what would later be called the Maccabean revolt. Mattathias and his five sons literally took to the hills, where they apparently joined other fugitives and quickly assumed leadership. They soon had other recruits; most important, a band of armed Hasideans ("Pious People") who intensified the religious tone of the resistance. Mattathias, already an old man, soon died, and his son Judas took over leadership of the group. Judas's nickname Maccabaeus (perhaps meaning "Hammer") gave a popular name to the movement and to the books written about it.

The violence that now swept Judea was both a revolt and a civil war. Syrian troops indiscriminately attacked any group they took for a gathering of dissidents, while the rebels terrorized any village they suspected of collaborating with the Syrian forces. Judas Maccabaeus proved to be a brilliant military commander. Within two years he had raised a considerable army of like-minded Judeans and defeated the Syrian troops in several engagements.

Antiochus and his generals were willing to negotiate. In 164 BCE Antiochus issued a decree reassuring the Jews of Judea that they were free to follow their dietary rules and other customs, and offering amnesty to rebels who would lay down their arms. But the insurrection had become more than a religious protest. Warfare continued, both between Maccabeans and Syrians and between Maccabeans and other Judeans.

Soon after, Antiochus died in battle against the Parthians on the eastern border of his kingdom. He was succeeded by his son, still a small child, under the regency of a powerful official. Thereafter the throne of Syria was always in dispute, and the contending parties sought support by granting more and more privileges to Judea. The result was that the Maccabeans were able to secure the complete autonomy of the province.

One of their first important acts was the purification of the Jerusalem temple. They removed all traces of foreign worship, and even built a new altar, since the old one had been profaned. This is the event commemorated every year as Hanukkah, the Festival of Lights.

In an important sense, religious persecution in Judea under King Antiochus IV may well have been accidental. From the king's point of view, he simply punished a rebellious province by instituting Seleucid law to replace local law. Unfortunately, that local law was also the holy scripture of a large portion of the population. When the

Torah was no longer the law of the land, people who tried to follow its commandments could be accused of treason. The Jerusalem temple and its priesthood no longer had a legal claim to authority. The sacrifices that all good citizens of the Seleucid kingdom were required to offer for their ruler's welfare looked like sacrilege to many Judeans. And the army of occupation that Antiochus left to keep the peace enforced the new rules so brutally that they alienated many more people and triggered a serious insurrection.

Judeans had very different perspectives. Many of them accepted the new rules, whether reluctantly or gladly. But many others saw the new rules as a direct attack on their religion, and some of them fought back. When these insurgents were killed or wounded, beaten, enslaved, or tortured—as many of them certainly were—their friends, families, and supporters could only see them as martyrs, victims of religious persecution. As the uprising spread, people who had not intended to rebel found themselves attacked from both sides, suspected of complicity with either the rebels or the oppressors. No doubt some were driven into the rebels' camp by army brutality, while others joined the rebels out of fear.

We know very little about what Judeans suffered at the hands of other Judeans. But we do know that Judeans suffered hideously at the hands of Syrian troops and officials. Mothers paraded through the streets with their murdered babies hung around their necks; old men held down while soldiers forced polluting meat into their mouths; young men tortured to death before their mothers' eyes— these scenes made an indelible impression on Jews in Judea and elsewhere. For those who experienced the king's wrath, it probably seemed that he had singled out the genuine Jews for punishment, and that those who were spared were not true worshippers of Yahweh. Many must have felt that the only reason for Antiochus to annul the Torah as Judea's law code was so that he could establish his own religion in its place. The authors of the books of Maccabees accepted that logic implicitly.

Judas Maccabaeus and his brothers founded a dynasty known as the Hasmonean, which lasted for roughly a century and scored impressive achievements. Reestablishing the Torah as the law of Judea was only the beginning. Hasmoneans became hereditary high priests of the Jerusalem temple and acknowledged rulers of Judea. Within a generation they had won de facto independence for the nation of Judea, for the first time in centuries.

In 104 BCE Aristobulus (a great-grandson of Mattathias) at last assumed the title of king along with his high priesthood. Capitalizing on their military success, the Hasmoneans set out to reconquer all the lands once ruled by Solomon. They succeeded brilliantly. During the long reign of Alexander Jannaeus (103–76 BCE) Judean territory grew to include approximately what is now the entire state of Israel, plus parts of western Jordan and Syria.

In the process of expansion, they conquered the Idumaeans and Ituraeans, whom they forced to become Jews. According to the Jewish historian Josephus, Alexander Jannaeus destroyed the Syrian city of Pella because its inhabitants refused to convert to Judaism. As priestly rulers of a theocratic state, the Hasmoneans saw no need to extend to others the religious freedom their ancestors had demanded and won for themselves. The sources' repeated references to "rooting the godless out of Israel" and destroying "lawless men" indicate that the Hasmoneans did not willingly tolerate religious diversity.

The Hasmonean dynasty had only a little longer to flourish. Rome was moving into the areas once controlled by the Hellenistic kingdoms. In 63 BCE the Roman general Pompey captured Jerusalem. Henceforth, despite spells of nominal independence, the ancient kingdoms of Judea and Israel would be part of the Roman sphere.

SOURCES AND FURTHER READING

The main ancient sources are 1 and 2 Maccabees, which were accepted by many Christians as part of the Bible. English translations can be found in Catholic editions of the Bible, and translation and extensive commentary in the Anchor Bible, volumes 41 and 41a (Garden City, NY: Doubleday, 1976 and 1983). Most modern scholars conclude that chapters 7–12 of the book of Daniel were written during the Maccabean revolt or the early Hasmonean period, and that its prophecies refer to contemporary events. Josephus's *Jewish Antiquities* gives the story of the revolt and the Hasmonean dynasty from the viewpoint of a Romanized Jew of the first century CE. Many editions are available.

John H. Hayes and Sara R. Mandell's *The Jewish People in Classical Antiquity: From Alexander to Bar Kochba* (Louisville, KY: Westminster John Knox Press, 1998) presents the Maccabean revolt and the Hasmonean period in their complex historical setting. (The title is misleading; the book does not deal with Jewish people outside Palestine.)

Chapter 6

Roman Empire

First and Second Centuries CE

It was Passover time in Jerusalem. The courtyard of the great Jerusalem temple was packed with worshippers. Jewish leaders and the Roman governor, Ventidius Cumanus, were in attendance. On the roofs of the porticoes overlooking the crowd, Roman soldiers stood guard.

Since the fall of the Hasmonean dynasty some eighty-five years earlier, Judea had been ruled directly by Romans or by a Rome-appointed client king. Just four years ago, in 44 CE, the emperor Claudius had declared Judea a Roman province. There were many people in the courtyard today who looked up resentfully at the armed men above them on the porticoes.

Suddenly one of those Roman soldiers turned his back, hitched up his tunic, and displayed his naked rear to the crowd—at the same time producing "a noise in keeping with his posture," as the historian Josephus put it.

Outrage swept the courtyard. The Jewish leaders turned to Ventidius Cumanus, and voices from the crowd yelled at him to punish the soldier who had mooned them. Some of the worshippers snatched up stones from the courtyard and hurled them at the guards. Cumanus called for reinforcements to clear the courtyard. Under an onslaught of soldiers with drawn swords, the crowd panicked, fighting for a way out. Thousands died, either trampled in the stampede or killed by Roman troops.

We do not know if the soldier who started the trouble was disciplined. But contempt for a subject people's religion was not Roman policy. When another soldier, tracking thieves who had robbed an imperial slave, tore up and burned a copy of the Torah, Cumanus had him executed for sacrilege. Cumanus's quick action in that case may have forestalled a revolt—for the time being.

Rome, once an insignificant town on the banks of the Tiber River, now ruled an impressive empire that included Arabs and Africans, Celts and Germans, Italians and Greeks. More and more of these diverse people had become Roman citizens, and more and more "old Romans" had moved into the new territories. There they often thought they found their own deities worshipped under other names, and they also learned to worship completely unfamiliar powers. Meanwhile, new Romans and subject peoples crowded into the city of Rome, swelling its population and bringing new religious practices. Roman religious horizons expanded. Inevitably, there were conflicts.

In 19 CE the emperor Tiberius had forbidden all foreign religious ceremonies in the city of Rome, specifically citing "Egyptian and Judaean rites." The Egyptian rites may have been those of Isis. Both Judaism and Isis worship were attracting many Romans at the time. Tiberius ordered followers of these "superstitions" to burn their religious vestments and equipment or leave the city. The penalty for disobedience was perpetual slavery. Several thousand Jews were drafted into the army and sent to Sardinia.

Some thirty years later, the emperor Claudius banished from the city of Rome "all the Jews, who were continually making disturbances at the instigation of Chrestus." Since "Chrestus" was a common Roman mistake for "Christus" (Christ), this may be an early reference to Christians. The disturbances might have been quarrels between Christians and Jews or between Christians and traditional Romans. The historian Dio, however, states that Claudius merely forbade Jews to hold public meetings.

Claudius might not have realized that the man known to his followers as Christ had been executed by a Roman governor in Judea little more than a decade earlier—but he probably did know of that governor's troubled tenure. Pontius Pilate had governed Judea during one of the periods of direct Roman rule, and he had been outstandingly unpopular. He had offended local religious sensibilities again and again, and one especially brutal mistake had led to his recall in 36 CE.

Jesus had been only one of the charismatic leaders imprisoned or executed under Pilate's governorship. Some had agitated against Roman rule, while others were purely religious dissidents. Pilate had also offended Judeans in a whole series of incidents. He had even financed a new aqueduct with money confiscated from the Jerusalem temple treasury, and had used club-wielding troops to quell protest demonstrations.

In 35 CE Pilate attacked a Samaritan procession with cavalry and heavy infantry. The gathering looked to him like a possible uprising. In fact the Samaritans were following the call of a prophet, who had announced that the time had come to dig up sacred vessels from the Israelites' original tabernacle. His followers believed that Moses had buried the vessels near Yahweh's temple on Mount Gerizim. Pilate's troops killed an unknown number of these pilgrims and took many captives. After the battle he executed not only the procession's leaders, but other prominent Samaritans as well.

The Samaritan community appealed to higher Roman authorities, and Pilate was recalled. Shortly after, the elderly emperor Tiberius died and was succeeded by his grandson Gaius, whose father had been a popular figure in Judea. It seemed that a new era of friendly relations had dawned.

Within a few years, Gaius (better known by his boyhood nickname, Caligula) announced that he was a god and demanded that his subjects worship him. That posed a serious problem for Jews, Samaritans, and Christians. They were faced with a choice between treason to the Roman state and treason to their god. Trouble broke out first in Alexandria, where Roman authorities forcibly installed images of Gaius in synagogues. Jews who protested lost their Alexandrian citizenship.

In Judea, non-Jews set up an altar to Gaius in the town of

Jamnia. Some of their Jewish neighbors demolished it. In response, Gaius decreed that the Jerusalem temple must be transformed into a temple of the imperial cult, complete with a life-size statue of himself. The "abomination of desolation" that rumor had ascribed to Antiochus IV (see chapter 5) was about to become real.

Luckily for the peace of the province, Petronius, the imperial legate in Syria, had taken pains to learn something about Jews and Judaism. He advised Gaius that pushing through the plan would probably trigger a serious revolt. Gaius agreed to a compromise. The emperor would leave the Jerusalem temple alone, and the Jews would leave his altars alone.

Not long after, Gaius was assassinated, and Claudius became emperor. The crisis had been avoided. No later emperor would demand that his subjects worship him as a god, although subjects sometimes did so voluntarily. But, as we have seen, there were other ways of offending religious sensibilities. In 49 CE came the incident of the "mooning" in Jerusalem and the expulsion of Jews and/or Christians from Rome.

Meanwhile, on the other side of the Roman world, Romans had encountered a widespread and sophisticated religious organization. In Gaul (roughly present-day France and northern Italy), Britain, and perhaps other Celtic societies, priests called druids were among the most powerful leaders. They were famous for their learning in almost every field, from medicine and astronomy to poetry and law. They were also educators for young Gaulish nobles and advisors to war leaders.

Unlike most priests and priestesses the Romans knew, druids underwent years of training. Druids from many different tribes came together for annual meetings at a central point, and acknowledged the authority of a chief druid. With such skills and such organization, they were well placed to lead the Gallic and British resistance to Roman conquest.

That would have been reason enough for Roman emperors, generals, and governors to suppress them—but there was more. Some of the rites at which druids officiated were sacrifices of human beings. The most spectacular example—presumably resorted to only in times of grave crisis—was the "wicker man." The Gauls would build a large wood-and-wicker cage in human shape, fill it with living animals and people, and burn it down.

Romans were far from squeamish. They were a military nation, with no qualms about bloodshed. As a slave-based society, they were accustomed to brutalizing other human beings. The bloody sports of their gladiatorial games and wild beast hunts are notorious. But most Romans found the idea of human sacrifice both weird and revolting. In his book on the conquest of Gaul, Julius Caesar had to explain the Gaulish theory to his readers: "Those who are afflicted with serious illnesses or engaged in battles and dangers either sacrifice human beings or vow that they will do so, and they employ druids for these sacrifices. They believe that unless a human life is offered for a human life, the power of the immortal gods cannot be placated."

Augustus, the first emperor, forbade Roman citizens to take part in the druids' rites. His successor Tiberius issued similar anti-druid decrees. Claudius went further, though we do not know what specific measures he took. The biographer Suetonius claimed that Claudius "completely abolished" the druids in Gaul. In Britain, on the far edge of the Roman frontier, they remained active longer. But their elaborate training and hierarchy, which had helped make druids powerful, now made them vulnerable to outside attack. When druids were driven underground, the whole system of lengthy education, public contests and performances, and regular convocations apparently came to an end.

Romans had long been intrigued by the odd customs that Jews practiced. Many Romans admired the Jews for being faithful to their ancient religion, and honored Moses as a lawgiver. Non-Jews attended synagogue services with their Jewish friends, and Jews sometimes partook of Roman holiday banquets where meat from sacrificed animals was served. In most places, Jews were accepted as eccentric but respectable Roman subjects.

Yet Jews were also "atheists"—that is, they refused to honor the deities of Rome. In fact, many Jews insisted that the gods and goddesses worshipped by other people were merely demons—a lower grade of supernatural power—or, even worse, that they did not exist at all. Some Romans, offended by these peculiarities, flatly declared that Jews were "enemies of humankind." In the first and second centuries CE, that attitude helped bring on a series of catastrophic wars.

In the province of Judea, old hostilities still smoldered and sometimes flared. From time to time, fighting broke out between Jews and Samaritans. Anti-Roman guerilla bands drifted through the countryside. Nationalist assassins whom the Romans called "dagger men" (*sicarii*) carried the cause of Judean independence into Jerusalem itself. In the mid-50s CE, one of them assassinated the high priest Jonathan, who had supported Roman rule. At least some of the *sicarii* were probably members of the Zealots, an activist group who opposed Roman rule for religious reasons. The Zealots were ardent Yahwists, who believed it was their religious duty to drive out the pagan Romans and establish an independent theocratic state ruled by God alone.

As one unpopular Roman governor followed another, Judea moved closer and closer to the point of explosion. That point was reached in 66 CE, when Florus, the most unpopular governor yet, confiscated the large sum of seventeen talents from the Jerusalem temple's treasury, apparently to cover overdue taxes. There were massive protests in Jerusalem. Some of the protesters loudly demanded Florus's ouster, while others made fun of him by taking up a collection. Florus demanded that everyone who had insulted him should be turned over to him for punishment. When they were not forthcoming, his troops massacred over three thousand men, women, and children in Jerusalem.

Many Judeans still feared that defying Rome would be suicidal. But a growing number of dissidents were coming around to the Zealots' position that only force could answer Rome's mistreatment. They persuaded the priests of the Jerusalem temple to stop making sacrifices for the welfare of the Roman emperor and the Roman state. A group of Zealots stormed the fortress of Masada and expelled the Roman garrison. The First Jewish War was under way.

A more accurate name is the First Judean Revolt. (The Latin and Greek words *Iudaeus* and *Ioudaios* mean both "Judaean" and "Jew" or "Jewish.") But certainly some Judaean Jews felt that they were fighting for their religion. As in the time of the Maccabees, religious convictions and political aspirations were inseparably tangled together.

Meanwhile Rome was undergoing its own upheavals. The year 69 CE is known as "the year of the four emperors," as one claimant after another followed Nero's overthrow and death. During this unstable period, a Roman army under the general Vespasian and his son Titus defeated the Judaean rebels. In late 69, Vespasian himself was declared emperor. He returned to Rome, leaving Titus the job of capturing Jerusalem.

To the tremendous shock of Jews everywhere, Titus's troops laid waste the city and destroyed Yahweh's temple, which rebels had used as a principal fortress. Elsewhere, a few rebel bases held out for two or three more years. The mountaintop fortress of Masada, defended by a force of Zealots that included women and children, was the last to fall.

Jews, both in Judea and elsewhere, had long paid an annual tithe for the upkeep of the Jerusalem temple. Vespasian replaced that payment with a Roman tax on all circumcised Jews in the Empire, at the rate of two drachmas per year. The money went to the temple of Jupiter Capitolinus at Rome, and thus Jews were forced to give financial support to what they considered idolatry.

In 115 CE a Jewish revolt broke out in Alexandria and spread to other Jewish communities in Egypt, Cyrene on the coast of Libya, the island of Cyprus, and Mesopotamia. It took two years to quell this widespread Jewish uprising.

Fifteen years later, the Second Judean Revolt began. Simon bar Kosiba, the leader, was said to be a descendant of David, king of ancient Israel. Simon's followers hailed him as the Messiah, and he became known as Bar Kokhba ("son of the star"). This was a far more unified and better organized uprising than the previous ones. The rebels set up an alternate government and issued coins and documents dated by years of Simon's rule (132–135 CE). The Bar Kokhba Rebellion, as it is also called, was unabashedly a fight for national liberation.

The emperor Hadrian had inadvertently set off the revolt. He had promised to rebuild Jerusalem, still in ruins from Titus's devastation in the First Judean Revolt—but to rebuild it as a Roman city, complete with temples to Roman gods. He had also issued a decree against genital mutilation. That decree's purpose was to outlaw commercial castration—some slave dealers had specialized in turning out eunuchs for the market—but it also had the effect of making circumcision illegal. Once again, the Romans had demonstrated to Judea's strictly observant Jews the Roman lack of understanding and respect for their religion.

The Second Judean Revolt ended like the first, in defeat and devastation. Hadrian not only rebuilt Jerusalem as a thoroughly Roman city, renamed Aelia Capitolina; he even made it illegal for Jews to enter the city or the district around it. Antoninus Pius, Hadrian's successor, legalized circumcision for Jews by granting them an exemption from the genital mutilation law. But it would be centuries before Jews could legally enter Jerusalem again.

To the Roman authorities, every private club or organization was potentially subversive and had to be carefully watched. Purely local clubs could be tolerated, but a group that was connected to a widespread network of similar groups aroused the gravest suspicions. And if those groups held secret meetings, only open to initiates, where they practiced a foreign cult, then their actions were clearly criminal.

That described the Christians. In Roman law, they constituted a subversive organization. By the time of Nero, it was clear that Christians were not Jews, though their religion had sprung from Judaism. To conservative Roman eyes, it seemed that Christians had abandoned their ancestral faith for a new, "invented" religion. Yet they had kept the Jewish scriptures and the Jewish rejection of all deities but their own.

When the great fire of Rome ravaged the city in 64 CE, Nero blamed Christians for starting it. He had hundreds of suspected Christians crucified, burned alive, or killed by wild beasts. This slaughter set a grim precedent for more than two hundred and forty years. Although Christianity was illegal, Christians could safely be ignored—until something went wrong. Christians were often blamed for fires, earthquakes, epidemics, famines, or simply hard times. Even if they had not caused the disaster with their own hands, they had certainly angered the gods.

But after the disastrous "year of the four emperors" the Roman Empire enjoyed long periods of peace and prosperity. For most people in most parts of the Empire, most of the time, life was tolerable or better. The gods seemed to be reasonably pleased with Rome. There was no need to root out Christians or other "atheists."

During those periods, Christianity made converts and became increasingly respectable. In many places, Christians met openly, and even built churches. Nevertheless, being a Christian meant knowing that at any time you might be arrested, thrown into prison, tortured, exiled, sent to labor in the mines, or executed. Christianity was not a faith to be accepted lightly.

When the laws against Christians were enforced, it was a local matter. The central government adhered to a type of "don't ask, don't tell" policy. Imperial instructions to provincial governors and local officials were clear and consistent, if not necessarily logical: Christians were not to be hunted down; but if they came to a magistrate's attention for any reason, they should be punished.

Times were not always good. Marcus Aurelius, the philosopher emperor, spent most of his reign dealing with crises beyond his control—war against the Parthians in the East, massive invasions of Germanic tribes from northern Europe, and plague. In parts of the Empire, all kinds of tensions, fears, and hostilities came to the surface.

In the northern Rhone Valley, where Christianity was still relatively new, many Christians seem to have been Easterners—Greek-speaking merchant families from Syria and Phrygia. Popular opposition to these newcomers boiled over into mob violence in the city of Lugdunum (present-day Lyons, France) in 177 CE. That attracted the attention of the authorities, who arrested, imprisoned, tortured, and finally executed a large number of Christians. Part of the evidence against them was the testimony of some of their own slaves, confirming the charges that Christians engaged in ritual cannibalism and incest—not very surprisingly, since the testimony of slaves was valid only if obtained under torture.

Convicted Christians were beheaded if they were Roman citizens. Otherwise they were executed in the most grisly way known to Roman law—killed by wild animals in the arena, to the cheers and catcalls of a holiday crowd. Many of them had been intensively tortured first. With dramas like this played out again and again, at scattered localities around the Empire, Christians' only protection lay in keeping a low profile. The time would come when that was not enough.

SOURCES AND FURTHER READING

For the reigns of the first- and second-century emperors, we have the *Lives of the Twelve Emperors* by Suetonius, the *History* and *Annals* of Tacitus, and the *Roman History* of Cassius Dio. Josephus's *Jewish War* gives a detailed account of the First Judean Revolt. Julius Caesar's *Gallic Wars* includes information on the druids, as seen by a Roman general. All these sources are easily available in English translations. The *Ecclesiastical History* of Eusebius, written in the early fourth century from an ardently Christian viewpoint, includes much information on persecutions of Christians and preserves many documents from earlier periods, including an eyewitness account of the persecution in Lugdunum in 177. The most recent English translation is *Eusebius—The Church History: A New Translation with Commentary* by Paul L. Maier (Grand Rapids, MI: Kregel, 1999). *The Acts of the Christian Martyrs*, edited and translated by Herbert Musurillo (Oxford: Clarendon, 1972), is a collection of some of the most important contemporary or near-contemporary accounts of individual martyrdoms.

Perhaps the best general account is still W. H. C. Frend's *Martyrdom and Persecution in the Early Church: A Study of a Conflict from the Maccabees to Donatus* (Garden City, NY: Anchor Books, 1967). Peter Schäfer's *Judeophobia: Attitudes toward the Jews in the Ancient World* (Cambridge, MA: Harvard University Press, 1997) discusses anti-Jewish feeling in Greco-Roman culture.

Chapter 7

Roman Empire
Third and Fourth Centuries

Historians know the period from 235 to 284 CE as "the crisis of the third century" or "the age of the barracks emperors." Repeated invasions shook the Roman Empire. One army commander succeeded another in a continual series of short and savage civil wars. It was somewhat as if "the year of the four emperors" had been stretched to half a century.

In 249 the emperor Decius made a special effort to unite the Empire's population behind him and the dynasty he hoped to found. He ordered all Roman citizens to offer a sacrifice to the deities of Rome. There had always been public sacrifices to celebrate the beginning of a new emperor's reign, but this was different. Never before had all citizens been told to contribute their individual sacrifices. Mobilizing the religious force of millions of Romans for a single purpose would surely have a powerful effect.

Jews were exempted from the requirement. Their long-standing arrangement with the Roman government allowed them to avoid

ust have been surprised and alarmed by the Christian reaction. His
tempt at unity had divided the Empire. The certifications quietly
ded in 251. A few months later, Decius was dead—the first Roman
mperor ever killed in battle against a foreign enemy. His plans for
dynasty came to nothing.

Decius was not the only one surprised by Christianity. His
ecree had revealed the extent of Christian penetration into Roman
ociety. Though they were only a small minority of the Empire's
opulation, Christians seemed to turn up everywhere and at every
ocial level. The next emperor, Valerian, decided that they were a real
ireat.

Valerian's first law against Christians required Christian clergy to
cknowledge the gods of Rome. If they refused, they were subject to
xecution, exile, or servitude in the imperial mines. In the North
frican province of Numidia, Christian laymen, women, and even
hildren accompanied their clergy to the mines, and some of them
ied in the harsh conditions there.

A second law abruptly intensified the pressure. Christian clergy
were to be executed at once. Upper-class Christians were to lose their
ank and any government positions they held. Their property could
be confiscated. If they still refused to renounce Christianity, women
were to be exiled, men executed. Christians on the imperial household staff were to lose their goods and be sent in chains to labor on
imperial estates.

When Valerian was captured in battle by the Parthians, his son
and co-emperor Gallienus reversed his father's policy. In a letter to
the Christian bishops of Egypt in 262 CE, the emperor assured them
that they were entitled to the undisturbed use of their places of worship. Christians would be unmolested—for a time.

Roman authorities had another religious menace to worry about,
perhaps even more dangerous than Christianity. This one came from
Rome's age-old rival and neighbor, Persia. By the late third century,
the new religion of Manichaeism had won converts across the
Roman Empire. Like Christianity and Judaism, it was an exclusivist
religion that left no room for Rome's traditional gods and goddesses. More than that, it claimed to replace both Christianity and
Judaism, as well as Persia's native Zoroastrianism. It was the fulfill-

sacrifices to idols on condition that their synagogues (
for the emperor's welfare. But Christians had no su(
What were they to do?

Christians had never been secure. Through the fi
third century, there had been scattered bursts of per
emperor Septimius Severus (reigned 193–211 CE) l
decree forbidding new conversions to Christianity. A gr
tians had been thrown to the beasts in the arena at Car
Maximinus Thrax, the first of the "barracks emperors,"
have exiled Pontianus, the bishop of Rome, and to h
other Christians. But there had never been a threat like
decree issued by Decius required every adult citizen to a
a local official, make a small sacrifice on behalf of state a
and receive a certificate to prove it.

Christian response varied widely. In some places, e
performed the sacrifice without objection. Apparently t
a onetime, token sacrifice for an essentially secular pur
damage to their religious convictions. Usually, their co
followed their example.

Some Christians managed to get their certificates wi
ally sacrificing. Local officials might allow one member
or household to sacrifice for the whole group. Christian
respected members of the community might persuade ma
with or without the aid of a tactful gift—to sign their
without a sacrifice. Many others, including some leadin
avoided the problem by arranging to be out of town (
period of the sacrifice, which conveniently varied from
place. Some Christians were frightened into abandoning
gerous religion. But there were many for whom the sac
unthinkable. They would rather die.

Some of them did die. The edict had not specified a p
noncompliance, and punishment was left to the discretio
magistrates. In some places, recalcitrant Christians were im
for a time and then released. Elsewhere, they were publicly
burned alive, or beheaded.

Christians often concluded that Decius had planned h
as a device to ferret them out. His reign is still sometimes cit
first Empire-wide official persecution of Christianity. In fac

ment of all their prophecies, the solution of all their theological conundrums.

Manichaeism had other attractions. It came with its own holy scriptures, lavishly illustrated, its own beautiful hymns, and its own devoted corps of missionaries. There were colorful myths and satisfying rituals, full of images of light and sweetness. And unlike the dominant forms of Christianity, Manichaeism did not instill feelings of guilt. According to Mani, prophet and founder of the religion, the essence of every human soul was purely good.

From a Roman emperor's point of view, Manichaeism had all the faults of Christianity. It took people away from the proper worship of the Roman deities. It encouraged people to neglect—even despise—their social duties. And it had one uniquely threatening aspect—it came from Persia. In conservative Roman opinion, that meant it was morally dubious and almost certainly subversive.

In 284 one more army commander, fresh from victory in the recurring civil wars, was recognized as emperor by the weary and intimidated Senate. Diocletian had worked his way up from the army's lowest ranks. He was certainly not the first tough, shrewd soldier to take the imperial throne in the past half century, but he was the first one to turn his powers immediately to the job of reorganizing the government and the army. He was determined that no other general would be able to do what he had done.

Both the armed forces and the civil service had been badly overstrained during the long crisis. To defend the Empire, make its administration easier, and keep the army under control, Diocletian instituted a whole new system. The sprawling Empire was divided into an eastern and a western area. Each part was ruled by a senior emperor assisted by a junior emperor. The haphazard system of provinces that had grown up piecemeal over the centuries was reorganized and rationalized, with a view toward smaller administrative units and clearer chains of command. Manpower of both the army and the civil service was dramatically increased. The tax system was overhauled.

Diocletian's reforms were radical, but his ideas were thoroughly conservative. The Empire's recent troubles could be cured by a return to old-fashioned Roman values. The growth of those modern, foreign religions, Manichaeism and Christianity, must be stopped.

Their adherents were now so bold that they worshipped openly in most of the Empire's cities. They had even infiltrated the imperial service. Something must be done.

Probably in 296, the four joint emperors issued their first edict of persecution. Manichaean leaders were to be burned alive, together with their sacred books. Upper-class Roman converts to Manichaeism were to be condemned to slavery in the mines, and their property confiscated. Ordinary Manichaeans were subject to the death penalty. Probably in 299 or 300, Diocletian purged the army and the imperial staff of Christians. He went no further at the moment, but his junior emperor Galerius urged a more aggressive policy. In 303 Diocletian obliged.

At dawn on February 23, 303, a procession of soldiers and officials approached the principal church in the city of Nicomedia, capital of the eastern Roman Empire. The doors were locked, but they broke in. Inside, they searched for incriminating evidence, looted or smashed everything of value, and burned the scriptures they found. While Diocletian and Galerius watched from the neighboring palace, the soldiers attacked the church with crowbars and axes. Before dark it was only a pile of rubble.

Thus began the first and last deliberate, Empire-wide persecution of Christians in Roman history. In Christian tradition it is rightly known as the Great Persecution. It lasted for roughly eight years. A series of four imperial edicts in 303 and 304 progressively tightened the noose. The first was issued the morning after the church in Nicomedia was demolished. It called for all Christian churches to be destroyed, and stripped upper-class Christians of their privileges. As with any imperial edict, anyone who defied it was subject to the death penalty.

Not all Christians were willing to turn the other cheek to persecution. Suspiciously soon after the demolition of the church at Nicomedia, a fire broke out in the imperial palace there. Disturbances in Syria and elsewhere may have been related. These events seemed to have triggered Diocletian's second edict, ordering the arrest of all Christian clergy. So many were packed into the prisons that a third edict soon offered amnesty to any who were willing to sacrifice to Roman deities. Some were coerced into sacrificing by threats, torture, or general mistreatment. Others died under such abuse. Local officials were often eager to find legal ways of releasing their prisoners. In some cases, clergy were physically pushed and pulled through the motions of offering sacrifice, and then released.

But these measures were not producing the wholesale rejection of Christianity that Diocletian had hoped for. Finally, in 304, he issued a fourth edict. This one repeated the ill-fated try for unity that Decius had made. All citizens—Jews excepted—were now required to offer sacrifice in the presence of a magistrate. Decius had not been looking for Christians, but Diocletian was. For the first time, imperial agents, court officers, and soldiers sought out and arrested Roman citizens purely on the grounds of their religion.

By the nature of Diocletian's reorganization, however, there were differences between the Eastern and Western parts of the Empire. Maximian and Constantius, the senior and junior emperors in the West, destroyed churches but may not have implemented the later edicts. Only a few Christians are known to have been executed in their territories. In 305 Diocletian and Maximian abdicated—the first time a Roman emperor had voluntarily retired—and Galerius and Constantius became the senior emperors in East and West respectively. The junior emperors appointed were Maximin Daia in the East and Severus in the West. All except Constantius pursued the persecution.

But now Diocletian's carefully planned system of collegial emperorship began to break down. Constantius' son Constantine (later to be known as Constantine the Great) had counted on being chosen as his father's junior emperor. Maximian had actually abdicated very unwillingly—and his son Maxentius also wanted to be emperor. Civil war broke out.

Constantius had long been in poor health. In 306 he died, and his army proclaimed his son Constantine as his successor. The other three emperors reluctantly accepted him as their colleague, but Constantine still had to fight Maxentius. Constantine would soon show himself to be a Christian sympathizer, and there is some indication that Maxentius was one as well. There were a few executions of Christians in territories controlled by Severus, the Western senior emperor, but overall the Great Persecution fell almost entirely on the Eastern half of the Empire.

Meanwhile, the civil war continued. Severus had been killed in battle and replaced by a new senior emperor, Licinius. Old Maximian, trying to regain power until the last, had switched sides several times and was finally driven to suicide. His son Maxentius, never officially recognized as a emperor, was still fighting to replace Constantine as junior emperor in the West.

In the spring of 311, Diocletian, the architect of the Empire's reconstruction and originator of the persecution, was living peacefully in retirement in his palatial villa at Salona on the seacoast of what is now Croatia. Galerius, his original second in command, was very, very ill, and clearly unhappy with the unsatisfactory results of the persecution. In April he issued a stunning decree:

> We had earlier sought to set everything right in accordance with the ancient laws and public discipline of the Romans and to assure that the Christians too, who had abandoned the way of life of their ancestors, should return to a sound frame of mind; . . . Very many, however, persisted in their determination and we saw that these same people were neither offering worship and due religious observance to the gods nor carrying out the worship of the god of the Christians. Bearing in mind therefore our own most gentle clemency and our perpetual habit of showing indulgent pardon to all people, we have taken the view that in the case of these people too we should extend our speediest indulgence, so that once more they may be Christians and build their meeting-places. . . . Consequently, in accordance with this indulgence of ours, it will be their duty to pray to their god for our safety and for that of the state and themselves, so that from every side the state may be kept unharmed and they may be able to live free of care in their own homes.

A few days later Galerius was dead.

As was normal for a general imperial edict, this one had been issued in the name of all four emperors, but only three complied with it. Maximin Daia, who had been junior emperor to Galerius, continued the persecution. He had now succeeded to the position of senior emperor in the East, directly controlling Egypt, Syria, and all of Asia Minor. Local officials in Tyre and some other cities petitioned him to suppress Christians in their localities, and he always responded positively.

In 312 the armies of Constantine and Maxentius met in a showdown battle at the Milvian Bridge into the city of Rome—a battle later hailed as the triumph of Christianity over paganism. Certainly Constantine, the victor, favored Christianity. In the following year, Maximin Daia was defeated by Licinius and committed suicide. Constantine and Licinius, the sole surviving emperors, issued a decree that not only confirmed the right of Christians to worship freely but even ordered restitution of their confiscated and destroyed property.

Yet Christians were still not entirely safe. Constantine was a genuine Christian sympathizer, but Licinius was not. From 320 to 324, Christians in the territories that Licinius controlled were sporadically harassed. It was no wonder that Christians throughout the Roman Empire hailed Constantine as their deliverer. In the years that followed, some of them would have cause to change their minds.

SOURCES AND FURTHER READING

Surviving sources are almost all written from an ardently Christian viewpoint. One unique treasure is the autobiographical account of her imprisonment by Vibia Perpetua, one of the Christians martyred at Carthage in 203, supplemented by an eyewitness account of her death. It is available with an English translation in Herbert Musurillo's *Acts of the Christian Martyrs* (Oxford: Clarendon Press, 1972), which also includes several other martyrdom accounts considered historically reliable. The *Ecclesiastical History* of Eusebius, bishop of Caesarea in the early fourth century, is highly biased, but very valuable as a contemporary account for much of this period, especially because it contains a number of official documents. *The Deaths of the Persecutors* by Lactantius recounts the unhappy ends of most of the emperors who persecuted Christians, as imagined by a fourth-century Christian. The surviving fragments of an anti-Christian treatise by the Neo-Platonic philosopher Porphyry have been collected and translated by R. Joseph Hoffmann as *Porphyry's Against the Christians: The Literary Remains* (Amherst, NY: Prometheus Books, 1994). *The Theodosian Code*, translated by Clyde Pharr (Princeton, NJ: Princeton University Press, 1952), contains some of the laws against Manichaeans.

Samuel N. C. Lieu's *Manichaeism in the Later Roman Empire and Medieval China* (Manchester: Manchester University Press, 1985) covers the history of Manichaeism. In *The Blood of Martyrs: Unintended Consequences of Ancient Violence* (New York: Routledge, 2004), Joyce E. Salisbury explores how Christians used the sufferings of Christian martyrs for their own purposes, and the psychological consequences throughout Western history.

Chapter 8

Persia

Second through Sixth Centuries

K artir, Chief of the Magi of Ormazd, Grandee of the Realm of Persia, Judge of the Empire, Master of Rites, had much to be proud of. He had served seven kings in succession, starting with the founder of the Sasanian dynasty, and each had honored him with higher offices and more power. He had restored the Mazdean religion throughout the lands conquered by Persian arms. Most admirably, he had destroyed the doctrines of Ahriman and the demons, namely, the doctrines of "Jews, Buddhists, Brahmins, Nasoreans, Christians, Maktaks, and Zandiks." To the everlasting glory of Mazdaism and himself, he had his accomplishments and the Mazdean doctrines carved on mountainsides.

Modern scholars have not certainly identified all the victims of Kartir's persecutions. The Zandiks were an unorthodox branch of Mazdeans. Nasoreans were probably some of the Judeo-Christian groups that had proliferated along the eastern borders of the Roman Empire. Maktaks may have been the gnostic Mandeans—or the

Manichaeans, whom Kartir certainly tried to suppress. In any case, it is clear that Kartir did his best to root out all false beliefs and to enforce what he considered the only orthodox form of the only true religion.

This was a change from ancient Persian policies. Cyrus the Great, founder of the earlier Achaemenid dynasty, had followed a deliberate policy of respecting and supporting the religious traditions of conquered territories (see chapter 2). Cyrus had welcomed the support of any deity. But already in Cyrus's time the seeds of change had been sown.

In many ways, ancient Iran was more akin to northern India than to the Near East. (The word "Iran" comes from the same root as "Aryan," the name of the dominant people of northern India in the second millennium BCE.) From time immemorial, the population of the Iranian plateau had worshipped a host of gods, goddesses, and lesser spirits. But sometime between the mid-second and the mid-first millennium BCE, a religious revolution began that would profoundly influence the world for thousands of years to come.

Zarathushtra—better known by the Greek form of his name, Zoroaster—may have belonged to the priestly clan of the Magi. According to later tradition, he lived from about 628 to 551 BCE— but the linguistic evidence of the hymns he apparently wrote indicates a much earlier date, perhaps around 1200 BCE. As a young man he began to preach a new revelation, received from the "Wise Lord," Ahura Mazda. The *ahuras* had long been known as a class of divine beings, but it is not clear whether Ahura Mazda had been worshipped as an individual god before Zarathushtra's time.

The new revelation provided one precocious solution to a dilemma that would bedevil all monotheistic religions—the problem of evil. How could an all-good, all-powerful, all-knowing creator make and maintain a world that contains evil?

In Zarathushtra's theology, Ahura Mazda was the creator. His first creation had been two mighty spirits, to whom he offered a choice between falsehood and truth. One chose truth, the other chose falsehood. With that beginning, the universe must inevitably be a battleground, but the creator bears no responsibility for the casualties. Evil and suffering result from the free choice of created beings.

Humans had the same choice to make. They could follow the

Bounteous Spirit (*Spenta Mainyu*) in truth, or the Destructive Spirit (*Angra Mainyu*) in falsehood. Zarathushtra's teaching was intensely ethical. As soon as people died, their deeds would be measured, and they would be rewarded or punished.

Yet Ahura Mazda was a good, just, and loving deity. In the universe he created, there could be no such thing as eternal punishment for temporal sins. The Mazdean equivalent of hell was temporary. At the end of time, the destructive Angra Mainyu would be vanquished, sinners redeemed, all humans who had ever lived resurrected, and there would be an endless realm of peace, virtue, and happiness for all.

Zarathushtra converted a local ruler in eastern Iran, and the new faith gradually spread westward. In the 540s BCE, Cyrus united the whole Iranian plateau as the kingdom of Persia, and pushed his conquests farther, building a great empire. That set the stage for the expansion of Mazdaism—or Zoroastrianism, as it is usually known.

The new faith was revolutionary in its combination of monotheism and dualism, in its emphasis on ethical behavior and bodily purity (rather than animal sacrifice and ecstatic worship), and in its picture of the afterlife. Yet it readily absorbed many elements of the old Iranian religious tradition, such as rituals of the sacred fire. Later kings of the Achaemenid dynasty accepted Ahura Mazda as their supreme god, and Zarathushtra's teachings became part of the common currency of Persian religion.

These stark and clear-cut concepts—the supreme creator, the cosmic battle between good and evil in which every human is required to enlist, the hellish and heavenly punishments and rewards after physical death, and the final resurrection of the body—are the Mazdean legacy to the world. Many scholars conclude that Jewish exiles met these ideas during the Babylonian captivity and transmitted them to the Western world.

It is not certain how much the Achaemenid kings understood and promoted Zarathushtra's doctrines. We do know that Xerxes I, who ruled from 486 to 465 BCE, destroyed "the temple of the *daeva*-worshippers." In Zarathushtra's system, *daevas* were spirits who had chosen falsehood. The "*daeva*-worshippers" whom Xerxes tried to suppress may simply have worshipped old Iranian gods in an old Iranian way. This was the first known case of religious persecution in Persia, and it was an isolated one.

෯

In the late fourth century BCE, the unthinkable happened. The great Persian Empire was conquered from one end to the other by the victorious army of Alexander the Great. Alexander may have hoped to unite his wide-ranging conquests in a harmonious whole, building on native institutions rather than destroying them. But conquest is conquest, and Mazdeans would remember Alexander as the great destroyer. We know that only about a quarter of the ancient Zarathushtrian scriptures have survived. According to Persian tradition, it was Alexander's troops who destroyed the rest, and killed the priests who could have reconstructed them.

On Alexander's death, his short-lived empire quickly broke up into the smaller Hellenistic kingdoms, but the conquest had lasting effects. New links had been forged between Central Asia and the Greek-speaking culture of the eastern Mediterranean. People, goods, and ideas flowed both ways. An inscription from the first century BCE records the worship of Zeus Oromazdes, a combination of the Greek high god Zeus with Ahura Mazda.

By that time, Mazdaism itself had changed. Without a centralized organization since Alexander's conquest, and with most of its sacred writings lost, beliefs and practices had evolved and drifted. Ahura Mazda (now known as Ormazd) had completely merged with the Bounteous Spirit. The Destructive Spirit Angra Mainyu was now called Ahriman. Believers thought of Ormazd and Ahriman as rival powers that had existed from eternity. Yet Ormazd was the stronger, and universal salvation was guaranteed at the end of time.

From 250 BCE another Iranian people, the Parthians, dominated the region. Popular Mazdaism absorbed or reabsorbed many deities, both from the West and from pre-Zarathushtrian religion. In the early third century CE, a political and religious revival changed the face of Iran again. A fiery leader named Ardashir overthrew the Parthian king in 224 and established the Sasanian dynasty of a revived Persia. He had the help of the young priest Kartir.

Together they set out to purify and strengthen the Mazdean religion. Ardashir had the surviving sacred texts collected and codified. Kartir organized the priesthood into an extensive hierarchy. The ancient Magi were now members of the Mazdean clergy. Doctrines and rituals were standardized, and deviations were labeled heretical. Under Ardashir's successors, Kartir's influence grew. He became convinced that the power of his king and his country—not to mention the good of the universe—required him to purge Persia of heretics and unbelievers.

Probably the worst of those, in Kartir's view, were the followers of a new prophet who had just appeared in Persian territory. Mani, the prophet, had been born into a puritanical Judeo-Christian sect in Mesopotamia. He began to receive his own personal revelations while still a child. Before he announced them to the world, he traveled as far as India, where he apparently studied Buddhist ideas. To make sure that his teachings would not be distorted by future generations, he wrote and illustrated several volumes, and established a carefully organized clergy from among his first converts. When he went public with his new religion, it was ready to sweep across continents—and it did (see chapter 7).

Manichaeism (or Manichaeanism), as it is called, was a fiercely otherworldly religion. The entire perceptible universe, Mani taught, was the result of a cosmic mistake. Bits of goodness had been torn from the eternal Kingdom of Light and stirred into the repulsive mass of evil known as matter. Human souls contained some of those bits of goodness. Salvation meant escaping from the body and returning to the light. Only a relatively few people—the "Elect" or "Perfect"—could manage the degree of abstinence and purity required to guarantee entrance to the Kingdom of Light when they died. Others were doomed to recycle through additional lifetimes, but with each lifetime they could get closer to salvation.

Meanwhile, their services were needed. The Elect lived as much like angels as physically possible. That meant they could not pollute themselves with gross activities like sex and physical labor. They ate only sparingly and of the most "light-filled" foods, such as honey and melons. The Manichaean "Hearers"—believers who had not attained perfection—supported and took care of the Elect. Thus there was a place for everyone.

Mani boldly took his message to the highest levels of society. He obtained an audience with King Shapur I, Ardashir's successor, and converted some of the king's family. With royal support, Mani made many more converts and established churches throughout the land.

One of the strengths of Manichaeism as a missionary religion was that it had the appeal of familiarity despite its newness. Like Zarathushtra, Mani taught that the universe was a battleground between good and evil, fought both in the supernatural realms and on earth.

Because of this resemblance, modern commentators sometimes lump Zoroastrianism and Manichaeism together as two varieties of the same basic dualism. But in fact, they were deeply opposed. Zarathushtra's dualism was purely ethical. He taught that the physical world was inherently good, and was to be enjoyed, respected, and cared for. His idea of evil was moral and spiritual.

In Mani's world, matter itself was irredeemably evil. Manichaeans were early advocates of birth control. It was sinful to produce children, since that meant imprisoning souls in matter. Manichaeans' object in life was to escape from life—an attitude that did not make for good citizenship.

Kartir must have been appalled that his king could support such a doctrine. For years he tried to discredit Mani. At last, in the 270s, King Bahram I allowed Kartir to arrest Mani. The prophet died in prison. Kartir was now free to pursue Manichaeans throughout Persian territory. And not just Manichaeans.

Shapur I (reigned 241–272 CE) had fought a series of successful wars against Rome. To strengthen the Persian border defense, he moved Roman inhabitants from the frontier zone deeper into Persia and replaced them with Persian settlers. That made for military security, but there was an unwanted side effect. Some of the resettled Romans were Christians, and Christians liked to make converts.

According to some accounts, one of the resettled Roman Christians was a beautiful young woman named Candida. King Bahram (probably Bahram II, who reigned from 276 to 293) enrolled her among his royal wives. Kartir disapproved. He persuaded the king that Christians were as subversive as Manichaeans—and that Manichaeans often masqueraded as Christians. When Candida refused to renounce her religion, she was tortured and executed. That was the beginning of a systematic persecution of Christians, along with all the other religious dissidents listed in Kartir's proud inscription.

Armenia, to the west of the Iranian plateau, had been part of the Persian Empire until Alexander's conquest. Zoroastrianism had spread easily among the Armenians. In the breakup of Alexander's empire, Armenia had fallen to the Seleucid kings of Syria. When the Romans defeated Antiochus III in 189 BCE, Armenia had achieved a precarious independence. In the following centuries, Persia and Rome maneuvered and fought for control over this buffer state. It was briefly annexed by Rome in the second century CE, a little less briefly by Persia in the third.

Meanwhile, Christians had migrated into Armenia from the west. Whenever there was an outburst of persecution in the eastern Roman Empire, Christian refugees crossed the border. By Kartir's time, there were well-established Christian churches in Armenia. Very early in the fourth century, King Tiridates III, a new convert, declared Christianity Armenia's official religion.

Although Kartir boasted of smiting Christians in the non-Iranian lands conquered by Persia, his purge was not as successful as he claimed. Decades after his lifetime, Armenia—now a Persian vassal state—was openly Christian. Worse, there were still Christians in Persia itself—and now they were much more dangerous.

Early in the fourth century, the Roman emperor Constantine began a policy of fostering Christianity (see chapter 9). Persia's greatest rival now took a protective interest in Christians everywhere, including those within Persia. Persian Christians all too readily looked to Rome for support and protection, making their political loyalty dubious. And even if Persian Christians themselves were not disloyal, there was always the possibility that the Roman government might use their safety as a pretext to attack Persia.

By the mid-fourth century, there were well-established Christian communities in the heart of Persia, with their own bishops and other clergy, and some Christians held responsible positions in Persian society. But for over forty years, starting around 336, Persia and Rome were almost constantly at war, and Christians attracted the highest suspicion. Simeon, bishop of the Persian capital Seleucia-Ctesiphon, was executed on a charge of spying and treason, probably in 344. Soon after, the queen of Persia fell ill, and a charge of sorcery was brought against Simeon's two sisters, together with a servant whom they had instructed in Christianity. All three were executed. Their bodies were dismembered and the queen walked between them in a healing ritual. We do not know if she recovered her health.

During the forty-year war with Rome, some fifty Christian bishops were executed, along with an unknown number of lower clergy and laypeople. Peace brought relief, but only for a time. In the next three centuries, the Persian government repeatedly tried to suppress Christian churches. Yet, as the charges against Simeon show, the Mazdean establishment had lost the righteous fervor of Kartir's day. Christians were persecuted not so much for their religious beliefs as for their supposed connection to a foreign power.

King Yazdegerd the Sinful (Yazdegerd I, reigned 399–420) earned his title in Zoroastrian tradition by his toleration of Christianity and Judaism, breaking the pattern of repression. He was even said to have married a Jewish woman. Both the Mazdean clergy and the nobles of his court opposed this softening. Christians took advantage of the respite from persecution to make new converts and pursue their internal disputes. Toward the end of his reign, Yazdegerd yielded to pressure and reinstituted anti-Christian measures.

Ironically, his successor was Bahram V, one of the nobles who had opposed him—and Bahram soon decreed freedom of worship for Christians. There were incentives for Bahram's generosity. His unsuccessful war against the Eastern Roman Empire had ended with a peace treaty that stipulated protection for Persian Christians. Bahram could safely guarantee that protection, since the dominant Christian church in Persia was now willing to declare its independence from all foreign hierarchies. These Christians were followers of Nestorius, the deposed bishop of Constantinople, who had been declared a heretic. Nestorians were persecuted in the Roman Empire, but in Persia they now found a safe haven.

Bahram's son Yazdegerd II (reigned 438–457) followed his father's tolerant policy for a time. Later in his reign he returned to Kartir's ideas and outlawed all religions but orthodox Zoroastrianism. In Persia itself, he enforced that ruling with some success. But Armenia, now administered by a Persian governor, had been Christian for a century and a half. Thousands of Christian Armenians took to the mountains. Others rose in revolt—a revolt so successful that after 451 Yazdegerd abandoned his attempt to enforce

Zarathushtra's doctrines in Armenia. In Persia his decree remained in effect.

Kavadh (Qobad) I (reigned 488–496 and 499–531) had religious interests of his own. A new movement had arisen in Persia. Mazdak preached doctrines somewhat like Mani's, but without demanding the rigorous discipline of Manichaeism. He called for an ethic of gentleness and communalism, and the populist overtones of his message attracted wide support among the people and fierce opposition from aristocrats. Kavadh became an early convert and enacted a number of social reforms. But in 528 the crown prince Khosrow, with the help of the Zoroastrian high priest, engineered a great massacre of Mazdakites. The survivors went underground, and Mazdakism was scarcely heard of again.

By this time, the Eastern Roman Empire had developed into what modern historians call the Byzantine Empire—Greek-speaking, Orthodox Christian, with its own elaborate and sophisticated culture (see chapter 11). But the age-old rivalry with Persia continued and even intensified. War was perennial. In the course of the sixth and early seventh centuries, Persia and Byzantium virtually exhausted themselves in mutual combat.

The timing was very bad. Arabs were on the move, empowered and excited by a new religion (see chapter 12). Neither Persia nor Byzantium was well prepared to resist their enthusiastic force. In the years 636 to 651, Muslim Arabs completely conquered Persia, destroyed the Sasanian dynasty that had ruled for almost four hundred years, and set up an Islamic government. The Zoroastrian priesthood were no longer in a position to persecute anyone. Like the Christians, the Jews, the Manichaeans, and the surviving Mazdakites, they could only wait and watch uneasily for what the conquerors would do with them.

SOURCES AND FURTHER READING

What remains of the Mazdean (Zoroastrian) scriptures is known as the *Avesta*, sometimes mistakenly called *Zend Avesta* (a *Zend* or *Zand* is actually a translation and interpretation in another language of parts of the *Avesta*). The oldest parts of the *Avesta* are the *Gathas* (hymns), which are believed to be the work of Zarathushtra himself. Their extremely archaic language makes them hard to read and hard to translate, but there are several renderings into English, notably *The Gathas of Zarathushtra: Hymns in Praise of Wisdom*, a complete translation and commentary by Piloo Nanavutty (Ahmedabad: Mapin, 1999; Middletown, NJ: Grantha, 1999). An anthology of representative texts, ranging from selected Gathas to accounts of modern worship practices, edited and translated by Mary Boyce, is *Textual Sources for the Study of Zoroastrianism* (Chicago, IL: University of Chicago Press, 1990). Mary Boyce is also the author of the standard survey, *Zoroastrians: Their Religious Beliefs and Practices* (London and Boston: Routledge & Kegan Paul, 1979), which has been republished several times. Paul Kriwaczek, *In Search of Zarathustra: Across Iran and Central Asia to Find the World's First Prophet* (New York: Vintage, 2004) is a handsomely illustrated historical travelogue.

Chapter 9

Roman Empire

Fourth and Fifth Centuries

When I, Constantine Augustus, and I, Licinius Augustus, happily met at Milan and considered all matters concerning the public welfare and safety, we thought that . . . the first things to be put in order were those insuring reverence for divine power, so that we might grant to Christians and to everyone the free ability to follow whatever religion each one wished.

I t was the world's first official statement of unqualified religious toleration.

It lasted less than a year.

The late emperor Diocletian's arrangement for orderly succession to imperial power had collapsed at the first test (see chapter 7). Constantine and Licinius were the survivors of a confusing civil war that had seen seven actual and would-be emperors struggling for a share of the Empire. The two winners met at Milan in 313, and warily agreed to split the Empire between them—Constantine in the west,

Licinius in the east. They also formulated the policy later called the Edict of Milan, quoted above.

By Constantine's own account, he had received a vision before the crucial battle of the Milvian Bridge, telling him to put a Christian symbol on his soldiers' shields and promising, "In this sign you will conquer." (One contemporary source says that he saw a cross. Another says that the symbol was a *chi rho*, the Greek abbreviation for "Christ.") Licinius, on the other hand, seems to have preferred the traditional Roman religion. The Edict of Milan was a compromise, ending the persecution of Christians without committing the Empire to a pro-Christian stance.

When the agreement between the two emperors broke down and fighting resumed, so did persecution of Christians in some areas controlled by Licinius. In 324 Constantine defeated Licinius for the last time and took over the whole empire. He ruled as sole emperor for thirteen years.

Constantine had long since been handing out special favors to Christians, and he continued the practice enthusiastically. One of his first laws exempted Christian clergy from serving on city councils—an expensive duty, since councilors financed the upkeep of a city's infrastructure. He restored confiscated church property, built and endowed new churches, and subsidized churches and clergy. Other favors included tax exemptions for clergy, their families, their servants, and any businesses they might operate.

Bishops were no longer subject to the Roman court system. Any lawsuits or criminal charges against them could be judged only by other bishops. Constantine also gave them extraordinary judicial power. Either party in any lawsuit could have the suit transferred to the local bishop's court. That applied to non-Christians as well as Christians. The bishop's judgment could not be appealed, and the civil authorities were charged with carrying it out.

Within a few years, Constantine crossed the line from religious favoritism into persecution. He confiscated gold and silver treasures from temples all over the Empire, even stripping gold plate from statues, and demolished some of the more notable temples. More important in the long run, one of his laws forbade sacrifices—the basic act of traditional Roman worship. Though this law was impossible to enforce widely at the time, it set a precedent for future Christian emperors. And with one exception, all the emperors after Constantine were Christians.

For the most part, Romans—Christian and non-Christian—lived together peaceably. But there was a strong aggressive streak in Christianity, based on scriptures inherited from Judaism. "Break down their altars, smash their statues, and cut down their groves. . . . The Lord, whose name is Zealous, is a jealous God" (Exodus 34:13–14). Over and over, preachers told their congregations that their pagan neighbors and relatives were the slaves of Satan. Christian writers urged emperors to destroy temples and suppress pagan worship.

Christian emperors responded to this pressure, but slowly. A complete program of destruction and suppression would have meant using imperial troops, who were needed elsewhere to meet foreign attacks and put down uprisings. And emperors were not eager to antagonize the great pagan majority of the Roman population.

At first, laws specified that temples and their images should be maintained as art treasures and public meeting places. Bit by bit the imperial decrees grew harsher. Subsidies to public priesthoods and festivals were cut off. Country temples could be torn down. Monumental urban temples were stripped of their images and closed to the public.

By November 392 even private worship of pagan deities was declared a crime. People who worshipped their household gods in their own homes could see those homes confiscated. Hanging wreaths or ribbons on trees, cutting sod to make a simple altar, pouring wine to your personal guardian spirit, or burning incense to the gods of your storeroom were all punishable offenses. Anyone could denounce a neighbor for pagan practices.

By 415 all pagan temples and shrines, with the land they stood on, were declared imperial property, and officials were ordered to convert them to other uses. Idols and pagan altars were to be destroyed wherever found. The traditional sacred banquets at tombs were declared illegal. Bishops were authorized to use force to prevent or break up any pagan religious service. Pagans were barred from holding government positions. Yet as citizens they were still protected by law—at least in theory.

That year, Christians and non-Christians alike were scandalized by the murder of Hypatia, a mathematician and philosopher at Alexandria. She was not only a renowned scholar and teacher, but one of the chief advisors to the city prefect. She was also a pagan, and Bishop Cyril of Alexandria resented her influence. In March 415 a group of Cyril's followers pulled her from her carriage and brutally murdered her. No one was ever punished for the crime, but Cyril was told to reduce his staff. Pagans were encouraged to keep a low profile.

By 435 the law required officials to destroy all temples and shrines, setting up crosses on the "polluted" sites. The penalty for practicing pagan rites—or knowingly permitting them—was now death. From 472 owners of property where such rites took place were held responsible. Upper-class owners could lose their rank and property, while the lower classes could be tortured and sentenced to hard labor in the mines.

Yet most of the violence perpetrated against non-Christians in the Christian Roman Empire was not official persecution. The people who burned, looted, and tore down temples and synagogues, abused and murdered non-Christians, desecrated sacred sites and defaced sacred images, were usually not government agents or soldiers, but pious Christian congregations inflamed by zealous Christian preachers.

Such mob action was illegal, but in most cases the Roman government permitted or even encouraged it. Christian agitators and rioters were rarely punished. Restitution was almost out of the question. Individual emperors might deplore illegal violence, and in 423 the imperial government even instructed local officials to prosecute overeager Christians who attacked law-abiding pagans. But in fact such violence was often the Christian emperors' most effective tool against paganism.

Historians used to say that Roman religion was a hollow façade of empty ritual, which crumbled at the vigorous touch of Christianity. Modern scholars point out that this could hardly be true. People do not risk their lives or livelihoods for something that is not deeply important to them. Paganism survived century after century of mob violence and government persecution, in some places even living on into the Middle Ages. But when faced with an aggressive and intolerant faith backed by government force, traditional Roman religion did have certain inherent weaknesses.

Pagans tended to be relatively easygoing about their religion. No god had instructed them to break down other people's altars. That very fact put them at a disadvantage in the "culture war" with Christianity. So did paganism's lack of structure. There was no organized hierarchy to direct a strategy of resistance, and no doctrines, creeds, or scriptures for people to rally around. And, when other factors were equal, it was easier to coerce a pagan than a Christian. Unlike Christianity, the belief systems of most pagans did not promise after-death rewards for martyrdom.

The Roman government offered incentives of cash, land, and advancement for converting to Christianity. Increasingly dire punishments were threatened for not converting. Since upper-class careers depended on imperial favor, the upper classes gradually assumed at least a nominal Christianity. The public side of paganism—civic festivals, publicly funded temples and priesthoods—was destroyed bit by bit. Government crackdowns and Christian hooliganism whittled away at the pagan population.

But people's habits of worship were not so easily changed. Converts to Christianity often continued to worship in the only ways they knew, even if the object of their worship had a different name. Thus Christianity involuntarily absorbed much of the style of traditional Roman religion—lighting lamps and candles, singing hymns, parading with sacred objects, dedicating votive offerings, giving gifts at religious holidays, eating and drinking to commemorate dead relatives and friends. Pagan festivals became Christian holidays, and Christian martyrs and saints were often revered at times and places where pagan deities had been worshipped.

Yet something very basic had changed. Belief—*right* belief—was now more important than worship or conduct. And everyone was now assured of eternal life, either in bliss or in agony. The world had become an anxious place, where thoughts as well as deeds were driven by the fear of hell.

Manichaeans had fared little better. In 372 a law ordered their meeting places confiscated and their teachers punished. In 381 Manichaeans were denied the right to make wills or inherit property. Their meetings were now completely forbidden. The next year, another decree made it illegal to support Manichaean monastics or hermits—presumably the "Elect," whose stringent ascetic lifestyle did not allow them to earn their own living (see chapter 8). In 398 Manichaeans were expelled from Rome and threatened with exile from all Roman territory. In the fifth century, Pope Leo I conducted a purge of Manichaeans from Italian churches, where some had passed as Christians. As a result of such measures, Manichaeism virtually disappeared from the Roman Empire, taking refuge in Persia and farther east. The last known Manichaean congregation lived in sixteenth-century China.

For the Roman authorities, Jews were a special case. Christians might see Jews as God's original chosen people—or as God's ungrateful children, who had rejected Christ. No Christian emperor could bring himself to declare the religion of Abraham and Moses illegal. From time to time, emperors' decrees reminded their Christian subjects that Judaism was *not* illegal, and that Jews should not be attacked or harassed for practicing their religion. Nevertheless, Jews were increasingly restricted.

From 339 on, it was illegal for a Christian to convert to Judaism, and the convert's property could be confiscated by the government. Despite laws protecting synagogues, zealous Christians often took matters into their own hands. In 388 a Christian mob, incited by the local bishop, burned down a synagogue in the Syrian town of Callinicum. The emperor Theodosius I ordered the bishop to rebuild the synagogue—but quickly rescinded the order under pressure from his own powerful bishop, later known as St. Ambrose.

Not only were laws protecting synagogues ineffectual, it was illegal to build new ones. Jews were forbidden to purchase Christian slaves, or to convert slaves they already owned. Well-intentioned decrees meant to reduce friction between Jews and Christians added new restrictions. Thus a law of 408 forbade Jews to burn the symbolic "gallows of Haman" during their Purim festivals. Some Christians had mistaken it for a cross.

But the principal victims of Christian persecution were other Christians.

With imperial support, Christianity had flourished—at a price. The number of Christians had grown explosively, from perhaps 10 percent of the population in 313 to a strong majority two centuries later. Church leaders complained that too many halfhearted or insincere converts joined the church, looking for economic and social benefits or evading punishment. And the government that promoted Christianity inevitably wanted to regulate it. Laws limited the appointment of clergy, their financial dealings, and sometimes their behavior. A law of 390 even decreed that women who cut their hair short were not allowed to enter a church.

Constantine had called for, and presided over, the first general church council—the Council of Nicaea in 325, which defined basic Christian doctrines. Thereafter, emperors took a leading role in all major church councils. Emperors often had their own theological and political axes to grind, and put pressure on the bishops to reach the "right" conclusions.

"Heretical" Christian groups—what modern Americans would call other denominations—were denied the privileges of "true" Christians. From Constantine on, Christian emperors named certain bishops as teachers of the true faith, and declared that all Christians who did not agree with those bishops were heretics. For the first time, imperial power was brought to bear on a problem that had dogged Christians from the beginning.

The earliest Christians had been certain that there was only one god, and that Jesus was the son of that god; but most of them were also sure that Jesus was more than a man. He was the Anointed— "Christ," the Greek translation of the Hebrew "Messiah." People prayed to him, pictured him in heaven at his father's side, felt that he ruled the world. How could he not be a god? And then there was the Holy Spirit, whose role and nature were obscure. Thoughtful Christians, from the time of Paul onward, struggled to put their beliefs into rational order.

Inevitably, different individuals and groups came to different conclusions. This might not have been a serious problem except for one belief all Christians shared—that there could be only one "right way." Salvation—a peculiarly Christian concept—depended on right belief as well as right action. If your ideas were wrong, you were a candidate for hell. If you taught other people wrong ideas, you condemned them to eternal torture. But how could a Christian know which way was the right one?

There were many answers. Some Christians (later labeled Gnostics) relied on secret teachings that Jesus had confided to only a few insiders. Others thought that Jesus had conferred special authority on the twelve apostles, who had passed that authority on to their successors, the bishops—especially bishops of important cities, like Alexandria, Antioch, and Rome. Some churches accepted new revelations from contemporary prophets, while others held that God had stopped giving revelations. All agreed that "Holy Writings" (scriptures) had the authority of divine inspiration—but which writings were the holy ones?

Modern Christians may name "the Bible" as their chief or only authority, confident that what they know as the Bible is complete and consistent—no holy scriptures left out, no uninspired writings included. Early Christians did not have that luxury. They were still trying to decide which writings were authoritative enough to include in a Bible.

By the mid-second century, four gospels and ten letters of Paul were widely accepted as scripture; but some Christians added other books, including additional gospels, "acts" of various apostles and disciples, letters ascribed to Paul and other church leaders, and several "revelations." The first known list of writings that corresponds to a modern New Testament dates from 367, thirty years after the death of Constantine. Even after that, the status of several books, including Revelation and the Epistle to the Hebrews, was fiercely debated.

By the mid-fourth century, some major problems had been resolved. It was agreed that Christ was not merely the Son of God— he was God the Son, who had been incarnated in the man Jesus, and somehow he, his Father, and the Holy Spirit constituted a single god. But many knotty questions were still disputed. Most Christians fell into one of two main groups. One held that God the Son and God the Father were equal in every way, including eternal existence, without beginning or end. The other group believed that God the Father had existed alone before producing God the Son.

The fieriest champion of the "equal in every way" school was Athanasius, bishop of Alexandria. The leader of the other was the theologian Arius. It was the version of Athanasius that ultimately won. It became known as the "catholic" (literally, "universal") doctrine. Virtually every mainstream Christian denomination now states as a primary doctrine the belief in a Holy Trinity of Father, Son, and Holy Spirit, completely equal and co-eternal (although it has been suggested that most American Protestants actually believe something much closer to the teachings of Arius). Throughout the fourth century, however, the lead in this race for orthodoxy continually seesawed.

When a Catholic emperor ascended the throne, Arian bishops were deposed, often by force, and replaced with Catholics. Arian churches were confiscated for Catholic worship, and Arians became criminals under imperial law. When an Arian emperor came to power, the process was repeated in reverse.

The one exception was the emperor Julian, known as "the Apostate." He was brought up as an Arian Christian, but his studies of Greek philosophy led him to reject Christianity as a young man. For self-protection, he kept his convictions secret until he became emperor in 361.

Then he began dismantling the privileges that Christians and Christian institutions had accumulated. Knowing from experience that Christians' bitterest enemies were other Christians, he recalled exiled Catholics and other "heretics," and left the various Christian communities to sort out their differences without government help. He revived the traditional state religion, subsidizing official priesthoods and encouraging public sacrifices. His most specifically anti-Christian act was to deny Christians the right to teach in public schools, declaring them unqualified because they rejected the myths that were the basis of Greek and Latin literature.

No one knows whether this pagan restoration could have reversed the tide that Constantine had set in motion. Julian reigned only two years before his death in battle against the Persians. His successors returned to the policy of supporting Christianity and repressing all other religious activity.

In 380 the emperor Theodosius I defined Catholic Christianity as the official religion of the Empire. All other schools of Christian thought were outlawed as "heretical dogmas." Heretics were forbidden to build churches or hold worship services. They were subject to fines, beatings, or exile. Their books were burned. Any official who allowed them to practice their religion could be fined one hundred pounds of gold. Such laws were repeated over and over— between 378 and 394, at least fourteen times.

A new precedent was set in 385 by the trial of several heretics—the first time a secular court had convicted Roman citizens on religious grounds. Priscillian, the controversial bishop of Avila in what is now northwest Spain, had attracted many followers to his ascetic lifestyle and unconventional worship practices. He and some of his prominent supporters, arraigned on a charge of sorcery, were convicted and executed. Even some bishops objected to this use of state power to enforce church discipline, but the precedent had been set. It would soon be endorsed by the church itself.

Aurelius Augustinus, better known today as St. Augustine, was one of the most brilliant Christian thinkers of all time. His autobiographical *Confessions* show him as an appealing character—human, sincere, and warm. He has also been called "the prince of the persecutors"—a title he earned by providing the first reasoned justification for invoking the power of the state against dissident Christians. North Africa had suffered heavily during the Great Persecution from 303 to 311 (see chapter 7). As elsewhere, many clergy had handed over their copies of Christian writings to government agents. When the persecution was over, these "collaborators" often hoped to return to their former positions in the church. But more puritanical Christians were outraged. How could a priest who had betrayed his church possibly serve as a minister of God? In the early fourth century these puritans, called Donatists, broke away from the Catholic hierarchy and formed their own church.

A century later, North African Christianity was still split, with Donatists probably outnumbering Catholics. As a leading African Catholic bishop, Augustine wrote, preached, debated, and organized councils in his efforts to convince Donatists that they were wrong—without success.

Faced with antagonists as devout and uncompromising as himself, Augustine appealed to force. He reasoned that Donatists, in spite of their generally orthodox religious beliefs, were heretics, because they refused to obey the Catholic authorities. If they were forced into the Catholic Church against their wills, they might sooner or later accept it and be saved—while if they remained Donatists, they would certainly be damned. Therefore, government persecution and forced conversions were desirable.

This was the rationale, for centuries to come, that church authorities used to justify calling on governments to support church rulings with secular force. The finest fruit of that doctrine would be the Inquisition.

SOURCES AND FURTHER READING

This period is rich in contemporary sources, most but not all of them heavily biased toward an orthodox Christian viewpoint. Among the most important is the *Life of Constantine* by Eusebius, of which the most recent English translation is by Averil Cameron and Stuart G. Hall (Oxford: Oxford University Press, 1999). The *Theodosian Code* contains many of the laws referred to here. The *Ecclesiastical History* of Socrates Scholasticus, book 7, chapter 15, gives the best account of the death of Hypatia. There is an English translation by A. C. Zenos in *A Select Library of Nicene and Post-Nicene Fathers of the Christian Church*, second series, volume 2 (Grand Rapids, MI: Eerdmans, 1957). This series also contains many other relevant writings from the period, as does the more modern translation series *The Fathers of the Church* (Washington, DC: Catholic University of America Press, 1947–).

For the viewpoint of educated pagans, important works are available as volumes of the Loeb Classical Library, with original text and English translation on facing pages. These include the *History* of Ammianus Marcellinus, whose books 23–25 give an admiring portrait of the emperor Julian; Julian's own surviving writings; and orations and letters of the orator and teacher Libanius. A convenient collection of readings from Christian and pagan sources is Brian Croke and Jill Harries' *Religious Conflict in Fourth-Century Rome: A Documentary Study* (Sydney: Sydney University Press, 1982). Eberhard Sauer's *The Archaeology of Religious Hatred in the Roman and Early Medieval World* (Charleston, SC: Tempus, 2003) examines the archaeological evidence.

Among modern books, an excellent survey is *Christianity and Paganism in the Fourth to Eighth Centuries* by Ramsay MacMullen (New Haven, CT: Yale University Press, 1997). More specialized works include W. H. C. Frend's *The Donatist Church: A Movement of Protest in Roman North Africa* (Oxford: Clarendon, 1971) and James Everett Seaver's *Persecution of the Jews in the Roman Empire (300–428)* (Lawrence: University of Kansas Publications, 1952).

Chapter 10

The Germanic Kingdoms
Fifth through Eighth Centuries

When the fifth century began, most of Europe and North Africa was ruled—at least in theory—by the Western Roman Emperor from his capital of Ravenna in northern Italy. By the end of the century, there was no emperor in the West. The king of the Ostrogoths ruled Italy from Ravenna; the kings of the Franks, the Visigoths, the Alans, the Burgundians, the Suevi, and others quarrelsomely shared the rest of what had been Roman Europe; and the king of the Vandals held all North Africa west of Egypt.

There had been no epic conquest. For the most part, these were the same peoples who had lived on the outskirts of the Roman Empire for centuries. They had traded with the Empire, fought the Empire, enlisted in the Empire's armies—and when the Empire weakened, they had settled within its boundaries as army auxiliaries, refugees, or squatters. Before long, they carved out independent states in Roman territory. When the last Western Emperor was gently deposed by one of them in 476, most Romans hardly noticed the change.

Most of these encroaching groups were already Christians when they entered the Empire. Unluckily for them, the version of Christianity that had reached them first was Arianism—the losing side in the great theological struggle of the fourth century (see chapter 9). Wherever they settled in the Empire, Romans saw them as both barbarians and heretics.

The majority of these groups spoke Germanic languages. The first Germanic group to be formally recognized as a sovereign state were the Vandals. Under a shrewd and capable king, Geiseric, they assembled a fleet and crossed the Strait of Gibraltar into North Africa. There they conquered the Roman provinces of Africa Proconsularis, Tripolitana, Byzacena, and part of Numidia, set up a kingdom, and sealed a treaty with the Roman government.

North Africa had long been one of the most thoroughly Christian parts of the Western Roman Empire. In the years before the Vandal conquest, it had been torn by the controversy between Catholics and Donatists (see chapter 9). To the Arian Vandals, both were heretical sects. Vandal forces confiscated cathedral churches and sent many African clergy into exile. Worse, Geiseric refused to allow the installation of new Catholic or Donatist bishops—and only bishops could ordain new priests and deacons. By attrition, the non-Arian churches were slowly running out of clergy.

The Vandals had simply taken over the Roman administration of the provinces and their thriving cities, including Carthage. Although many Roman officials and civil servants had fled or died in the bloody conquest, many others remained and kept their jobs. Geiseric was happy to use the administrative skills and political knowledge of educated Africans, whatever their religion might be. More than a few Catholics held high positions in the government and the royal household. From time to time, however, the king might invite them to accept the Arian faith—and if they refused, they might be demoted, flogged, or tortured.

At the same time, Geiseric was extending his power at Roman expense. The Vandal fleet harried the islands that lay between Africa and Europe, conquering Sardinia, Corsica, the Balearics, and part of Sicily. According to one report, Geiseric tried to coerce Sicilian Catholics to become Arians, and executed those who refused.

Geiseric's greatest military feat came in 455. The Western

emperor Valentinian III had just been assassinated, and Rome was in turmoil. Geiseric took advantage of the confusion to attack southern Italy and pillage the city of Rome itself. Content with this spectacular show of force, he retired with his booty—including Valentinian's widow and two daughters, one of whom was already betrothed to his son Huneric. By the time Geiseric died in 477, Huneric's Roman princess had married him, left him, and retired to Jerusalem, where she spent the rest of her life, apparently still a Catholic.

Soon after Huneric succeeded his father as king, he received a letter jointly signed by the Eastern emperor Zeno and Placidia, widow of the Western emperor Olybrius. They asked him to allow the appointment of a Catholic bishop for Carthage. Huneric agreed—but only on condition that Arian bishops could freely practice their religion in the Eastern Roman Empire.

Hard-line Catholics in Africa denounced this agreement. They would rather have no bishop themselves than allow Arians to worship freely somewhere else. But ordinary Catholics in Carthage were ecstatic. Their great cathedral had closed for lack of clergy, and they wanted it back. The agreement was sealed, the bishop was appointed, and the cathedral of Carthage reopened. Catholic relations with the Vandal king had never been better.

Manichaeans were not so favored. Huneric—more pious and less patient than his father—cracked down on Manichaeans, starting with those who practiced their religion openly. That led on to a purge of Arian churches, where a number of real or suspected Manichaeans were uncovered, some of them even deacons or priests. Those convicted of Manichaeism could be burned alive. The lucky ones were merely exiled.

Huneric might allow Catholic services for Romans, but he wanted to protect his Vandals from Catholic teachings. When he heard that men and women in Vandal dress had been seen entering the Catholic cathedral in Carthage, he stationed soldiers on the cathedral steps to arrest them. It was useless for the bishop to protest that all were welcome in the house of God, and that the people who looked like Vandals were really Romans and lifelong Catholics, wearing Vandal clothes simply because they worked in the royal household.

It seems likely that the Catholic cathedral services had attracted some genuine Vandals, since the king meted out severe punishments to some of the churchgoers. Some were publicly whipped, others sent to the countryside to do field labor. To prevent any further lapses, he decreed that the government bureaus and the royal household would employ only Arians. Thus many people were faced with the choice of converting to Arian Christianity or losing their jobs.

African Catholics later counted this as the beginning of a sustained persecution, and so it was. But for some time Huneric moved cautiously, to avoid retaliation against Arians in the Roman Empire. With a series of decrees and executive actions, he harassed Catholic clergy and monastics. Nuns were accused of sexual immorality and subjected to humiliating medical examinations. Some of them were tortured to make them confess to sleeping with bishops and other clerics. Priests and deacons were accused of trespassing on Vandal property and trying to convert Arian Vandals to Catholicism.

Victor, the bishop of Vita in what is now northern Tunisia, wrote a contemporary account of the Vandal persecutions. By his count, 4,966 Catholics, including priests and deacons, were literally herded into exile in the Moorish territories south of the Vandal kingdom. Guards with whips drove the procession forward in a crowded mass—soon stinking of urine and feces, since the guards did not allow comfort stops. At their destination in the wilderness, the exiles were apparently turned loose to fend for themselves.

In February 484 Huneric summoned all the Catholic bishops of his kingdom to Carthage, to debate with Arian bishops. The Catholics assembled reluctantly. Their worst fears were realized when they learned that the judge of the debate was to be the patriarch of the Arian Vandal church. The "debate" broke down in shouting, and—to no one's surprise—the judge declared the Catholic doctrine heretical.

Huneric now had what he wanted—an official declaration that Catholics were heretics. He adapted the Roman laws against heresy and added new ones of his own. Catholics in the Vandal kingdom were now subject to all the penalties that had been enacted against Arians in the Roman Empire, and Huneric applied them ferociously.

All Catholic churches were officially closed, their property confiscated by the government. Clergy were executed, exiled, or enslaved. Recalcitrant Catholics were tortured, sometimes to death. Relief did not come even with Huneric's death later in 484. His nephew and successor Gunthamund continued the persecution, but gradually relaxed its severity.

The next king, Gunthamund's brother Thrasamund (reigned 496–523), adopted a less violent policy. Instead of using torture and execution to coerce conversions to Arianism, he rewarded converts with gifts and official positions. But he did continue the practice of closing Catholic churches and exiling Catholic bishops.

In 523 the new king, Hilderic, finally ended the persecution. For a little while, the Vandal kingdom was one of the safest for dissident Christians of any variety. Catholic churches were reopened and Catholic property restored, and many Catholics returned from exile.

Ten years later, there was no more Vandal kingdom. The Eastern emperor Justinian had sent his general Belisarius to reconquer the former Roman territories of the West. In 533 the Vandal forces crumbled before the imperial army. A new Eastern Roman (Byzantine) administration was set up in North Africa, and Roman law replaced Vandal law. Arian Christians were heretics again. So were the Donatists who had managed to survive a century of persecution and had rejoiced in the tolerant atmosphere of Hilderic's reign. At first, Catholics welcomed the Byzantine conquest. They would soon learn that the Eastern and Western churches had been moving in different directions.

Meanwhile, in Italy, the Western Roman government had been replaced by another Germanic kingdom. Theodoric, king of the Ostrogoths, had brought his branch of the Gothic people to Italy in 488 with a commission from the Eastern emperor Zeno—to get rid of the barbarian coalition that had deposed the last Western emperor in 476. Theodoric succeeded very effectively, and set up his own kingdom in Italy, with a nominal allegiance to the Eastern Empire.

Theodoric and his Ostrogoths were Arian Christians; but he had spent much of his boyhood at the imperial court in Constantinople. There he had received a Greek education and learned the art of getting along with other kinds of Christians. Freedom of worship was a mainstay of his domestic policy. There might be unfriendly feelings between Goths and Romans, between Arians and Catholics, but the law protected all. Probably unintended beneficiaries of this tolerance were all the other kinds of Christians and non-Christians in Theodoric's kingdom.

Theodoric died in 526. His daughter Amalasuintha continued his policies, but many of the Gothic nobles opposed her, and she was murdered in 535. Belisarius had just conquered the Vandals in North Africa, and Justinian took the opportunity to send him with an army to Italy. The emperor was determined to bring the homeland of the Roman Empire back to Roman rule.

But Italy was not the easy conquest that the Vandal kingdom had been. A destructive war dragged on for almost twenty years. The city of Rome was captured and recaptured, and almost every part of Italy was fought over. Local economies and local administrations were devastated. In the end, Justinian had his wish: Italy was declared a Roman province, with its capital at Ravenna. It took Italy centuries to recover.

In practice, Ravenna did not control very much. Still another Germanic tribe, the Lombards, had set up their kingdom in northern Italy. Rome and the region around it were chiefly controlled by the pope, as the bishop of Rome was now called. Farther south, Italy broke into local duchies that tended to ignore orders from Ravenna. In the seventh century, the Lombards succeeded in taking over a number of these duchies, isolating Ravenna still more.

When they entered Italy in the late sixth century, most Lombards still followed their tribal religion. But Christianity was the key to acceptance as a civilized people. Kings and their immediate followers allowed themselves to be baptized, and more and more subjects imitated the leaders. At first, kings changed easily from Arian to Catholic and back again as politics and war suggested. But in the seventh century, under the joint influence of Rome and Ravenna, Catholicism won out. King Aripert I (reigned 653–661) outlawed Arianism.

In northern Europe, continual wars and shifting alliances bound the new Germanic kingdoms in an ever-changing net. Religious differences played an important part. The Franks were pagans when they entered the Roman Empire, but around the year 500 King Chlodovech (better known as Clovis) converted to Catholic Christianity. Catholicism gave Clovis the support of the pope and of the Gallo-Roman churches already within his territory. The Franks became known as the only Catholic nation among the new kingdoms.

Starting with Clovis and his queen Clotilda, Frankish kings and queens supported the Catholic Church enthusiastically, and most

Frankish nobles followed suit. Ordinary Franks were less willing to give up their ancestral habits of worship. The Roman provinces of Gaul and Germania, where the Franks settled, had never been more than half Christian. There was a well-established church organization and a widespread network of Christian communities, but much of the rural population was either openly pagan or only nominally Christian. The church hierarchy embraced the newly converted Frankish rulers, and quickly persuaded them to use their power in the fight against paganism.

Kings and queens encouraged and subsidized the founding of monasteries, which became centers of missionary activity. Rulers and clergy alike urged landowners to correct their pagan tenants, by force if necessary, and to destroy pagan shrines and sacred trees. Royal decrees backed up this advice. Thus Childebert I, whose reign stretched from 511 to 558, ordered the destruction of "idols dedicated to demons" and prescribed one hundred lashes for peasants caught worshipping them. King Dagobert I (reigned 623–639) decreed that pagans who did not voluntarily convert could be forced to accept baptism.

The result was often a hybrid form of religion. People learned not to make offerings and prayers to demons; instead, they made them to Christian saints. Church authorities recognized that much of their flock's devotions amounted to baptized paganism. A church council at Auxerre in the late sixth century declared, "It is forbidden to make offerings or keep vigils of the saints' festivals in private houses, or to discharge vows in woods or at sacred trees or at springs."

Although Frankish rulers had little tolerance for pagans, they were more accepting of Jews—perhaps because they found Jewish merchants and scholars useful. Indeed, the early Frankish kings relaxed much of the anti-Jewish legislation of the Romans. Jewish courts were allowed jurisdiction not only over Jews but in any case covered by Roman law if all parties preferred the Jewish court.

The Arian kingdoms—Burgundians, Visigoths, Ostrogoths, and others—were just as enthusiastic about their own faith. Sooner or later, however, Arian Christian rulers felt the advantage that the Franks had acquired by joining forces with the Catholic Church. In 589 the Visigothic king Reccared converted to Catholicism and ordered all his Arian Christian subjects to do the same. Other Arian kingdoms followed similar patterns. By the end of the eighth century, Arianism had been well rooted out of western Europe—a feat the Christian Roman Empire had never achieved.

Meanwhile, both Catholic and Arian rulers tried ceaselessly to suppress paganism. Traditional pre-Christian religion was driven underground. In both legal and popular opinion, it fused with magic. A sixth-century law in Visigothic Spain lumped together "magicians and invokers of tempests" with "those who disturb people's minds by the invocation of demons or celebrate nocturnal sacrifices to devils." Such evildoers were to be publicly whipped with two hundred lashes, then scalped, then dragged through ten villages, and finally—if they were still alive—thrown into prison. People who consulted them got off with two hundred lashes.

In seventh-century Lombard Italy, traditional worshippers were luckier. A person who "worships at a tree which the rustics call holy or at springs, or performs sacrilege or incantation" was merely fined and compelled to do Christian penance.

The Visigothic territories of southern Gaul and Spain were home to many prosperous Jewish communities dating from Roman times. The Arian kings of the Visigoths had been generally tolerant of their Jewish subjects. They kept the repressive Roman laws limiting Jewish rights, but seldom enforced them. Reccared and his immediate successors protected Jews against the anti-Jewish decrees of local church councils and pressure from the pope to enforce anti-Jewish laws.

In 612 a new Visigothic king, Sisebut, broke with this tolerant policy. He gave the Jews of his kingdom some four months to free all their Christian slaves, restored the death penalty for converting Christians to Judaism, and forbade Jews to hold government positions. In many places local authorities were reluctant to enforce these decrees, prompting Sisebut to announce that all Jews must convert to Christianity or leave the country. An unknown number of Jews, including some prominent leaders, submitted to baptism. Others went into voluntary exile rather than give up their religion.

Sisebut's ruling was never completely enforced. For the following century, until the end of the Visigothic kingdom in 711, royal policy toward Jews alternated between support and suppression. Almost every king reversed his predecessor's policy. Jews went on living in Visigothic territory, doing business, practicing their religion, and even holding official positions and accepting Christian converts—but they lived under certain legal disabilities and suffered periodic bursts of renewed persecution.

If every law and every decree of church councils had been enforced, there would have been no Jews at all in the Visigothic kingdom. At various times, Jews were forbidden to keep the Sabbath or Jewish holidays, own or study anti-Christian books, or practice circumcision or Jewish dietary rules. In fact, Jews were forbidden to "avoid baptism," and Jewish children were to be taken from their parents and brought up as Christians. Christians who converted to Judaism were subject to especially horrendous penalties. In the mid-seventh century, the royal Visigothic law code insisted that any Christian found guilty of practicing circumcision "or any other Jewish rite" should be tortured to death "under the most ingenious and excruciating tortures that can be inflicted." It was the best incentive the lawmakers could devise.

SOURCES AND FURTHER READING

Victor of Vita's vivid *History of the Vandal Persecution* is available in an English translation by John Moorhead (Liverpool: Liverpool University Press, 1992). The basic source for the history of the Frankish kingdom is the contemporary *Histories* of Gregory of Tours, translated by Lewis Thorpe as *History of the Franks* (Harmondsworth, UK, and Baltimore: Penguin, 1974). Several of the Germanic kingdoms issued their law codes in Latin. Examples of laws relating to religion are found in *Christianity and Paganism, 350–750: The Conversion of Western Europe* (Philadelphia: University of Pennsylvania Press, 1986), edited by J. N. Hillgarth, a collection of representative documents in English translation, including laws, church rulings, sermons, letters, and biographical accounts, many of which touch on aspects of persecution in this period.

Useful modern works include *Before France and Germany: The Creation and Transformation of the Merovingian World* by Patrick J. Geary (New York: Oxford University Press, 1988) and *The Coming of Christianity to Anglo-Saxon England* by Henry Mayr-Harting, third edition (University Park: Pennsylvania State University Press, 1991).

Chapter 11

Byzantine Empire

Sixth through Tenth Centuries

There had been a riot in Antioch, one of the Byzantine Empire's most important cities. Excited Christians had accused their bishop of pagan sympathies and taken the law into their own hands. They had burned the bishop alive. The emperor Tiberius II (reigned 578–582) had sent troops to quell the disturbance. Now he had to quell charges that he was soft on paganism.

Tiberius summoned Constantinople's senate and all the Empire's highest officials to the imperial palace. All day, they listened while secretaries read aloud the current administration's record on protecting and fostering the true faith. It was impressive. Under Tiberius, local officials, army commanders, and imperial agents had repressed not only suspected pagans but also all kinds of non-Christians and deviant Christians.

At Baalbek (also known as Heliopolis), a still largely pagan city in Phoenicia, Tiberius had empowered his officer Theophilus to punish the pagans as they deserved. (Theophilus had already proved his merit by the savage way he had put down a revolt of Jews and

Samaritans.) Pagans condemned to beheading could consider themselves lucky.

Constantine, the first Christian emperor, had abolished crucifixion. The resemblance to the death of Jesus was too close for comfort. But in the more than two centuries since Constantine, crucifixion had slipped back into the list of legal penalties, and new ones had been added. Blinding and mutilation were routine. Since Christian judges were reluctant to condemn anyone to death without a confession of guilt, people charged with capital crimes were often simply tortured until they confessed or died.

Theophilus applied all legal measures, including crucifixion for those guilty of worshipping the wrong deities. Results at Heliopolis were so successful that he broadened his inquiries to other cities. A pagan high priest at Antioch committed suicide rather than submit to judgment by Theophilus. Informers denounced suspected pagans, including some highly placed individuals—even Anatolius, vice-prefect and governor of the province.

A governor was too big a bite for Theophilus to chew. He could do nothing worse than arrest Anatolius and one of his aides and send them to Constantinople. There the governor was stripped of his offices, tortured, and thrown to wild beasts. Since he survived all that—though his aide had died under torture—the emperor had him crucified.

Many people who had openly worshipped the old gods and goddesses were willing to accept Christianity when the alternative was torture and execution. Unfortunately, that kind of conversion gave suspicious Christians the grounds they needed to look for closet pagans among churchgoers, and even among the clergy.

The bishop of Antioch had adopted a "live and let live" attitude toward the pagans in his city. Some of his parishioners felt that such a nonaggressive policy could only be a cover for secret paganism, or at least a sign of far too much sympathy with pagans. They denounced the bishop to Theophilus—and when he seemed too slow in acting, they collected a mob, seized the bishop, built a fire, and threw him into it. This was the bit of overenthusiasm that had prompted the emperor Tiberius to declare a cease-fire in the war on paganism.

It was only a brief truce in a long campaign. Some fifty years earlier, the emperor Justinian had already made the suppression of non-Christians one of his priorities. Early in his reign, from 527 to 531, Justinian produced a series of laws against pagans and heretics. He affirmed all previous anti-pagan legislation and instituted a search for wealthy pagans. He confiscated their property, executed several prominent individuals, and decreed that no pagan could hold public office.

At the same time he gave Christian heretics a three-month grace period. If they had not embraced the orthodox faith by the end of the three months, they were to be exiled. Orthodox Christians who had lapsed into heresy were liable to the death penalty. So were Manichaeans. Threatened by Justinian's persecution, heretics in some towns locked themselves in their churches and set fire to the buildings.

On the far edge of the Empire, at Philae on the southern border of Egypt, a famous temple dedicated to Isis was a center of pagan pilgrimage. There was even a treaty with the African nation of the Blemmyes that guaranteed them the right to worship there every year. Justinian disregarded the treaty and closed the temple in 537. The priests of Isis were arrested, the cult statues and all the temple treasures confiscated, the carved and painted images defaced, and the temple transformed into a church dedicated to St. Stephen. In Libya, Justinian closed at least two temples of Ammon.

Although pagan worship had been illegal for more than a century, pagan philosophy was thriving. Even Christian intellectuals sometimes studied at the Academy, the famous Platonic school at Athens. Neoplatonist thinkers went on producing books and lectures for eager students throughout the fifth century and into the sixth. Brawls between Christian and non-Christian students were common, and non-Christian professors were sometimes harassed, but the school continued to function—until Justinian closed it in 529. His laws forbade pagans to teach. Many of the professors fled to Persia, or to Carrhae (Harran), a city on the eastern Roman border that was still proud of its traditional religion and its intellectual level. Many students followed their teachers.

People in the Byzantine Empire never used the term "Byzantine"—
a purely modern label. In their opinion, they were Romans. Most of
the Western Empire had been replaced by Germanic kingdoms,
Greek had replaced Latin as the language of government in the East,
and church and state were so closely intertwined that it was impossible to think of one without the other. But the Empire was still the
Roman Empire, and it was perfectly natural for Justinian to reclaim
the lost territories in the West.

When Justinian's army conquered the Vandal kingdom in North
Africa, Catholics there were delighted (see chapter 10). They soon
learned, however, that Byzantine Christianity was often different
from their own. Bishops who refused to accept the emperor's edicts
on church doctrine were imprisoned or exiled. Because many Jews
had resisted the Byzantine conquest, Justinian ordered all North
African synagogues confiscated. Heretics were ruthlessly suppressed.

Shortly before he ascended the throne, Justinian had engineered
a change in the law to allow him to marry a well-known (not to say
notorious) actress, some twenty years younger than he. The scandal
was juicy. But Justinian himself had come from a lower-class background, and he knew how to recognize merit. Theodora proved to
be a magnificent empress—intelligent, practical, and courageous.
Her advice and encouragement pulled the emperor through some
difficult crises. But they had one perennial disagreement.

The orthodox Justinian accepted the Council of Chalcedon's
decision that Christ had two complete and distinct natures, united
in a single person. To many people, including Theodora, that
sounded like an impossibly split personality. Instead, they felt that
Christ's divine nature had completely absorbed his human nature.
Their position, called Monophysitism ("single-nature-ism") had a
wide appeal.

Theodora used all her power and influence to support the Monophysite cause. When Justinian decided to finance a major missionary
effort to the pagan areas of rural Asia Minor, he accepted Theodora's
choice for the missionary—the Monophysite John of Ephesus. Over
the course of some twenty years, John and his staff of deacons claimed
to have founded ninety-two churches and ten monasteries, and baptized more than seventy thousand new Christians. Besides any spiritual rewards they might expect, each convert received a substantial

cash bonus. The missionaries also demolished temples, smashed idols and altars, and cut down sacred trees. If they could destroy the pagan infrastructure, people would have nowhere to turn for religious consolation and help except the Christian church.

Ironically, in 564 Justinian himself accepted one of the most extreme offshoots of Monophysitism—the doctrine that Christ's body was divine and therefore incorruptible. The old emperor issued a decree approving that doctrine, and was apparently ready to declare anyone who disagreed a heretic. Perhaps fortunately, he died the next year, and the decree lapsed.

After Justinian's long reign (527–565), pressure against the old religions eased for a time—but not for long. Tiberius II came to the throne in 578, and quickly reinvigorated the war on paganism. The pause in persecution that followed the murder of the bishop of Antioch was brief. Soon after the interminable reading of reports at the imperial palace, active persecution began again. When Tiberius died in 582, his anti-pagan policy was continued by his successor, Maurice, who reigned until 602.

It was the last great anti-pagan campaign. From the seventh century on, the imperial government no longer considered paganism a serious threat. Heresy took priority—and there was no shortage of heresies. Christians obstinately persisted in thinking, and thinking produced differences of opinion. That was unacceptable.

An especially unacceptable opinion had turned up in Armenia. A group called the Paulicians, led by Constantine Silvanus, rejected the Old Testament and some of the New Testament. They revered the apostle Paul and modeled their church organization on his. But they accepted the Gnostic idea that the creator of the physical world was an evil god, while Jesus Christ was the Savior.

By 668 the movement had blossomed into revolt. Imperial troops were repeatedly sent to suppress the rebels and stamp out the heresy. Constantine Silvanus was arrested and stoned to death, and his successor was burned alive. Many other Paulicians were executed. Undeterred, a group of Paulicians set up their own government on the border of the Empire, strengthening their position by forming alliances with nearby Muslim emirs. They thrived until a Byzantine army destroyed their military power in 872. Surviving Paulicians sought refuge in Muslim territory, where their ideas may have contributed to the origins of the Bogomil heresy (see chapter 12).

The earliest Christians had inherited the Jewish disapproval of "graven images." How could there be a statue or painting of God? God was a spirit, with no bodily form. And besides, any physical image could tempt devout people into idolatry—worshipping a created thing instead of the Creator.

Yet there was another, opposing factor for Christians. The essence of their religion was that God had been embodied in Jesus. According to early Christian tradition, the resurrected Christ had told his doubting disciple Thomas to touch him, urging him to "put your hand in my wound." It would be hard to get more physical than that. Even the Holy Spirit, the most ethereal person of the Christian Trinity, was said to have appeared in the form of a dove. Jesus had been a real man. It was natural to want to know what he had looked like. The Old Testament objected to idols not because they were images, but because they were images of false gods. Since Christians worshipped the true God, they were never idolaters, even when they used images.

From at least the second century, Christians had been making and cherishing pictures and carvings of Jesus and his disciples, and other Christians had been condemning them for it. When Christianity "came out of the closet" in Constantine's reign, churches and church decoration proliferated. Many of the artists and handicrafters who had carved and painted and woven and molded Greco-Roman goddesses and gods for a living now produced Christian scenes and portraits. Although some bishops and a few regional church councils spoke out clearly either for or against religious images, for the most part the custom developed from the grass roots.

In western Europe, religious art was generally thought of as illustration. Images were simply artists' renderings of scenes from the Bible and church history, or imaginings of heaven and hell, to help believers visualize these things. In the Byzantine Empire, images had taken on mystical qualities. They had become icons.

An icon is not simply a picture. For a believer, it is the true representation of a holy personage. As such, it partakes of holiness, almost as if the personage were present in it. For Orthodox Christians in the early eighth century, having an icon of the Virgin Mary on the wall, or on the city gate, meant that the Virgin Mary herself was there, giving care and protection.

Protection was needed. It was a hard time for the Empire. The Arabs had burst out of Arabia in the seventh century, and had not stopped advancing (see chapter 12). They had already cut away most of the Empire, and now they threatened Constantinople itself. In 717–18, Constantinople weathered an Arab siege, in part thanks to a storm and a volcanic eruption that destroyed most of the Arab fleet. It was clear—at least to the emperor Leo III—that God had given the Empire a warning and a chance to repent. But repent of what? How had they angered God so much that he had let the infidel Arabs come within a hair of destroying the Christian Empire?

Leo suspected that the Empire had tolerated Jews too much. In 722 he ordered all Jews in the Empire to become Christians. Naturally enough, Jews failed to comply. Harried officials, already coping with the economic and social effects of war and natural disasters, apparently did not even try to enforce Leo's edict. (Ninety years before, the emperor Heraclius had issued a similar decree, with a similar lack of effect.)

Leo tried again. Perhaps the general level of public morality was too low. He enacted new laws against abortion and homosexuality. At the same time he tried to make the penal system more merciful by reducing the penalty for many crimes, from death to mutilation.

These measures were not enough. Another volcanic eruption alarmed Leo, and he began to suspect that there was something wrong with the way Byzantine Christians worshipped God. Islam, the new religion of the Arabs, was very strict in forbidding the use of religious images—and under the shield of Islam the Arabs seemed to be on their way to conquering the world. Perhaps it was time for Christians to learn from their enemies.

There was a prominent icon of Christ above one of Constantinople's gates. As an experiment, Leo had it removed—and touched off a riot. To most citizens, taking Christ's picture down meant taking Christ's protection away from the city. But Leo had found a number of bishops who agreed with him, and he persevered. He issued an edict against icons, though he made little effort to enforce it against a hostile populace. And his armies drove back the Arabs.

Encouraged, Leo persuaded a council of officials to endorse his policy in 730. Armed with this approval, he set about removing all public icons. The patriarch of Constantinople resigned in protest. Leo's army won another victory.

The iconoclastic controversy would trouble the Byzantine Empire throughout the next century. Leo's son Constantine V finally began a real persecution of "image-worshippers" in the 760s. He required bishops and officials to take an oath swearing that they would not venerate icons. Since icons were especially popular among monks and nuns, he closed many monasteries, confiscated their property, and burned their books.

To the iconoclasts (the "image-breakers"), Christians who venerated icons were either pagans or heretics. Iconoclasts reasoned that since a portrait of Christ could only show his physical body, it completely misrepresented him and could only mislead beholders. In the same way, pictures of saints could not show saintliness. The true image of Christ, or of a saint, was a virtuous life. The cross, the Eucharist, and the church building were the only acceptable symbols.

Most Orthodox Christians did venerate icons. As they saw it, iconoclasts clung to a Jewish superstition and rejected the true Christian experience. It was not only foolish to claim there could be no physical image of the divine, it was heretical.

For more than a hundred years, icons were alternately set up and taken down, depending on the beliefs of the ruler. Religious paintings and mosaics were scraped off church walls or covered with whitewash. Both sides managed to convene church councils that endorsed their views and condemned their opponents. Clergy and laity alike were fined, whipped, exiled, imprisoned, tortured, or mutilated, and occasionally executed or forced to commit suicide. Monks and nuns were publicly humiliated and abused, and many monasteries were closed by iconoclast emperors.

In the end, the iconoclasts lost the struggle. Public icons were definitively restored by the emperor Michael III in 843. In the meantime, both the pope and the patriarch of Constantinople had declared iconoclasm a heresy. But the restoration of images did not mean religious freedom. Artists no longer had to worry about being imprisoned and tortured if they painted icons, but a church council in 870 ruled that painters could not work in churches unless they subscribed to a long list of church canons.

✿

Meanwhile, the Byzantine Empire expanded again, as the conquering Arab caliphate broke up into rival smaller states. In 934 the great Byzantine general John Curcuas conquered the Arab emirate of Melitene in east central Asia Minor. He gave the Muslim inhabitants a choice— either be baptized as Christians or be driven out of the country. That became a standard practice for Byzantine expansion to the east. Muslims who refused to convert were expelled, and Christians were brought in from neighboring territories to take over their vacated lands.

Byzantine armies faced not only Arab Muslims but also the newly Christianized Bulgars. Boris I, khan of Bulgaria (reigned 852–889), was a willing convert to Christianity. He intended to accept the Roman Catholic version, but political and military considerations led him to join the Eastern Orthodox Church instead. When he tried to force his nobles and the general populace to accept baptism, a pagan rebellion erupted. Boris succeeded in suppressing the revolt, and executed fifty-two nobles together with their families.

After that show of force, many Bulgarians accepted Christianity more or less voluntarily. Boris had also learned a lesson, and thereafter he relied more on nonviolent methods. He supported the efforts of missionaries and the building of churches and monasteries. But Bulgaria's Christianization did not go smoothly. The great Bulgarian heresy of the Bogomils may have been influenced by Paulician refugees from Byzantine persecution. In turn, it spread into the Byzantine Empire. Everywhere, Bogomils were outlawed, imprisoned, tortured, and sometimes executed.

Kievan Russia was the last major pagan state on the Empire's eastern frontier. In the late 980s the Byzantine emperor Basil II made peace with the Grand Duke Vladimir of Kiev on condition that Vladimir and his people accepted Christianity. As an incentive, Vladimir was allowed to marry the emperor's sister Anna—a major concession, since ordinarily Byzantine princesses did not marry "barbarians."

Vladimir agreed enthusiastically. His grandmother Olga had been a Christian, and his envoys were impressed by the splendor of Byzantine cathedrals. He informed his nobles and all his people that they were about to become Christians, and had them herded to a river for mass baptism. Any who refused were killed. His soldiers pulled down the statues of the ancient Slavic gods, mutilated and abused them, and "drowned" them in the river. Vladimir is still revered as a saint in the Russian Orthodox Church.

SOURCES AND FURTHER READING

Principal sources for Justinian and his wars are the works of Procopius, available in the Loeb Classical Library edition. A number of contemporary sources on the iconoclast controversy have been translated into English, including *Icon and Logos: Sources in Eighth-century Iconoclasm: An Annotated Translation of the Sixth Session of the Seventh Ecumenical Council (Nicea, 787)* by Daniel J. Sahas (Toronto: University of Toronto Press, 1986); *The Letter of the Three Patriarchs to Emperor Theophilus and Related Texts*, translated and edited by J. A. Munitiz et al. (Camberley, UK: Porphyrogenitus, 1997); and *Three Treatises on the Divine Images* by St. John of Damascus, translated by Andrew Louth (Crestwood, NY: St. Vladimir's Seminary Press, 2003). Sources on the Paulicians, Bogomils, and other heresies are usefully sampled in *Christian Dualist Heresies in the Byzantine World, c. 650–c. 1450: Selected Sources*, translated and annotated by Janet Hamilton and Bernard Hamilton (Manchester: Manchester University Press, 1998).

The standard work on early Monophysites is W. H. C. Frend's *The Rise of the Monophysite Movement: Chapters in the History of the Church in the Fifth and Sixth Centuries* (Cambridge: Cambridge University Press, 1972). For the Paulicians, there is *Paulician Heresy. A Study of the Origin and Development of Paulicianism in Armenia and the Eastern Provinces of the Byzantine Empire* by Nina G. Garsoïan (The Hague: Mouton, 1967). Though it is misleading to single out a few among the many good modern works on the Byzantine Empire, a good place to begin is with J. A. S. Evans's *The Age of Justinian: The Circumstances of Imperial Power* (London: Routledge, 1996). Charles Barber's *Figure and Likeness: On the Limits of Representation in Byzantine Iconoclasm* (Princeton, NJ: Princeton University Press, 2002) examines the relationship of theology and art in the iconoclast controversy. J. M. Hussey's *The Orthodox Church in the Byzantine Empire* (Oxford: Clarendon, 1986) is a good overview.

Chapter 12

Islamic Empire

Seventh through Fifteenth Centuries

Around the little building, men strode triumphant through the debris of gods. Inside, others were sweeping out more broken deities. This ancient shrine had housed and been surrounded by the images and symbols of hundreds of gods and goddesses—three hundred and sixty, by some counts. People had come here from all over Arabia to worship every year. Here now lay the shattered remains of the warrior god Hubal, here the goddesses al-Uzza and Manat. This mutilated fragment was all that was left of a divinity so sacred that she was known simply as "the Goddess"—in Arabic, Allat. All these had forfeited their powers to "the God"—Allah.

Along the coasts of the Red Sea and the Persian Gulf, and in the north where the Arabian Peninsula merges into the Syrian desert, there were kingdoms and city-states. Elsewhere in Arabia, there were no governments as such. The desert clans managed their own affairs. They lived from their flocks and herds, from trade, and from raiding each other and the more settled communities on their outskirts. Scattered through the peninsula were shrines where sacred stones and simple images manifested the divine powers.

Such shrines were meeting places where rival clans could come together in peace at certain times of the year. There they paid their respects to local deities, and traded with each other and with the resident merchants. The most famous of these shrines was the Kaaba in western Arabia. The city of Mecca grew up around it. Each year pilgrims from all over Arabia worshipped and conducted business there. As Mecca's fame grew, more and more images were set up in the Kaaba. But the greatest attraction was a black stone, said to have fallen from the sky. To touch it brought good luck.

Around the end of the sixth century, a young Meccan married a wealthy widow and launched a successful career as her business manager. He belonged to a branch of the holy clan in charge of the Kaaba and its pilgrimage, and he could look forward to respect and prosperity. Then, in the opinion of most Meccans, he went wrong. He began to tell his wife and relatives that he was receiving revelations from a divine power. Within a few years he created a new religion that he called "Submission" (*Islam*) and attracted dozens of converts.

That might have been harmless—perhaps even good for Mecca—except that he claimed the gods and goddesses of the Kaaba were evil demons. Such an idea was not only impious, it was bad for business. Muhammad and his flock were hounded out of Mecca.

Luckily they had a place to go. The oasis town of Yathrib—later known as Medina—had invited Muhammad to act as arbiter among their quarreling clans. With some seventy followers, Muhammad made the move in 622 CE—a date that would be commemorated as Year One of the Muslim era.

Three of the clans at Medina were Jewish. A good deal of Jewish and Christian religious tradition had found its way into Arab thought and culture. In Muhammad's opinion, his own revelation completed what Abraham and Moses had begun. He had hoped for an enthusiastic acceptance from Jews and Christians, but they had disappointed him. Now the Jewish clans in Medina opposed his authority as arbiter.

When a brawl between Jews and Muslims left one dead on each side, Muhammad decreed death for a whole Jewish clan. Other Medinans protested, and the sentence was reduced to banishment. The entire clan was forced to abandon their homes and leave the city with only what they could carry. Their houses and fields were distributed to Muslims. Not long after, Muhammad accused another Jewish clan of plotting against him, and forced them too out of Medina.

During the next few years, Muhammad turned his attention back to Mecca. With no agriculture of its own, the city depended entirely on commerce for its survival. Besides trade with pilgrims, Meccans carried on a large-scale caravan trade across the desert. Muhammad's warriors harassed the caravans, and when the Meccans struck back, he won a series of victories. Mecca's business fell off rapidly.

In 627 a Meccan army attacked Medina, but withdrew after a short siege. Muhammad feared that if the Meccans tried again, the remaining Jews in Medina might support them. To forestall this internal threat, he attacked the Medinan Jews. When they surrendered, Muhammad appointed a Muslim judge to decide their fate. The judge ruled that all adult male Jews should be executed and the women and children sold into slavery. Again, Jewish property was distributed to Muslims.

Meanwhile, Muhammad was still receiving revelations from Allah, which gave his message a very immediate appeal. Many desert clans joined forces with him. Part of any alliance with Muhammad was an agreement to accept Islam unconditionally. The new Muslim community absorbed clans and settlements one after another, sometimes with the threat or exercise of armed force, sometimes without. Muhammad was clearly a winner, and many people were eager to join his side.

The Meccans were willing to negotiate. Their economy could not take much more abuse, and their allies were defecting. They agreed to a truce, and Muhammad won the right for Muslims to enter the holy city as pilgrims. Allah had revealed to him that the Kaaba had been built by Abraham and was still sacred, though now polluted with idols.

By 630, Muhammad had amassed an army that Mecca could not resist. When he advanced on the city, the Meccans capitulated in return for an amnesty. Muhammad and his disciples systematically purged the Kaaba, smashing one image after another. Only the sacred black stone was spared. Perhaps it could be safely kept because no one knew what, if anything, it represented—only that it was ancient and holy and extremely good luck to touch.

For some pagans, the destruction at the Kaaba showed that Muhammad's message was sound. The old deities could not stand against Allah. For others, it was sacrilege. Muhammad declared the Kaaba and its surrounding area off-limits to anyone who did not accept his religion. More than that, he and his people had not stopped smashing idols. Wherever they found shrines in outlying towns, villages, or countryside, they destroyed the images and did their best to make the shrines unusable. Although pagan clans resisted, Muhammad and his converts fought with supreme conviction. Within Muhammad's lifetime Arabian paganism was essentially destroyed in all the territory he controlled.

Like any other Arabian tribal leader, Muhammad ruled his people with the advice and consent of a group of his friends and relatives. The difference was that Muhammad was also the mouthpiece of God—not just a god, but the supreme and only God. Among believers, his authority could not be challenged. His counselors could still advise and suggest, but in the end they must always consent. Since there was no distinction between religion and government, God had the last word in every argument.

Muhammad had been ruthless to the Jews of Medina, but he later worked out a way to accommodate both Jews and Christians within his Islamic state. If they did not choose to be Muslims, they could be *dhimmi*—"protected people." Dhimmis paid special taxes that entitled them to the state's protection. In return, they were freed from military service and allowed to practice their own religion.

But dhimmis were not equal to Muslims under the law. They could repair existing churches and synagogues, but not build new ones. Their testimony was not valid against Muslims. Crimes against them, including murder and rape, were not punished as severely as crimes against Muslims. As Islamic law developed, dhimmis were often forbidden to own real estate. And the special tax they paid was explicitly designed to humiliate them.

By the time Muhammad died in 632, he had changed Arabia. The clans and areas that had accepted Islam were under his direct rule, while others were subordinate allies. Arabian paganism had all but disappeared. At his death, his counselors chose one of their own number to replace him as leader. Abu Bakr had been one of Muhammad's earliest supporters. He took the title of *caliph* ("successor" or "deputy"). The pattern for orderly and peaceful succession seemed to be set.

But Muhammad had forged his unified movement from a collection of proud and strong-willed individuals with their own family connections and ambitions. His commanding personality, his diplomatic and military skills, and the power and simplicity of his message had kept rivalries and cross-purposes from tearing the new Islamic community apart. After his death, those factors came to the fore.

Most Muslims look back on the first thirty years after Muhammad's death as a golden age—the time of the four "rightly-guided" caliphs. Nevertheless, Abu Bakr was the only one of the four who died of natural causes. During his short reign (632–634) he established two principles that would guide the development of Islam for centuries: First, that Muhammad was the final prophet, and there would be no new revelations. Second, that Muslims had a mission to bring Islam to the world—and the most direct way to bring it was by war.

Under Abu Bakr and his successor Umar, Muslim armies finished the pacification of the Arabian Peninsula and pushed out beyond its borders to conquer Syria, Iraq, and Egypt—until then, territories of the Byzantine Empire—and to begin the conquest of Iran. For the first time, Arab conquerors found themselves dealing with non-Arab populations and completely different languages. And in Iran they found a puzzlingly different native religion (see chapter 8).

Zoroastrians were not like Arabian pagans. Zoroastrians had no idols. They worshipped one supreme God. They even had scriptures and a revered prophet. After some uncertainty, the conquerors decided that Zoroastrians who declined to convert could be accepted as dhimmis. Nevertheless, Muslim rulers in Iran repeatedly took repressive measures. In the early eighth century the general Ubaidallah bin Abi Bakra put out sacred fires and confiscated temple treasures, reportedly to the amount of forty million silver dirhams. Many Zoroastrians fled the country. Some of them eventually arrived in India, where they became known as Parsis, "Persians."

Caliph Umar was killed in Medina by an Iranian slave, said to have been a Magian. The killer may have been trying to defend his ancestral religion against the Muslim takeover. Umar's successor was Uthman, another close associate of Muhammad. He is best known for collecting the separate bits of Muhammad's teachings that believers had written down. Gradually an authorized version of Muhammad's revelations was produced—the holy Qur'an. In 656 dissidents attacked and killed Uthman in his own house in Medina.

Ali, the next caliph, was both Muhammad's cousin and the husband of his daughter Fatima, but his position was insecure from the beginning. He left Medina to seek support in Iraq. There the first battle was fought between Muslims and other Muslims. Ali's forces won, but in 661 he was assassinated in a mosque by a member of a militant group. The golden age was over.

The next caliph was Ali's chief rival—Muawiya, who founded the Umayyad dynasty. Disputes continued. Ali's son Hussain was killed at the battle of Karbala, becoming a martyr in the eyes of Ali's partisans. In the next four centuries those partisans developed into a distinct branch of Islam, whose members are called Shiites.

Meanwhile the Umayyad dynasty continued the Arab/Muslim expansion. Their armies pressed farther into what had been the territory of the Persian Empire. The caliphs founded new cities to serve as military garrisons and centers of administration. From these bases, they sent expeditions deep into Central Asia and as far as what is now Pakistan. In the West, they pushed beyond Egypt, completing the conquest of North Africa and most of Spain. From there, they raided deep into France, until a raiding party was defeated at the battle of Poitiers in 732.

Muhammad had made the point that religious faith could not be coerced. No one could be a Muslim except by free choice. Nevertheless, the choices that Muslim conquerors offered their new subjects were stark. Become a Muslim, become a dhimmi (if you were eligible), leave the country, or die. There were many conversions.

The Islamic Empire had grown so rapidly that the Arab conquerors were spread very thin. In many places, they had taken over much of the administrative structure—and the personnel—of conquered territories. The Umayyad caliphs undertook a serious reorganization. Arabic became the language of government throughout the empire. Byzantine and Persian civil servants were replaced by

Arabs, and more Arabs were settled in the conquered lands. Most important, the Umayyads developed a war fleet, which enabled them to attack Constantinople—attacks that helped trigger the iconoclast controversy (see chapter 11).

The rapid expansion brought other problems. Many second- and third-generation dhimmis converted to Islam. Muhammad had taught that all Muslims were equal—yet Muslim society had always been essentially Arab. How could large numbers of non-Arabs be incorporated into it? And how to make up for the lost dhimmi taxes?

The Umayyad government compromised. Converted dhimmis were released from the poll tax, but still had to pay special property taxes. And, though theoretically equal, they were treated as second-class citizens in many ways. Their discontent made them potential allies for any rebel leader.

And there were rebels. As the momentum of conquest died away, internal discontents absorbed more and more of the conquerors' energy. The Byzantine emperor Leo III had stopped the Muslim offensive against Constantinople, and Muslim expansion in the west had reached its limit. Hostile Berbers in North Africa and advancing Turks in Central Asia tied down the frontier armies. In the interior, Arab clans still disputed for power and prestige. In 750 rebels defeated the last Umayyad caliph and proclaimed Abu al-Abbas as-Saffah first caliph of the Abbasid dynasty. Only one of the Umayyad family escaped to Spain, where he founded a new Umayyad dynasty at Cordova.

The Abbasids drew support from a variety of dissatisfied elements. Many religious Muslims felt that the worldly Umayyads had forgotten the real message of Islam. Non-Arab Muslims wanted equal rights. The Abbasid caliphs set out to base their law and government squarely on the Qur'an and the traditions handed down about Muhammad. At the same time, they adopted much of the culture of the former Persian Empire, employed many non-Arabs, and fostered learning and the arts. They founded a new capital, Baghdad. This is the Islamic culture that would be immortalized in *The Thousand and One Nights*.

But the Abbasid caliphs' power and glory was temporary. Beginning in the tenth century, the caliphs employed units of Turkish soldiers, bought as slaves when they were boys and raised for warfare.

They were highly effective fighters—too effective to control. The caliphs became puppets in their hands. The vast Islamic Empire crumbled into a collection of virtually independent states, although the caliph was recognized almost everywhere as the leader of Islam.

By this time the rift between the two great branches of Islam was clear and deep. Ali's partisans had become the Shiites. They believed that Ali should have been Muhammad's original successor, and thus they condemned the first three caliphs as usurpers. Because they held that only direct descendants of Ali and Fatima could be legitimate caliphs, they also rejected the Umayyad and Abbasid dynasties.

To the basic Muslim statement of faith—"There is no God but God, and Muhammad is God's Prophet"—Shiites added "Ali is God's Friend." They developed festivals of their own, and the tombs of Ali, Hussain, and other saints of Shiite tradition became their shrines. Most Shiites looked forward to the return of the "Twelfth Imam"—the rightful leader of Islam, hidden from humankind since 874 CE but still living. Henceforth, Muslims had to take a stand; they were either Sunni or Shiite.

Arab traders had reached the Indian subcontinent long before Muhammad's time. Much of the Indian Ocean trade was carried in Arab and Persian ships, and these merchants had permanent settlements on the west coast of India and especially in the Indus River valley in what is now Pakistan. With the spread of Islam, these trading centers served as gateways through which the new religion entered India. Some Indians were converted to Islam in this peaceful way, but large-scale conversion had to wait for armed conquest.

That was not long in coming. In 711 the Umayyad caliphate sent a small army under Muhammad bin Qasim, a remarkable seventeen-year-old general, to push Islam's authority farther east. He conquered much of what is now Afghanistan and the neighboring Indus valley and set up a Muslim regime. Islamic control expanded slowly at first, pushing east and south in a long series of raids and minor invasions by Turkish Muslim rulers. The next major wave of conquest began in the eleventh century, and for the next six hundred years a series of Muslim dynasties extended their power farther and farther. Indian rulers and officials were invited to accept Islam, and some of them did. By 1605 Afghanistan and virtually all of northern and central India had been consolidated into the Mughal Empire, ruled by Turkish Muslims.

In the process of conquest, Muslim armies had deliberately destroyed temples and often killed temple personnel. This systematic destruction reached its peak during the conquests of the eleventh through thirteenth centuries. The new rulers sometimes used stones from demolished temples to build mosques on the same sites. In other places, they merely removed statues of gods and goddesses, mutilated them, or polluted them with cow's flesh or excrement. Whole cartloads of idols were shipped to Baghdad as tribute to the caliph.

The city of Mathura had long been a religious center for Hindus, Buddhists, and Jains. It was reportedly home to a thousand temples and many thousands of sacred images. In 1018 Sultan Mahmud of Ghazna ordered the temples and images stripped of their gold, silver, and jewels, and the temples demolished and burned. The following year Mahmud took the city of Kanauj, a major religious center and the capital of the local dynasty. His soldiers slaughtered the people who had taken refuge in the thousands of temples, and destroyed the holy statues.

A colossal statue of Somnath, lord of the moon, stood on India's western seacoast. Hundreds of thousands of pilgrims came here, and a city had grown up beside the great temple. In 1025, Mahmud ordered the temple destroyed, the thousands of lesser images in gold and silver confiscated, and the main idol cut into pieces that were sent to Mecca, Medina, and his home city of Ghazna in Afghanistan. For the next four centuries, Hindus repeatedly rebuilt a lesser version of the temple, and Muslims repeatedly destroyed it.

But if Somnath could not stop the destruction, the sheer size and dense population of India could tame it. By Islamic standards, the Indians were clearly idolaters of the worst sort, but they far outnumbered the Muslim conquerors. If the new Islamic states wanted an adequate population to farm the land and do all the other necessary work, they needed mass conversions—or else a way of accommodating idolaters. As a matter of practical necessity, non-Muslim Indians were accepted as dhimmis, just as Zoroastrians had been.

And like the Zoroastrians in Iran, non-Muslim Indians found that they were only precariously tolerated within Muslim states. On the one hand, they were allowed to worship freely, to repair their temples and images, and even to construct new ones—most of the time. Some Muslim rulers even subsidized temples. On the other hand, all tolerance and support might be withdrawn at any moment. Devout Muslim rulers sometimes destroyed temples, broke up religious festivals, and executed priests. From time to time there were forced conversions to Islam. In the mid-fourteenth century, Firuz Shah, ruler of northern India, was said to have converted 180,000 slaves.

Even under Muslim domination, Hinduism remained a resilient tradition. So did Jainism, although many Jain temples were destroyed. Buddhism was more vulnerable. Buddhists had no clergy except for monks and nuns, and no centers except monasteries—some of which, like the huge library and school of Nalanda, had become virtual universities. Muslim conquerors routinely destroyed the monasteries, and Indian Buddhism never recovered from the blow. By the twelfth century, Buddhism had essentially withdrawn to other parts of Asia, where it played out a strangely varied history (see chapter 14).

SOURCES AND FURTHER READING

Like the Qur'an itself, Arabic sources for the early history of Islam were oral traditions that were written down several decades or more after the events. Very few have been translated into English. Contemporary non-Muslim sources—Christian, Jewish, and Zoroastrian—are collected and discussed in *Seeing Islam as Others Saw It* by Robert Hoyland (Princeton, NJ: Princeton University Press, 1997).

The great majority of books on Islam have been written either to attack it or defend it, and even authors who tried to be impartial have often been handicapped by their preconceptions. Hugh Kennedy's *The Prophet and the Age of the Caliphates: The Islamic Near East from the Sixth to the Eleventh Century*, second edition (Harlow, UK: Longman, 2004) is a valuable historical overview. Akbar Ahmed's *Discovering Islam: Making Sense of Muslim History and Society*, revised edition (London: Routledge, 2002) gives a moderate insider's view. André Wink's *Al-Hind: The Making of the Indo-Islamic World* (Boston: Brill, 2002) covers the Muslim conquest of India in three detailed volumes.

Chapter 13

Europe

Eleventh through Fifteenth Centuries

The city of Béziers was prepared for battle. Like other cities in the south of France, it was used to taking care of itself. These cities governed themselves and paid little heed to commands from bishops or feudal lords, let alone the far distant king of France to whom they theoretically owed allegiance. The citizens spoke Occitan, not French. In their opinion, Frenchmen were barbarous foreigners. Now they faced an army of French crusaders—soldiers who fervently believed that God would thank them for attacking fellow Christians.

The original Crusades had begun as an attempt to reclaim some of the once-Christian territory that had been conquered by Muslims. Beginning in 1095, successive popes had authorized one crusade after another. But by the late twelfth century, crusades for the Holy Land had lost their momentum and much of their purpose. In 1208 Pope Innocent III decided that the Catholic Church's most urgent problem was heresy, not Islam. And the most notorious hotbed of heresy was the region of southern France where Occitan was spoken, centered on such cities as Albi and Béziers.

Much of this area owed allegiance to Raymond VI, count of Toulouse. Again and again, Raymond had promised to deal sternly with heretics—but even excommunication had not forced him to make good on his promises. A new religious order, the Dominicans, had been formed specifically to preach to these heretics, but with little success. As a last resort, Pope Innocent declared a crusade.

The leader of the attack on Béziers was Simon de Montfort, an experienced crusader, tough and devout. He came armed with a list of 222 known heretics thought to be in Béziers. If the city would give them up, it would be spared. The city fathers scornfully refused Simon's offer, and the attack commenced. The battle was fierce and short. Once inside the walls, crusaders massacred every living soul they could find.

This is the scene of one of the most famous quotations in the history of persecution. Asked by a crusader how to tell heretics from good Catholics, the papal legate who accompanied the army reportedly answered, "Kill them all! God will know his own." Whether or not the legate actually said it, the crusaders certainly acted on that principle. As the legate reported in a letter to the pope, "Divine vengeance raged miraculously. Our men spared no one, irrespective of rank, sex, or age, and put to the sword almost twenty thousand people." Afterwards they set fire to the city.

Two very dangerous heresies were involved here. From their beginnings in Lyons in the late twelfth century, Waldensians had preached against the wealth and secular power of churchmen and called for a return to a simple, apostolic lifestyle. They insisted on the right of any believer to preach, and they had translated parts of the Bible from Latin into the vernacular—in this case, a French dialect—so that ordinary people could understand its words.

Gradually the Waldensian message had become more radical. Citing Jesus' saying, "Swear not at all," they refused to take oaths—and oaths were part of virtually all legal transactions. Many Waldensians claimed that no sacrament was valid if the priest who administered it was sinful. For traditional Catholics, that was like saying that no one could ever administer a sacrament, since every mortal human was a sinner.

Some of the 222 heretics named at Béziers were Waldensians, but most were probably Cathars—also called Albigensians, from the town of Albi. Catharism had woven itself into the fabric of life throughout southern France. Its ministers, simply known as "Good Men" and "Good Women," traveled from town to town and village to village, holding small private meetings at which they taught a truly revolutionary doctrine: God had made souls, but the Devil had made the material world. Fashioned by Satan out of vile matter, the earth could only be an ordeal of pain and misery. God had sent his son to bring salvation to pure souls, but Christ was all spirit and therefore did not suffer and die. Sex was sinful because it produced babies, imprisoning souls in flesh.

This view of the universe is so reminiscent of Manichaeism (see chapters 7 and 8) that many scholars have tried to trace a connection across some eight hundred years—with dubious success. Catharism was not the only dualist faith to develop from a Christian background. The Paulicians and Bogomils of the Byzantine Empire had preceded them (see chapter 11).

Like the Manichaeans, Cathars recognized two levels of commitment. The Good Men and Women were fully committed to a celibate, ascetic life of service, and expected to go straight to heaven when they died. Ordinary believers were simply learning and accumulating merit. They would have to live at least one more life—unless, as they might hope, they attained the level of Good Man or Good Woman on their deathbeds.

Many cities surrendered to avoid the fate of Béziers. When Simon de Montfort captured Cathars, he burned them. Lavaur, close to Toulouse, fell in May 1211 after a siege of months. Simon had the commander of the garrison and more than eighty knights executed. About four hundred Good Men and Women, who had taken refuge in the town, were burned. Soon after, the crusaders seized some sixty suspected heretics at Les Cassès and burned them "with great rejoicing."

Crusaders quarreled about whether to burn heretics who had recanted. Simon reasoned that they might be lying—and if their repentance was sincere, the fire would purge their sins. At Minerve, the papal legate proposed to offer heretics their lives if they would convert to Catholicism. Simon agreed to the deal only after the legate assured him that very few would accept. The legate was right, and over 140 people were burned alive.

In 1228 Simon's army besieged St. Cyprien, a suburb of Toulouse. The townspeople resisted desperately, with women and children joining the defense. Reportedly, a crew of women fired a catapult stone that crushed Simon de Montfort's head. Without Simon's leadership, the first Albigensian Crusade was effectively finished.

Two more crusades followed, separated by stints of inconclusive diplomacy. The final significant battle was the capture of Montségur, the last fortified Cathar stronghold. When the crusaders finally penetrated the walled fort high on a crag, they found more than two hundred men and women who chose to be burned rather than recant.

By then the Albigensian Crusades had continued for almost thirty-five years. The French king had extended his power to the Mediterranean, far beyond his former reach. The count of Toulouse had been effectively broken. Heresy had not been eliminated, but it had definitely been driven underground. It would take a different sort of repression to finish it off.

In 1229 Pope Gregory IX applied new methods. Gregory's legate offered a bounty to anyone who reported a heretic. He also convened a council, which decreed that every man (fifteen or older) and woman (thirteen or older) must swear an oath to seek out and denounce heretics. The council tried and convicted a number of reported heretics, and set the frightening precedent of refusing to let defendants know who had accused them.

In 1233 Pope Gregory began the practice of sending specially appointed investigators—"inquisitors," as they were called—to areas where heresy was particularly rife. The inquisitors' technique was quickly perfected. First they preached a well-publicized sermon, outlining the true faith and inviting anyone who had ever held heretical beliefs to repent and be absolved. Anyone who knew of heretics—or people they suspected of being heretics—was urged to report them.

People who confessed to heretical thoughts or acts were asked to prove their repentance by listing all the other possible heretics they knew or had heard of. Suspicion carried a high presumption of guilt, and the best way to prove that you were not shielding heretics was to give the inquisitor more names. This chain reaction of accusations soon involved great numbers of suspects. In general, the testimony of accusers and the confessions of the accused were the only evidence considered. In 1252 the pope authorized the use of torture. The number of convictions was predictably high.

Penalties for the repentant ranged from a pilgrimage and a fine to life imprisonment and the confiscation of all property. Those who refused to repent were turned over to the secular authorities to be burned alive. (The Catholic Church maintained its benign image by abstaining from direct killing.) Over the course of a century, hundreds of committed believers were burned in southern France. Far more were sentenced to life imprisonment. Of 636 heretics convicted by the famous inquisitor Bernard Gui in the early fourteenth century, forty-two were burned, about three hundred were sent to prison, and the rest were given lesser penalties.

The Inquisition was new, but the burning of heretics was not. Already in 1022, one nun and eleven clergymen had been arrested for heresy at Orleans. Three of the men were respected scholars and teachers—one of them the former confessor of the queen of France. Queen Constance was outraged. When the defendants emerged from their trial, she walloped her former confessor with her cane, knocking out his eye.

All twelve were convicted, but the nun and one of the lesser clerics saved themselves from death by recanting their heresy. The other ten were burned at the stake. It was the first burning for heresy in medieval Europe. Some two hundred years later, the French Inquisition put the whole process of finding and punishing heretics on a systematic basis. Cathars and Waldensians were the most common heretics sought by the Inquisition, but far from the only ones. One manual for inquisitors listed ninety-six types of heresy to watch for.

The Inquisition followed fugitive heretics across borders. While the king of Navarre and thousands of spectators watched, 183 heretics were burned at Mont-Aime. Cathars flourished for a time in northern Italy, until they were suppressed by fire and prison. Waldensians managed to survive in remote communities in the Alps. Centuries later they would find their place among the churches of the Reformation.

England was no friendlier to heretics. In the mid-twelfth century, more than thirty men and women were tried for heresy at Oxford. They had first attracted suspicion because they were German-speaking immigrants. Examined before a panel of bishops, they claimed to be good Christians, but they rejected the sacraments of baptism and the Eucharist. The bishops concluded that they were "Publican"—that is, Paulician—heretics and handed them over to the king for punishment.

He had them all branded on the forehead, stripped to the waist, publicly flogged, and driven out of the city. The chronicler William of Newburgh reported that they all "perished miserably in the bitter cold, for it was winter and no one offered them the slightest pity." Similar heretics were punished in York in 1191, while in 1211 authorities in London burned a single "Ambigensian"—probably a garbled version of "Albigensian."

By the fourteenth century, the Catholic Church in England was in intellectual ferment. Renaissance ideas were penetrating the University of Oxford, and there were louder and louder calls for reforms within the Church. No scholar was more outspoken than John Wyclif (also spelled Wycliffe). Among other things, he called for a Bible that any literate Christian could read.

That alone was enough to get him into trouble. Church authorities held that the Bible was too potent for ordinary people to handle. If the laity were allowed to read the Bible freely, they would come up with all sorts of misinterpretations, damaging to their souls. Latin, that protectively obscure language, was a buffer between ordinary Christians and God's naked word.

In 1382 an English translation of the Bible began to be circulated under Wyclif's name. He probably did not translate it himself, but it had his blessing. In Wyclif's view, the Church did not have sole authority to interpret the Bible. Instead, the Bible was the authority by which the Church should be judged. Besides, every soul was predestined either to salvation or to damnation, and only God knew which. The Church had no power to absolve sins. Excommunication was meaningless. The royal government could rightly overrule the Church—and in fact, the king should strip the church hierarchy of its wealth.

This dizzying array of doctrines, produced in a stream of writings and sermons, brought Wyclif again and again into trouble. He consistently opposed the pope's power and supported the king's. Not surprisingly, Pope Gregory XI called for his arrest and King Edward

III protected him. Wyclif was twice prosecuted for heresy, but never convicted. He died peacefully in 1384.

After his death Wyclif was declared a heretic and his books were banned. Eventually his grave was dug up and his remains thrown into a river. The Oxford scholars who had supported his views were pressured into recanting. But Wyclif's tirades against the church hierarchy had triggered a popular protest movement, the Lollards.

During the reign of Richard II (1377–1399), inquisitors were appointed to seek out heretics in every county of England. Meanwhile the Lollards grew more radical. They preached that the Church had stolen the nation's wealth and should be forced to give it back. The pope was a foreign dictator. Monasteries should be abolished.

Henry IV was crowned king of England in 1399, after deposing and murdering Richard II. He intensified the crackdown on heresy. Anyone possessing heretical writings could be burned. Bishops could imprison suspects. Even so, Lollards managed to produce a new edition of the Bible in English. Copied and recopied, it became popular even among Catholics. Of the many Lollards arrested during Henry IV's reign, only two were ever burned. The others either recanted or stayed in prison.

Soon after Henry V succeeded his father in 1413, a genuine Lollard uprising broke out. The rebellion was easily put down, and the leaders were executed. Those who were proved to be Lollards were burned, the others hanged. Yet Lollards survived, despite occasional burnings and sentences of life imprisonment through the rest of the century. Like the Waldensians of continental Europe, they went underground until the Protestant Reformation allowed them to reemerge.

In the kingdom of Bohemia—ancestor of the modern Czech Republic—the University of Prague was a center for outspoken reformers. In the first years of the fifteenth century, the most popular and controversial preacher in Prague was Jan Hus (or Huss). What he advocated sounded increasingly like Wyclif or the Waldensians. The Church must give up its wealth. Sinful priests could not validly administer the sacraments. Any devout Christian had a right to preach. The Bible was the only source of true doctrine and church organization.

Few conscientious clergymen could agree with these propositions. The Church's institutions and methods were the fruit of centuries of experience and thought. Church problems should be solved through Church channels. When reformers called for scrapping the system, they bordered on heresy.

It was a difficult period in the history of the Catholic Church. Since 1378 there had been two rival popes—one in Rome, the other in Avignon in the south of France. In 1409 an attempt to straighten out the mess only produced a third pope.

In 1410 Hus was excommunicated by the archbishop of Prague, and in 1412 by the Roman pope Gregory XII. The pope sought to undermine Hus's support in Prague by placing the city under interdict while Hus was there. That meant, among other restrictions, that no church services could be held, and that people were denied Christian burial. To spare the city, Hus withdrew to the south of Bohemia, but he continued to write and agitate for reforms.

In 1414, in a last-ditch attempt to resolve the problem of too many popes, a church council met at Constance in southwestern Germany. Hus was summoned to attend and defend himself against charges of heresy. He was happy to go, with a safe-conduct from the Holy Roman Emperor for his return to Bohemia.

But the Council of Constance ignored Hus's safe-conduct. He was imprisoned, tried, convicted of heresy, and burned at the stake in 1415, still protesting his innocence. A year later one of his fellow reformers, Jerome of Prague, was also convicted and burned. The council did succeed in solving the papal crisis. It deposed the two "antipopes" (one of whom was found guilty on seventy-two counts, including sodomy, fornication, and murder), Gregory XII resigned voluntarily, and a single new pope was elected.

Bohemians were outraged by the burning of Hus and Jerome. Henceforth, the church reform movement was deeply entwined with Bohemian patriotism. Regardless of their exact theology, Bohemians refused to take orders from the pope—any pope. Reformers themselves disagreed on many points, but most of them accepted the basic Hussite principles: free preaching of the Gospel, frequent communion with both bread and wine for all believers, no material wealth for the Church or clergy, and punishment of notable sinners.

Some offshoot groups from the Hussites went much further. The Taborites held that all Church tradition could be discarded.

Taborites were literally militant about their faith. Under the leadership of John Zizka, they burned and looted monasteries, which they considered parasitical growths on the Christian body. That militancy proved useful for Bohemia. Between 1420 and 1432 five separate crusades were launched against the Bohemian separatists. Zizka and his forces, supported by many Bohemian nobles and townspeople, handily defeated them all.

But reformed Bohemian Christians were not necessarily more lenient than orthodox Catholics. Thus in 1421 and 1422 Zizka had a number of prominent Taborites executed for heresy. He also established the use of forced conversion, and suppressed a group known as Adamites. They had shed their clothes in imitation of life in the garden of Eden—though in a more aggressive mode, they sometimes assaulted and killed priests.

In 1434 the Taborites were defeated by a more moderate branch of Hussites, who returned to communion with the Catholic Church but did not give up their basic principles. Jan Hus and his fellow reformers had won their point, at the cost of many lives.

Heresies came and went, but there were always Jews to remind Europeans that Europe was not perfectly Christian. And while it took the power and authority of church and state to suppress heretics, anyone could have a hand in suppressing Jews.

In 1096 armies were gathering for the First Crusade to the Holy Land. People who could not afford the time and expense of joining the crusade wanted to show that they too could kill Christ's enemies. They simply attacked their Jewish neighbors. In Rouen, Mainz, Cologne, Trier, Metz, Bamberg, Regensburg, Prague, and many other cities, Jews were rounded up. They were given an opportunity to accept Christianity. If they refused, they were slaughtered. There were more massacres of Jews in Germany in 1298, in 1336 through 1338, and in 1394.

No government ordered or officially approved these massacres, but no government made a move to stop them. Governments did their own persecuting as well. King Edward I of England expelled all Jews from his kingdom in 1290. French rulers expelled Jews from French territory three times in the fourteenth century—and always readmitted them after a time.

In the so-called Shepherds' Crusade of 1320, thousands of shepherds and other poor people converged on Paris. Joined by some of higher status, they called on King Philip V to lead a crusade to the Holy Land. Philip declined the honor. The would-be crusaders turned south, plundering their way through France. They massacred Jews in more than a dozen cities. Most notably, 337 Jews who had taken refuge in the castle of Montclus were slaughtered. Some children were spared, to be forcibly baptized and brought up as Christians. Here, as in many other places, local authorities gave at least tacit approval to the killers.

Jews were routinely the prime suspects when things went wrong. In an epidemic, Jews were often charged with poisoning wells and springs. They were imprisoned and offered the choice of being burned alive or confessing their "crime" and accepting baptism. Some committed suicide—forty at once, in one case—rather than make that choice. During the Black Death in the mid-fourteenth century, when plague killed at least a third of Europe's population, Jews were often executed or simply lynched.

Beginning in the fourteenth century, Jews in most European cities were segregated into separate areas, later called ghettos. These were virtually separate cities with their own walls, within which Jews were autonomous. Outside, they were usually required to wear distinctive yellow badges.

Jews found a slight measure of security in Spain, which was split between competing Christian and Muslim kingdoms. Both were willing to tolerate Jews—with certain conditions. In the words of King Alfonso X of Castile, Jews were permitted to "live forever as in captivity and serve as a reminder to humankind that they are descended from those who crucified our lord Jesus Christ." In other words, they were allowed to exist in Christian countries only to remind Christians to hate them. That approach was not likely to discourage religious violence.

One of the worst outbreaks came in 1391, when mobs attacked Jewish neighborhoods in cities across Christian Spain, killing thousands of Jews and looting synagogues, homes, and businesses. Some estimates run as high as fifty thousand Jews murdered.

In the early fifteenth century a papal edict forbade Spanish Jews to study the Talmud and required them to attend Christian sermons.

Under this unrelenting pressure, thousands of Jews saw the advantages of accepting Christian baptism. Finally, in 1492 the remaining Spanish Jews were given an ultimatum: convert to Christianity now, or leave Spain immediately.

Thousands converted. Thousands more left, abandoning most of their property. Some went to neighboring Portugal, where King Manuel soon insisted that they must become Christians. In 1497 he resorted to force. Jewish children were taken from their parents to be raised as Christians. Soldiers drove thousands of Jews to a gathering in Lisbon, where they were forcibly baptized.

For Catholic Spain, this was a glorious time. The marriage of Isabella of Castile and Ferdinand of Aragon had united the whole country under one rule. The last Muslim kingdom in Spain had just been conquered. The peace treaty guaranteed toleration for Muslims, but that quickly changed. In 1501 Isabella ordered all copies of the Qur'an to be burned. Early the next year, Muslims were given the same ultimatum the Jews had received: convert, get out, or die.

Now Spain had been purged of both Jews and Muslims. Ferdinand and Isabella had achieved their goal—a united, totally Christian nation. Or had they? In the past century, tens of thousands of Jews and Muslims had been pressured, coerced, and sometimes physically forced to become Christians, at least in name. Could they be trusted? What was to prevent them from secretly practicing their old religions? What could stop them from spreading heretical ideas among "old" Christians?

The Spanish Inquisition, accountable only to the pope, had been set up to deal with this perceived problem. People who had accepted Christianity to escape persecution quickly found themselves persecuted again. Converts from Judaism—and even the children and grandchildren of converts—were automatically suspected. Tomás de Torquemada, the first Grand Inquisitor for Castile, condemned about two thousand people to be burned alive. They died in spectacular public ceremonies—the *autos-da-fé*, or "acts of faith." Presumably the spectators learned wholesome lessons.

Again and again, medieval authorities in both Church and government tried to root out unorthodox ideas and practices. Repression often succeeded, at least in the short run. Some divergent groups were wiped out entirely. Others were driven underground or into more hospitable lands. But the religious ferment that had begun in the twelfth century could not be contained forever. In the sixteenth century it would boil over as the Protestant Reformation—opening a whole new age of persecution (see chapter 16).

SOURCES AND FURTHER READING

Two contemporary accounts of the Albigensian Crusade have been translated into English by W. A. Sibly and M. D. Sibly: *The History of the Albigensian Crusade: Peter of les Vaux-de-Cernay's Historia in Albigensis* (Woodbridge, NY: Boydell, 1998) and *The Chronicle of William of Puylaurens: The Albigensian Crusade and Its Aftermath* (Woodbridge, NY: Boydell, 2003). A few of the extensive Latin writings of John Wyclif and Jan Hus are available in English translation. Other sources from the period include many surviving letters and church and government decrees and records. A good collection in English is *Heresies of the High Middle Ages: Selected Sources*, translated and annotated by Walter L. Wakefield and Austin P. Evans (New York: Columbia University Press, 1969).

Among modern works, Gordon Leff's *Heresy in the Later Middle Ages* (Manchester: Manchester University Press, 1967) is a classic analysis. R. I. Moore's *The Formation of a Persecuting Society: Power and Deviance in Western Europe, 950–1250* (Oxford: Blackwell, 1987) is an important work that compares the persecution of Jews to the treatment of lepers, who were also persecuted. John Edwards's *Ferdinand and Isabella* (London: Pearson/Longman, 2002) puts the forced conversion and expulsion of Jews and Muslims into the context of Spanish history.

Chapter 14

Asia

Fifth through Seventeenth Centuries

By the eleventh century CE, mainstream Chinese society recognized three pillars of civilization: Confucianism, Daoism, and Buddhism. Buddhist and Daoist temples and shrines often housed each other's deities and saints. Daoist priests and Buddhist monastics took part in each other's ceremonies. Confucianism was a social and ethical system, not a theology. In Confucian practice, any respectable deity was worthy of honor, and Confucius himself was revered in countless shrines.

This comfortable coexistence had not been reached easily. Buddhism—introduced to China a thousand years earlier—was long under suspicion because of its foreign origin. Thus when government troops discovered a cache of weapons at a Buddhist monastery in 446 CE, the emperor Tai Wu Di of the Northern Wei dynasty outlawed Buddhism in his territory. Buddhist monks and nuns were to be executed, Buddhist temples and shrines destroyed, images defaced, and books burned. This reign of terror continued for eight years.

But popular resistance persuaded the emperor to back down a

little, allowing people to practice Buddhism in their own homes. On Tai Wu Di's death in 454, his successor quickly repealed the anti-Buddhist decree. Temples were rebuilt and scriptures recopied. In 574 a similar situation produced a similar response. The emperor Wu of the Northern Zhou (or Chou) dynasty tried again to suppress Buddhism. As before, his successor reversed the persecutor's decree.

Two hundred years later, such persecution seemed unthinkable. After a long period of troubles and fragmentation, China had been reunited. The powerful Tang dynasty presided over a golden age of prosperity, artistic achievement, and social development. Hereditary government offices and political patronage had been largely replaced by a system of civil service examinations. Religious toleration was complete. Buddhism was widely popular, while Daoism and Confucianism were especially associated with the imperial court and aristocracy. Even fringe religions like Zoroastrianism and Christianity were practiced freely.

Yet the golden age had a tarnished side. Revolts and foreign attacks shook the fabric of Tang society. The tax-exempt Buddhist monasteries and temples had become ostentatiously wealthy. Furthermore, some schools of Buddhism preached doctrines that no government could like. The "Three Ages School" taught that the present age was so degenerate that governments were incapable of doing justice and deserved no respect. In 713 the empress Wu Ze Tian declared the Three Ages School heretical and confiscated its head temple's wealth.

At last, in the 840s the emperor Wu Zong decreed the third great persecution of Buddhism. According to Chinese records, 4,600 monasteries and 40,000 Buddhist shrines were destroyed. This time monks and nuns were not executed, but 260,500 of them were forced to withdraw from their religious orders. The government confiscated all temple lands and treasures.

Chinese Buddhism never fully recovered. As in the previous cases, Wu Zong's successor reversed the anti-Buddhist measures, but he did not return the confiscated land and wealth. Impoverished, Buddhism settled into the coexistence with Daoism and Confucianism that characterized Chinese society for a thousand years to come.

In Tibet, the shamanist religious tradition called Bon had been practiced from ancient times. Buddhism apparently reached Tibet in the seventh century CE, when Tibetan culture was welcoming goods and ideas from India. At least one eighth-century king tried to suppress Bon in favor of Buddhism. In the following century, it was Buddhists who were persecuted. In the long run, Tibetan Buddhism adopted many practices and ideas from Bon, and vice versa. By the twelfth century, the two religions had arrived at a state of mutual toleration.

Buddhism reached Korea from China, probably in the fourth century CE. At the time, the Korean Peninsula was divided into three kingdoms. Two of them, Koguryo and Paekche, welcomed Buddhist missionaries. The third, Silla, emphatically did not. Some of the early missionaries were executed, and their converts kept a low profile. Still, the traditional shamanistic religion practiced throughout the Korean Peninsula readily accommodated Buddhism. By the mid-sixth century the rulers of Silla had accepted Buddhism and made it the official national religion. It remained so for the next millennium of Korean history.

The thirteenth-century Mongol conquest of Korea was a blow to Korean pride and Buddhist prestige. Though nominally independent, Korea became a Mongol satellite. Organized Buddhism came to be seen as a tool of foreign control. When Mongol domination was shaken off at the end of the fourteenth century, Korean Buddhism suffered from a backlash. In the next century, Korean rulers closed hundreds of Buddhist temples, leaving only thirty-six open. Perhaps more damaging, they forced the many Buddhist sects to reorganize, forming two government-defined schools.

Then, in 1659, a royal edict prohibited anyone from joining a Buddhist monastic order. The next year, monks and nuns were forbidden to enter the capital, Seoul, and some Buddhist schools were closed. Clearly the government intended for Buddhism to die out. Instead, it went underground. In 1675 officials uncovered an esoteric Buddhist sect that was allegedly plotting against the king. The leaders were executed and the group disbanded. But much Buddhist tradition had been absorbed into Korean popular religion, and survived in that form.

The late first century BCE was a troubled time in Sri Lanka. Buddhist monks were involved in some of the rebellions and coups that plagued the island. For fifteen years, a series of strict Hindu rulers persecuted Buddhism. Many monks and nuns were killed or fled. In 29 BCE the Buddhist king Vattagamani returned to power, but the trouble was not over. In the following centuries, rivalry between two Buddhist monasteries escalated to such a point that the government became involved. In the mid-fourth century CE, King Mahasena destroyed one of the monasteries and confiscated its land.

In 1017 the south Indian Chola kingdom conquered Sri Lanka, and its Hindu rulers began a new persecution of Buddhism. The Chola domination lasted less than a century, and Buddhism was restored with the help of monks from Burma, but the order of Buddhist nuns had been wiped out.

Beginning in the early sixteenth century, a new threat appeared, this one coming from the other side of the world. Portuguese ships reached Sri Lanka, and Portuguese soldiers and adventurers began to conquer and plunder the island, while Portuguese missionaries tried to turn the Sri Lankans into Christians. Buddhist monasteries and temples were looted, Buddhist women and children sold into slavery and prostitution. In the eighteenth century the Portuguese were ousted by the Dutch. In 1795 the British took over the island, and active persecution ceased.

The most ancient Japanese religion—Shinto, the "Way of the Gods" —recognized a world full of living powers. These *kami* ranged from the indwelling power of a particular stone or tree or mountain to such national deities as Amaterasu, the sun goddess from whom the Japanese emperors traced their descent.

Buddhism was introduced from the Korean kingdom of Paekche in the mid-sixth century CE. At the end of the century, Prince Shotoku, the imperial regent, proclaimed Buddhism Japan's official religion. He established a temple and school at Nara to study and spread Buddhist teachings—an enterprise so successful that in the next two hundred years a half-dozen varieties of Japanese Buddhism developed.

There was little conflict between Shinto and Buddhism. By the eighth century, Japanese Buddhism had accepted Shinto deities, and Shinto priests and Buddhist monks often shared holy sites and participated in each other's ceremonies. There was no danger of persecution. That did not mean there was no killing.

One of the basic doctrines of Buddhism was strict nonviolence.

Believers were taught not to harm anything that breathed. But Japan's society was military to the core. A feudalistic system of government, and recurring periods of lawlessness, meant that there were many small private armies. Buddhist monasteries wanted their own.

By the twelfth century, there were thousands of monasteries, many of them wealthy in land and treasure. They were deeply involved in politics, and often in disputes with neighboring monasteries and local aristocrats. Monasteries defended themselves and their interests by maintaining troops of warrior monks who were not bound by vows of nonviolence. At times, their armed demonstrations brought pressure on the government. At other times, there were outright battles between monasteries.

In late twelfth-century Kyoto, the monk Honen began to preach an appealingly simple faith. "Pure Land" Buddhism already taught that any believer could reach the paradise where Amida Buddha presided—the Pure Land—by sincere prayer and devotion. Honen simplified the process. According to his doctrine, merely repeating a three-word mantra would guarantee salvation. Thousands of people welcomed the message.

But if salvation was so easy to attain, what was the point of temples and rituals and regulations? The whole system of organized Buddhism seemed unnecessary. And if, as Honen also taught, the present age was hopelessly degenerate, then government and the feudal structure of society were unnecessary, too.

The shogun exiled Honen from Kyoto and had him defrocked, but did not dare to take more extreme action against him. The man and his ideas were simply too popular. His disciples continued to spread the saving word, with the result that within a few generations the "True Pure Land" sect, as it was called, took its place as one of the most powerful and militant Buddhist orders, with its own warrior monks.

The late thirteenth century ushered in a still more militarized period of Japanese history. From their base in Korea, the Mongols repeatedly tried to invade Japan. Storms—presumably sent by divine powers—twice wrecked Mongol fleets, and the Japanese drove off every invasion attempt. In the centuries that followed, Japan was wracked by continual civil wars, some of them between rival Buddhist sects. In 1537 True Pure Land monks, allied with other sects and the forces of the shogun, savagely defeated the powerful

Nichiren sect. Some fifty thousand Nichiren monks and supporters were killed, and many of their temples were destroyed.

In the late sixteenth century, a trio of warlords emerged from the chaotic power struggle that Japanese society had become. Oda Nobunaga, Toyotomi Hideyoshi, and Tokugawa Ieyasu formed a three-way alliance that gave them control of most of Japan. Both Nobunaga and Hideyoshi were openly contemptuous of religious claims, especially of Buddhism. In 1571 Nobunaga burned some three thousand temples and monasteries of the Tendai sect and massacred the survivors. In 1580 he accepted the surrender of the True Pure Land sect after a long siege of their last stronghold. In 1584 Hideyoshi defeated an army of the Shingon sect, killing four thousand.

Meanwhile, another religion had begun to make itself known. Dutch and Portuguese ships had recently reached Japan, and trading relations were quickly established. The first Christian missionaries had arrived in 1549—Jesuits led by Francis Xavier of the newly founded Society of Jesus, a Catholic order established for the express purpose of educational and missionary work. Quickly sizing up the structure of Japanese society, the Jesuits concentrated their efforts on the upper classes. They reasoned that when a feudal lord converted to Christianity, his vassals and dependents would follow.

It worked. Within twenty-five years, there were some thirty thousand Japanese Christians. Many people found Christianity a good alternative to Buddhism, which had been badly discredited by its excesses of violence. One feudal lord actually ceded the town of Nagasaki (then a small fishing village) to the Jesuits. Within a few years, Nagasaki was the center of a thriving Christian community. It also had an excellent harbor. With a little prodding by the Jesuits, it became the major port for European commerce.

Both Nobunaga and Hideyoshi welcomed the Christian missionaries and made no objection to their preaching, baptizing, and church building. Hideyoshi entertained a Jesuit at his own palace, listened to his exposition of Christian doctrine, and assured him that he himself would become a Christian if he could get an exemption from the rule against having more than one woman.

The honeymoon did not last. The Japanese were delighted to learn from the West—they were making their own firearms within a year of first contact—but not to give up their way of life. Japan had just achieved a hard-won degree of stability. The rulers were not willing to endanger that. And what they were learning about Europeans was not reassuring.

In the Philippines, in Southeast Asia, and apparently everywhere, Christian missionary activity went hand in hand with European commercial and strategic interests. It was supported and protected by European governments, using money, threats, and ultimately armed force, and it culminated in European takeovers. Hideyoshi did not like the prospect. In 1587 he ordered the missionaries to leave Japan, and began the systematic destruction of churches and Jesuit schools.

But having caught the missionaries' attention, Hideyoshi quickly compromised. The anti-missionary decree stayed on the books, but he indicated that he would not enforce it so long as the missionaries and their converts behaved themselves. They must not insult Shinto or Buddhism, nor destroy or damage shrines and temples. And they must by no means preach disobedience to feudal lords.

The compromise held until 1597, when Hideyoshi ended it dramatically. Twenty-six Christians, including six Franciscan friars, were crucified. On Hideyoshi's orders, about a hundred and twenty churches were destroyed. Yet hundreds remained untouched, and of more than a hundred Jesuits in the country, only eleven were forced to leave. Christianity was still—very precariously—tolerated.

The next year Hideyoshi died. Supreme power now rested in the hands of Tokugawa Ieyasu, the new shogun, a much less colorful personality. Ieyasu refused to rescind Hideyoshi's anti-Christian decrees—that would have shown disrespect for the dead—but he assured the missionaries that they could safely continue their work. He believed, he said, in every individual's right to free choice of religion—with the exception of feudal lords, who were forbidden to convert.

In 1605 one of the most prominent Christian aristocrats renounced Christianity and expelled the Jesuits from his territory. Other feudal lords occasionally persecuted Christians in their areas. But the faith still grew. In 1606 the Jesuits counted 750,000 Christians in Japan, and claimed to be adding thousands every year. They also admitted that some thirty thousand had renounced Christianity as a result of the various anti-Christian decrees.

Those decrees were nothing compared to the one that Ieyasu issued in January 1614. In effect, it established Buddhism as the state religion of Japan, with a theocratic control mechanism. Every Japanese must register as a member of one of the recognized Buddhist sects. Local Buddhist priests were to visit each family annually and make sure that no one defected to an alien religion. All missionaries and their assistants, as well as certain prominent Japanese Christians, were ordered to go to Nagasaki. From there they would be deported.

To keep the peace, missionaries obeyed the order—or at least pretended to. At Kyoto, five of the eight resident Jesuits promptly went underground, and much the same thing happened at other missionary centers. Sympathetic local authorities made it possible in many places. In October 1614 Japanese officials formally took possession of all church property, and the deportees took ship for Macao and Manila. Christianity would be illegal for Japanese citizens for the next two and a half centuries.

The persecution that followed was sporadic and patchy, but harsh where it struck. Japanese authorities knew well that disguised missionaries were in hiding under their official noses. As a result, they increasingly restricted the activities of all foreigners in Japan. Foreign ships were limited to two ports—Nagasaki and Hirado—and foreign traders and diplomats were closely supervised.

Missionaries were beheaded when found. Feudal lords charged with being Christians or concealing missionaries could be executed or deprived of their fiefs. Most of the remaining churches were destroyed, and Christian cemeteries were sometimes desecrated. At least five hundred Japanese Christians died in the persecutions of 1614 through 1622. Not all were executed outright. Some died in prison, others under torture.

The surviving Christians became outlaws. Substantial rewards were offered for turning them in. Many fled from their homes and set up crypto-Christian groups in remote parts of Japan. Others recanted. By 1637 Christianity had outwardly been purged from the country, even around Nagasaki—but only outwardly.

In 1637 the peasants of the Shimabara Peninsula, near Nagasaki, rose in revolt. The stimulus may have been mistreatment by a harsh landlord, but the driving force quickly became religious. These farmers and fishermen had renounced Christianity years before, but most of them remained Christian at heart. Now they came out of the closet with a vengeance.

To the amazement of Japan's warrior aristocracy, these virtually unarmed peasants proceeded to win several battles and take possession of an abandoned castle, which they refortified. It took a large army and a siege of several months to suppress the rebellion. On April 15, 1638, all the rebels, including women and children, were massacred. The death toll was estimated at thirty-seven thousand. Japan's remaining Christians became invisible, though in a few places Christian families managed to pass down their secret faith for generations.

For the Japanese government, and the feudal aristocracy it represented, Shimabara was traumatic. The rebellion demonstrated just how subversive Christianity could be. Peasants rising against their lords, farmers defeating samurai in battle—this was the poisonous fruit of welcoming foreigners into the country. The government was determined not to repeat that mistake. Starting in 1637, all foreigners were banned from Japan, with the exception of a few carefully supervised Chinese and Dutch traders, and Japanese were forbidden to leave the country. Thus began more than two centuries of Japanese isolation.

SOURCES AND FURTHER READING

Most of the extensive historical records from countries covered by this chapter are not available in English. A small but important exception is *Japanese Traditions of Christianity* (London: Kegan Paul, 1929), edited by Montague Paske-Smith, a collection of Japanese accounts of missionary activity and the Shimabara rebellion in English translation.

C. R. Boxer's *The Christian Century in Japan: 1549–1650* (Berkeley: University of California Press, 1967) is a detailed account of the rise and fall of Christianity in Japan. Noble Ross Reat's *Buddhism: A History* (Berkeley, CA: Asian Humanities Press, 1994) is both a good introduction to Buddhist thought and a country-by-country survey of its history. James Huntley Grayson's *Korea: A Religious History*, revised edition (New York: Routledge, 2002) covers the interactions of different religious traditions throughout Korea's past.

Chapter 15

Africa

Eighteenth and Nineteenth Centuries

The kingdom of Kongo was in trouble. Portuguese expansion from Angola had driven King Antonio to resist, but he had been killed in battle and his army crushed. Kongo had broken into fragments. Now, in 1704, after almost forty years of virtual anarchy, King Pedro IV was struggling to reunite the once prosperous kingdom and restore its shattered economy. But devastation, poverty, and fear were still widespread. Luckily, St. Anthony had just arrived from heaven.

Kongo had long been a Christian state. King Nzinga Nkuwu had been baptized by a Portuguese missionary in 1491. His successor took the baptismal name of Afonso and began a program of Christianization. He built churches, encouraged his nobles and their followers to be baptized, and corresponded tirelessly with Portuguese royalty and Catholic dignitaries, always appealing for more priests.

According to at least one account, he also burned idolaters along with their idols. Certainly European missionaries burned idols, fetishes, and all the paraphernalia of "heathenism" they could confiscate, both in Afonso's time and later. That sometimes got them into difficulties. One friar died from the beating he received from outraged villagers when he burned their sacred images and utensils.

Hundreds of thousands of adults and children were baptized by Portuguese and French Catholic priests. The Christian cross became part of the royal insignia, and large crosses were set up in towns and villages. Even in the absence of permanent clergy, converts continued to practice the new religion, and were delighted whenever a priest turned up to hear confessions and administer baptisms.

In general, Kongolese cheerfully accepted the Christian God and all the saints they heard of. However, that did not mean they were ready to give up their tried-and-true religious practices and symbols. Christianity penetrated deeply into Kongolese religion and changed it profoundly, but the result was not always what the missionaries had intended.

Thus, when a young woman named Kimpa Vita announced in 1704 that she was St. Anthony come from heaven, the missionaries were shocked. Her messengers, called "little Anthonies," traveled throughout Kongo, calling the people together to hear her preaching. She designated her male assistant "St. John."

As the movement swelled, the missionaries grew more alarmed. Kimpa Vita taught that all the outward manifestations of religion—even baptism—were insignificant, because "God considers the intention." She also held that Jesus and his mother, Mary, had been born in Kongo. In 1706 she and "St. John" were arrested, tried, and burned as heretics.

Kimpa Vita (also known by her Portuguese name Dona Beatriz or Beatrice) was a striking example of how Africans dealt with foreign religions. Christianity and Islam, the two great missionary religions, were welcomed by most people—except when the representatives of those religions insisted on completely disrupting African lifestyles. And where Christianity and Islam were popularly adopted, they were also changed. Africans reshaped alien creeds and practices to their own needs and purposes.

From the Africans' point of view, there was nothing wrong with honoring a new deity alongside the powers they had always worshipped. But to strict Christians and strict Muslims those ancient

African powers looked like devils and evil demons. Sooner or later, there would be trouble.

Islam had come to North Africa by conquest. In the rest of Africa, Islam arrived peacefully. The first Muslims that black Africans met were not soldiers but businessmen—seagoing Arab traders in eastern Africa, Berber merchants farther west. Everywhere, they set up trading stations that grew into cities, and they brought new commercial opportunities, new jobs, new styles, and new goods. Eventually they brought Muslim preachers, teachers, and scholars. Conversions were by example and education, not the threat of force.

As a result, the first native Islamic communities in most of sub-Saharan Africa practiced a mixed Islam. They accepted Muhammad and his transcendent God. They built mosques and adopted Muslim festivals and fasts. But they also went on consulting their ancestors and negotiating with the spirits they knew.

In certain ways, Islam could adapt to African life more easily than Christianity could. For one thing, both Muslims and traditional Africans practiced circumcision, which was anathema to most Christian missionaries. For another, in many African societies it was important for a man to have as many wives as he could afford, and Islamic law allowed polygamy. True, a Muslim husband was limited to no more than four wives at one time, but concubines were also acceptable. These customs scandalized Christian missionaries.

Another advantage for Islam was that for the most part it entered Africa from the East. Elsewhere in the world, Muslims burned temples and smashed idols. In East Africa, they found neither. East Africans' religion centered on the spirits of their ancestors, who remained very much part of family tradition and society. There were charms and talismans, healers and mediums, festivals and rituals, but nothing that looked obviously like "false gods" to the Muslim merchants.

From the eighth to the fifteenth century, Islam spread through vast tracts of eastern, central, and finally western Africa. Many states and peoples declared their allegiance to the new faith. Most of them practiced the mixed Islam that resulted from absorbing Muslim ways into the traditional lifestyle. Even within such areas, many people did not adopt Islam at all.

All this changed when African scholars began to graduate from

Islamic schools. They had studied not only the Qur'an and its com-
mentaries, but also Islamic law, theological treatises, and moral
exhortations. These new Muslims were dismayed to find that the
practice of Islam in their own countries was sadly lacking by classical
Islamic standards. They became reformers. They preached, wrote,
and lobbied their governments to enforce a stricter kind of Islam.

Some of them went farther.

In 1794 a scholar and preacher named Usuman dan Fodio
announced that he had received the "Sword of Truth" in a vision
and was ready to unsheathe it against the enemies of God. To dan
Fodio, those enemies included not only pagans, but also Muslims
who failed to meet his rigorous standards. He had already tried to
reform Muslim West Africa by preaching. Now he collected an army
of followers, and in the first decade of the nineteenth century they
conquered a whole series of small West African kingdoms. Dan
Fodio was installed as caliph of Sokoto, a city he founded east of the
Niger River. Within his territory he strove to enforce Islamic law and
root out the vestiges of paganism.

Besides judicial punishments, people in dan Fodio's caliphate
faced another powerful incentive for accepting his strict version of
Islam. By Islamic law, Muslims were forbidden to enslave Muslims.
Thus—at least in theory—Muslims could only take part in the thriving
slave trade by continually finding non-Muslims to enslave and sell to
European or North African dealers. When dan Fodio identified the
nominal Muslims he conquered as infidels, he made them fair game
for Muslim slave dealers. Bewildered longtime Muslims confessed
their sins and burned their fetishes to avoid enslavement.

Catholic missionaries had often protested against the abuses of
slavery, but seldom against the slave trade as such. In fact, it was
fairly common for priests and friars to take part in it. The Portuguese
slave trade was a major factor undermining the kingdom of Kongo.
In 1684 Lourenço da Silva, a black Kongolese Christian, traveled to
Rome and protested to the pope against the slave trade. The pope
did respond with a blanket condemnation of the trade, but it had no
noticeable effect. By dan Fodio's time, slave trading was an important part of the economy in many nations.

Inspired by dan Fodio, other Muslim reformers unleashed a
whole series of jihads. Most of them were against nominally Muslim

rulers and peoples who practiced an "impure" form of Islam. Some went on to attack populations that had never been Muslim. Everywhere, the rule of Islamic law was declared.

The major European penetration of Africa began on the west coast, but there were some exceptions. Seventeenth-century Portuguese traders were active on the east coast as well. The city of Mombasa, in what is now Kenya, was a leading trade center. There the king chose to be baptized as a Christian, and a small Christian community developed.

In 1631 the king changed his mind. He renounced Christianity and ordered his subjects to do the same. More than a hundred of them, led by the king's own brother, refused. The king had the Christians massacred. One hundred and forty-nine Portuguese men, women, and children were honored as martyrs by the Catholic Church. At least as many black Africans, massacred along with them, were officially ignored.

In one corner of Africa, a Christian state had survived since the fourth century. Ethiopia (including modern Eritrea) was the major kingdom in the Horn of Africa, just across the Red Sea from southern Arabia and Yemen. The major ruling dynasty liked to trace its ancestry to the Queen of Sheba and King Solomon. From very early times there was a considerable community of native Ethiopian Jews—the Falasha, or Beta Israel.

There was also an Islamic connection. A group of Muhammad's early followers had taken refuge in Ethiopia to escape persecution in Mecca. The Ethiopian king Armah had protected them until they could safely return to Arabia. In later centuries, considerable areas in southern Ethiopia had a largely Muslim population, and Muslims and Christians intermarried freely.

Christian Ethiopia thus had a background of friendly involvement with the other great monotheisms of the Middle East. Ethiopian Christianity even shared what most other Christians condemned as "Jewish" customs, including circumcision and keeping the Sabbath (as well as Sunday). At the same time, many Ethiopian communities still held to a traditional African belief system and "pagan" practices.

Ethiopian tolerance ended in the fifteenth century. The emperor Zara Yakob (or Zar'a Ya'qob), who ruled from 1434 to 1468, decreed that every Ethiopian must wear an amulet stating, "I belong to the Father, the Son, and the Holy Spirit." The penalties for failure to comply included confiscation of property and possible execution. A magistrate called the "Keeper of the Hour" was appointed to oversee a hunt for idolaters. The system was much like the European Inquisition.

Zara Yakob did not spare even his own family. He had one of his wives and several of his sons and daughters flogged to death for allegedly participating in pagan practices. He also persecuted one order of Christian monks, whom he accused of false teaching. Their leader Estifanos was flogged and exiled, and some of their monasteries were closed.

A number of provincial officials who had converted to Judaism raised a revolt against the emperor's repressive measures. Zara Yakob put down the revolt and instituted a persecution that earned him the title of "exterminator of the Jews." He also declared that it was no sin to kill a pagan—a royal opinion that could only encourage mob violence. His successor Baida Maryam (son of the executed queen) found no fault with his father's violent religious policies. He supported forced conversions of pagans, and continued the persecution of Jews, especially converts from Christianity.

Ethiopia was sandwiched between Muslim North Africa and an increasingly Muslim East Africa. In 1529 the Islamic kingdom of Adel attacked. Ahmad Gran, the leader of this jihad, quickly defeated the Ethiopian army in a major battle. He spent the next eleven years extending his conquests across Ethiopia, systematically demolishing churches and monasteries. Government archives and religious manuscripts were destroyed or carried off. Willingly or unwillingly, thousands of Ethiopians accepted Islam. In 1541 Gran defeated a small Portuguese force that had come to Ethiopia's aid.

The next year, the Ethiopians rallied under the leadership of King Gelawdewos (Claudius) and the Queen Mother, Sabla Wangel. Gran was defeated and killed, and the Muslim armies retreated. Peace was restored—but not for all Ethiopians. Subsequent emperors made outright war on Ethiopian Jews, exterminating some tribal groups and forcing others to convert to Christianity. Most of the survivors retreated into inaccessible mountain areas.

Ethiopian Christianity had its own internal disagreements. At the beginning of the seventeenth century, a prophet proclaimed himself the new Christ, and won the support of many disciples. He was executed, but his movement survived for years. The emperor Susenyos (Sisinius), who ruled from 1607 to 1632, finally wiped them out, driving many to suicide.

Meanwhile, Catholic missionaries had been trying to "reclaim" the Ethiopian Church for Catholicism. Susenyos became a devout Catholic and used his authority to impose his new faith on the country. That was no easy task. The bishops of Ethiopia had always been ordained by the patriarch of Alexandria, and the Ethiopian Church followed the ritual and doctrine of the Egyptian Coptic Church. Unlike Catholics and Protestants, Coptic and Ethiopian Christians had always been Monophysites (see chapter 11). In its long isolation, Ethiopian Christianity had also developed characteristics of its own.

Susenyos forbade circumcision and Sabbath observance. He instituted a program to reordain all priests, reconsecrate all churches, and rebaptize all Christians. It was a program doomed to failure. Ethiopian Christians rose in a series of rebellions. Again and again Susenyos crushed them, and went on reconsecrating and reordaining—but in the end he gave up. In 1632 he abdicated in favor of his son Fasilidas (Basilides). The Ethiopian Church was restored.

As his last royal act, Susenyos had declared complete freedom of religion. That was also doomed to failure. Fasilidas banished or executed all Catholic missionaries and forbade any more to enter the country. He also executed or banished a number of prominent Catholic Ethiopians. But the Catholic community, and even a few surreptitious missionaries, survived.

So did internal dissensions. The monastic orders of the Ethiopian Church had separated into two competing camps, each accusing the other of heresy. In 1720 the emperor David (Dawit) III unleashed his army against one of the two competing schools. His soldiers attacked several monasteries and massacred the monks.

In the late eighteenth century, there was a new wave of Muslim invaders. Although their attacks were not nearly as devastating as Ahmad Gran's jihad, they were destructive enough. Monks were massacred and churches desecrated. Some of them were turned into mosques.

In the 1850s the emperor Theodore (Tewodros) II decided that Catholicism threatened his sovereignty. He exiled the head of the Catholic mission and began arresting Ethiopian Catholic monks. Their leader, Ghebra-Mika'el, was tortured to death in 1855. Tewodros, increasingly paranoid, expanded his persecution. He imprisoned the few Protestant missionaries, and then turned against segments of the Ethiopian Church itself, burning and looting churches in areas he considered disloyal. In 1868 a British expeditionary force arrived to rescue the European hostages. Tewodros fought and lost a battle, released the hostages, and committed suicide.

The emperor Yohannes IV (reigned 1872–1889) did much to restore Ethiopia's stability, prosperity, and prestige. He soundly defeated an Italian invasion, and improved communications within his country by building railroads and installing telegraph and telephone systems. In an attempt to unify the country religiously, he ordered Muslims, Jews, and pagans to become Christians, on pain of losing all their property. In practice, the decree was applied almost exclusively against pagans. Churches were built in areas where populations clung to traditional African religions. People were coerced into baptism, and required to pay tithes and observe Christian fasts and holy days.

Outside of Kongo and the small state of Warri, Christianity had made little headway in West Africa. To become Christians, Africans had to renounce their gods, and much more as well. African clothing, dances, and marriage customs all struck the missionaries as un-Christian and uncivilized. Christianity and civilization, they believed, went hand in hand, and might even be identical. Christian missionaries assured Africans that railroads and steam power were among the benefits of accepting Christianity.

In many places, Christianity seemed no more than an aspect of European colonialism. Kings and their families might be baptized and churches were sometimes built, but they served primarily European settlers and slave traders. As a result, anti-European resistance sometimes took an anti-Christian form. Thus in 1693 a little community of Christians in Zimbabwe was massacred and its Portuguese priest was flayed alive.

In the island kingdom of Madagascar, Queen Ranavalona I

(reigned 1828–1861) outlawed Christianity in 1837. She expelled missionaries and other foreigners, and during the next twenty years she executed several hundred native Christians. But in 1857 she ended the persecution. Twelve years later, Ranavalona II became a Christian convert. Here, as elsewhere in Africa, Christianity was welcomed as a new faith but condemned for its foreign connections and its intolerance of older faiths.

In the early nineteenth century, Muslims in Yorubaland (partly equivalent to modern Nigeria) suffered similar persecution, for similar reasons. Yet by midcentury they were fully tolerated. Then it was the turn of Christians. In 1848 two Christian converts were put into the stocks for refusing to take part in their families' traditional religious rites. More and more Yoruba people complained that family members were rejecting their ancestral religion to join Christian churches, but local authorities insisted that the new religion should be tolerated.

In 1849 that toleration was stretched to the breaking point. The first funeral and burial of a Christian convert in Yorubaland infringed on the burial monopoly of an important Yoruba society, the guardians of the earth cult. Several Christians were arrested, beaten, and fined. A mob attacked other Christians, beating them and shaving their heads in an attempt to shave away the effects of their baptism. Under popular pressure, local authorities arrested as many as eighty Christians, inflicted heavy fines on them, and forbade them to attend church services. Christian women, and the wives of Christian men, were barred from the public market. A few cities refused to allow Christians within their territories.

But public repression soon lapsed. Missionaries went on preaching, and the number of converts grew steadily, provoking many family disputes. In 1867, partly as a means of putting pressure on the British government, European missionaries were expelled from the city of Abeokuta. Mobs attacked several mission stations. Christianity was officially prohibited, but the prohibition was withdrawn in less than a year.

In the late nineteenth century, King Mutesa of Buganda tolerated and even encouraged Muslim, Catholic, and Protestant missionaries. He died in 1884 and was succeeded by his son Mwanga. The young king feared that the new religions bred disloyalty, and he promptly began a persecution of Christians. An English bishop was murdered. Thirty-one Christians, including both Catholics and Protestants, were burned alive and some seventy others butchered. Many who were not killed were flogged, beaten, or castrated.

Christians and Muslims briefly joined forces to depose Mwanga. The ensuing power struggle between Christians and Muslims ended when Mwanga's Muslim brother Kalema seized power. He resumed the persecution of Christians, expelled Europeans from his domains, and began to force conversions to Islam. A civil war between the brothers followed. Protestant missionaries pleaded for British intervention, and in 1894 Britain took over the country as the protectorate of Uganda.

Religious persecution in Africa almost always involved Christians, Muslims, or Jews. They were sometimes perpetrators, sometimes victims, often both. Indigenous cults could be regulated by native African authorities—as when worship of the smallpox god was suspended in Abeokuta during an epidemic in 1884—but they were not persecuted except when Christians or Muslims took power.

SOURCES AND FURTHER READING

Much of African history is obscured by a lack of written sources and archaeological studies, and many of the written sources that do exist are in Arabic. The series *Fontes Historiae Africanae* consists of collections of sources in English translation, including *Corpus of Early Arabic Sources for West African History*, translated by J. F. P. Hopkins, edited and annotated by N. Levtzion and J. F. Hopkins (Cambridge: Cambridge University Press, 1981) and David William Cohen's *Towards a Reconstructed Past: Historical Texts from Busoga, Uganda* (Oxford: Oxford University Press, 1987). For the history of Christianity in Africa, there are journals, reports, and books by missionaries and explorers.

The Religious Traditions of Africa: A History by Elizabeth Isichei (Westport, CT: Praeger, 2004) provides the religious background. Specialized modern works include Adrian Hastings's *The Church in Africa:*

1450–1950 (Oxford: Clarendon, 1994); Taddesse Tamrat's *Church and State in Ethiopia, 1270–1527* (Oxford: Clarendon, 1972); and Steven Kaplan's *The Beta Israel (Falasha) in Ethiopia: From Earliest Times to the Twentieth Century* (New York: New York University Press, 1992).

Chapter 16

Europe

Sixteenth and Seventeenth Centuries

S ir Thomas More was an accomplished lawyer, diplomat, and author. His *Utopia* added a new word to the English language and created the genre of utopian fiction. It described an ideal society whose people "count it among their most ancient principles that no one should ever suffer harm for his religion." The Utopians suspected that God might "prefer to have varied and manifold forms of worship, inspiring different people differently."

That was fiction. Reality was something else. As Lord Chancellor of England from 1529 to 1532, More was charged with enforcing the laws against heresy. There were dangerous developments in continental Europe. Martin Luther had created a whole new heresy there, one that was producing upheaval in Germany and might do the same in England. During his three-year tenure, More presided over the burning of four alleged Lutherans.

Many heretics shared the subversive idea that all Christians should be allowed to read the Bible. The Englishman William Tyndale had moved to Germany in order to translate the Bible into English. Now copies of his English Bible were being smuggled into England, and Sir Thomas was busy confiscating them. Like a powerful drug that could cure or kill, the Bible was strong medicine, to be handled only by trained professionals. Punishment for importing or possessing an English Bible ranged from fines to burning at the stake.

Meanwhile, King Henry VIII was trying to shed his wife, Katherine of Aragon, daughter of the famous Ferdinand and Isabella (see chapter 13). After more than a decade of marriage and at least six pregnancies, Katherine had produced exactly one surviving child, a daughter. Henry wanted a son.

Katherine had been briefly married to Henry's late brother, and only a special dispensation from the pope had allowed her to marry Henry. Now Henry decided that their lack of a son showed that God did not approve. He asked the new pope to annul the marriage. When the pope refused, Henry appealed to an English court.

Meanwhile, a young nun named Elizabeth Barton, whom her admirers called the Holy Maid of Kent, prophesied that if Henry repudiated the queen he would lose his throne within six months. Sir Thomas More was dubious about the prophecy, but he was certain that Henry was wrong to defy the pope. He advised the king to abandon the annulment plan.

Henry persisted. If the pope would not annul his marriage, Henry would annul the pope's authority in England. Ignoring More's advice and Elizabeth Barton's prophecies, he persuaded Parliament to pass a series of measures freeing the English church from papal control. In 1533 he appointed Thomas Cranmer as archbishop of Canterbury, the highest church position in England. In quick succession, Cranmer annulled Henry's marriage, and the pope excommunicated Henry. Parliament declared the king supreme head of the Church of England, and recognized Henry's new wife, Anne Boleyn, as queen. Almost certainly, Henry never suspected the forces for change that he had unleashed.

Sir Thomas More was caught between conflicting loyalties. He had tried to remain true to both King Henry and the Catholic Church, but now he had to choose. A new law required every adult Englishman to take an oath accepting Henry's marriage to Anne as valid—which implied that Henry's break from the Catholic Church was also valid. To underline the point, Elizabeth Barton and some of her supporters were executed, and their dismembered bodies were displayed on London's city gates.

Sir Thomas might have been willing to recognize the marriage, but he could not in conscience disown the pope. His reward was prison and execution—technically on a charge of treason, but in fact for his religious convictions. He was not alone. Several prominent clergymen and monks also refused the oath and were executed.

In a sense, More's life is the story of the Protestant Reformation. It is the story of sincere believers who saw persecution from both sides, as perpetrators and as victims. Almost all sixteenth- and seventeenth-century religious reformers and their followers had to struggle against persecution. Sooner or later, almost all of them persecuted other Christians. The leading reformers were sincere, intelligent, deeply moral individuals, and many of them were humane and kindly by disposition. Only their religious convictions drove them to persecute. Since they were right and all other opinions wrong, and human souls hung in the balance, it was their duty to stamp out error.

In 1500 the greatest European power was the Catholic Church—a single, centralized organization that covered all of western Europe. In theory, the Holy Roman Empire was the political equivalent of the Church, and the emperor was the political head of all Western Christendom. In fact, that had never been true, and by 1500 the Empire had become a confederation of states with varying degrees of independence.

The early sixteenth-century Empire included Bohemia and Moravia, Belgium, the Netherlands, parts of northern Italy, and Switzerland, but its heartland was Austria and what is now Germany. The ruling Hapsburg dynasty was Austrian. Germany was a collection of small principalities and even smaller city-states, each with its own relationship to the imperial power. Other sections of the Empire were ruled by imperial governors.

This was the *Holy* Roman Empire—heir to ancient Rome, but self-consciously Christian, meaning Catholic. Jews were allowed—though their books were often burned—and even Muslims could be tolerated in small numbers. But heretics were always to be suppressed. France, Spain, and England—Europe's other great powers—were also solidly Catholic. No one dreamed that only fifty years later European Christianity would be split in half, and public officials in many places would openly curse the pope and the traditional sacra-ments. Sir Thomas More was not the only conscientious Christian caught up by religious ideas so powerful that people inflicted and suffered deadly violence for them.

"I am rough, boisterous, stormy, and altogether warlike, I am born to fight innumerable monsters and devils, to remove stems and stones, cut away thistles and thorns, and clear away wild forests." Not all the reformers were gentle scholars. Martin Luther was a monk by profession and a brawler by temperament.

He argued that individual Christians had the right and duty to study the Bible and work out their own understanding of this single source of Christian truth. More disturbingly, he taught that salvation could not be earned. No matter how diligently you did good works, you remained what you were born—a miserable sinner. No priest could absolve you from your sins. Only faith could justify you in God's eyes. Sacraments, such as baptism and the Eucharist, had no automatic, miraculous effect. They were valid only as aids to faith, and some of them (like the ordination of priests) were worthless. These ideas—summed up in the phrase "the priesthood of all believers"—made the whole structure of the Church unnecessary.

In spite of his revolutionary theology, Luther's own instincts were conservative. He wanted to change the Catholic Church, not break away from it. But the Catholic hierarchy rejected him. Pope Leo X repeatedly condemned the new teachings, and in 1521 he excommunicated Luther.

Ever a fighter, Luther devoted the rest of his life to the movement he had started. He vigorously organized his new church, translated the Bible into German, and produced a flood of books, controversial pamphlets, hymns, devotional and liturgical works, and sermons. Traveling preachers spread Luther's call for change far and wide.

Lutheranism quickly attracted followers among intellectuals, common people, and the ruling class. Semi-independent cities often embraced the new ideas, and so did aristocrats. Germany was soon divided between Catholic princes and Lutheran princes—some of them sincere converts, others who saw the new church as a lever they could use for political purposes.

To many ordinary Christians, Luther's doctrine sounded like a declaration of freedom—freedom of conscience, freedom from penances and tithes, freedom from the decrees of popes and bishops and the hypocritical meddling of priests. To some, it was a call for equality. German peasants had long struggled under economic and social oppression. Many of them took the Lutheran message to heart in ways that the preachers had not intended. Freedom from the tyranny of the Church? Equality of believers? Clearly, God was on the peasants' side. In 1524 they rose in revolt.

Luther was appalled. He published a pamphlet titled *Against the Robbing and Murdering Hordes of Peasants*, calling for their violent repression. "Let everyone who can, smite, slay, and stab, secretly or openly, remembering that nothing can be more poisonous, hurtful, or devilish than a rebel." Catholic and Lutheran princes put aside their differences to crush the revolt. An estimated one hundred thousand peasants were killed in less than two years of warfare. Luther shrugged off the carnage. As he pointed out, "It is a trifle for God to massacre a lot of peasants, when he drowned the whole world with a flood and wiped out Sodom with fire."

The Peasants' War was primarily the revolt of an oppressed class, but people on both sides saw it in religious terms. On the eve of the climactic battle of Frankenhausen, the peasant army sent a message to the noblemen arrayed against them: "We have not come here to injure anyone (see 2 John), but to receive divine justice." The princes replied that they came to punish blasphemers with the sword of God. Several thousand peasants died in the battle that followed. The radical Thomas Müntzer had enthusiastically supported the revolt, and had set up a theocratic state in the city of Mühlhausen. After the battle of Frankenhausen, the victorious princes had him tortured and executed, with thousands of his followers.

Luther had once believed that religion could not be coerced. He had not anticipated how hard it would be to convert the world. By the end of his life he approved of the death penalty for blasphemy and idolatry—usually meaning the teachings and practices of other churches. He also argued that synagogues should be burned and Jewish books confiscated. Reformation persecution was well under way.

Throughout western Europe, new religious groups proliferated. New reformers built on the work of Wyclif, Hus, and the Waldensians (see chapter 13). With the advantage of the printing press, their ideas spread much faster and farther. Reformers expelled from one state could always hope to find refuge and support in a neighboring one.

But virtually everyone agreed that any state needed religious unity. Many small-scale persecutions marked the early Reformation, as princes struggled to keep their rebellious subjects Catholic, or convert them to a newly discovered faith. Alliances and local wars turned on religious conversions. From this troubled chaos, a principle emerged at the Peace of Augsburg in 1555: *cuius regio, eius religio*—"whose realm, his religion." In other words, subjects must accept the religion of their ruler.

Among the most radical reformed Christians were the people whose opponents scornfully called them "Anabaptists," meaning re-baptizers. For centuries, Christian parents had been taking their babies to church to be baptized as early as possible. After all, unbaptized children could not get into heaven. But according to Anabaptists, infant baptism was meaningless. Babies had no way of understanding Christianity or making an informed choice. Their so-called baptism was a farce. If you had been baptized as a baby, you needed another, real baptism as an adult.

By the 1530s, there were several kinds of Anabaptists. The Mennonites, or followers of Menno Simons, were committed to nonviolence. Others were more militant. In 1534 a group of Melchiorite Anabaptists (followers of Melchior Hoffmann) succeeded in taking over the city of Münster. They burned all books except German-language Bibles, and expelled everyone who disagreed with their views. Anabaptists from other cities and rural areas flocked to Münster. The expelled citizens' property was shared out among them. Münster had become a revolutionary commune.

Prince-Bishop Franz von Waldeck, the Catholic ruler of Münster, besieged the city. Within Münster's walls, disagreements arose. Men and women who complained about conditions or questioned the Anabaptist leadership were thrown into prison or killed. Jan Matthias, the Anabaptist leader, was killed in a suicidal sortie against the bishop's forces. His successor was Jan Beukelsz or Bockelson, also called Jan van Leyden, whose ideas were still more radical. He ruled that every adult must be married, and that men should have as many wives as they could afford. He himself proceeded to take nineteen.

After putting down an uprising within the city, Jan declared himself king—not only of Münster, but of the whole world. God had chosen him as the successor to the biblical king David. Anyone who resisted would be put to death. He sent "apostles" to neighboring cities to call for reinforcements—without success. Some were betrayed to Bishop von Waldeck, who had them tortured and beheaded.

Martin Luther denounced Jan and called the Anabaptist teachings "blasphemous errors." Philip Melanchthon, another major reformer, recommended that all Anabaptists should be exterminated. The Anabaptists of Münster had nowhere to turn. Within the city, they were dying of starvation and disease. In spring 1535 King Jan announced that anyone who wished could leave Münster—but they could never come back. Hundreds of people left, only to find new horrors. The bishop ordered his soldiers to shoot the adult male defectors and drive the women and children back to the city walls.

The bishop's final attack came in June. The city was taken, Jan and other leaders captured, and most of the population massacred. Women who survived the first slaughter were allowed to live if they recanted their unorthodox beliefs. Some did so, but others preferred to die. Jan and two other prominent men were ripped apart with red-hot tongs, and their bodies displayed in iron cages hung on the city gates.

Jean (John) Calvin was a Frenchman who was not safe in France. He had studied Hebrew and theology and absorbed some of the ideas of Luther and other reformers. In the early 1530s he developed his own system of theology and morality. Church authorities condemned his ideas, and he wandered from city to city until he settled at the independent city-state of Geneva in 1536. Geneva had already expelled its Catholic bishop and accepted the teachings of the reformer Guillaume Farel. Here at last Calvin could freely work out his rigorous doctrines.

Luther had emphasized that salvation was God's gift, beyond human power to earn. Calvin added that nothing could happen in God's universe without God's will, including the salvation and damnation of souls. Not only were individuals helpless to achieve their own salvation, but their fate was already predestined. Good works were of no value in themselves, but anyone who had true faith in God would demonstrate that faith by living a life of virtue.

This bleak-sounding doctrine was a message of liberation for many people. If your fate was sealed and there was nothing you could do about it, a burden of responsibility was lifted from your shoulders. You had nothing more to fear from God. You did not need to earn your salvation. By believing the doctrine, you had already done all you could do. And since no one could know exactly who were predestined to salvation, you could trust that most believers were saved, you among them.

The city government of Geneva had vowed to follow "the holy law of the Gospel." But Calvin's stern vision of what that law was did not meet with universal approval. He wanted to impose his own creed on all citizens and give the clergy power to excommunicate anyone who failed to live by it. The dispute grew heated. In 1538 both Calvin and Farel were expelled from the city. In 1540 Calvin was invited back. For the next fifteen years the struggle between rival factions continued.

One thing all agreed on was that heresy must be punished. In 1553 Miguel Serveto (better known as Michael Servetus) arrived in Geneva, fleeing from the French Inquisition. Servetus was a unitarian. He rejected the concept of a three-personed God as unbiblical and illogical. He had corresponded with Calvin for years, and may have hoped to find toleration. But Calvin and the Genevan government decided to carry out the death sentence that had been passed on Servetus in France. He was burned at the stake, with wide approval from Protestants as well as Catholics throughout Europe.

In 1555 some of Calvin's opponents in Geneva rioted against his increasing power. Calvin's party charged the rioters with attempting a coup d'état. Four of them were beheaded. Others were exiled or fled the city. That was the last serious challenge to Calvin's theocracy.

Elsewhere, each country went through its own Reformation process, with varying degrees of bloodshed. In the early sixteenth century, Protestant ideas spread through the Netherlands, which then included Belgium. The local Inquisition made its first arrests of suspected Lutherans in 1525. In a grand public ceremony, eight men and two women were sentenced to prison for terms ranging from two to seven years. If they survived their imprisonment—on a diet of bread and water—they were to wear conspicuous red or yellow crosses for the rest of their lives. Such examples did not stop the spread of heresy. Within a few years, civil courts were burning Lutherans at the stake. By 1555 hundreds of people had been executed for heresy in the Netherlands.

In that year, the emperor Charles V presented the Netherlands to his son Philip, king of Spain. The pious Philip was distressed to learn that heresies were rife in this new addition to his kingdom. He installed Spanish governors, who knew how to deal sternly with dissidents. The Netherlands were soon at the point of rebellion. The duke of Alba (also spelled Alva) was appointed military governor in 1567, and set up what came to be known as the Court of Blood. It condemned some eighteen thousand people to death as heretics, rebels, or both. In 1581, after years of struggle, the Netherlands drove out the Spanish and declared independence.

Only a few countries of western Europe were immune to the Reformation's revolutionary changes. The vigilant Roman Inquisition executed about seventy-five heretics in Rome between 1545 and 1600, and lesser numbers were executed at other Italian cities. A few Waldensian communities survived in the mountain valleys of the Piedmont in northern Italy—even after a massacre in 1655 by troops from France and Savoy. But for the most part, Italy remained solidly Catholic.

So did Spain and Portugal. When the Spanish Inquisition uncovered a few small Protestant groups in 1557, it appealed to Pope Paul IV for emergency powers. Armed with these powers, the Inquisition could and did execute even repentant first offenders. Ten years and more than a hundred public executions later, Spanish Protestantism was virtually extinct. The heretics that continued to be executed on occasion were usually foreigners. The last was a French Huguenot in 1604. In Ireland, Protestantism was the religion of their oppressive English rulers, and therefore had no appeal for the vast majority of the population.

Unlike Germany and Switzerland, France was a unified, centralized nation ruled by a strong—and strongly Catholic—monarchy. But the reign of King Francis I (1515–1547) was a time of religious and intellectual turmoil. Though Francis himself was a tolerant and open-minded man, the French religious establishment was determined to resist dangerous new ideas.

In 1521 the Parlement (or high court) of Paris ruled that no religious books could be published without prior approval by the theological faculty of the Sorbonne. Bibles in French were burned, and new translations forbidden. The first Protestant was burned at Paris in 1523. In 1525 a special commission was appointed to prosecute suspected heretics. By 1526 it was a crime to read or possess any of Luther's works or any French translation of the Bible.

This was the persecution that drove first Guillaume Farel and then Calvin out of France. Many other Protestants also sought refuge in free cities or Lutheran principalities of the Holy Roman Empire— but more stayed in France. By the 1530s there were small groups of Protestants scattered throughout the country. For the most part they adhered to the doctrines of Calvin. They came to be called Huguenots.

On the morning of October 18, 1534, people in Paris and several other cities woke to find provocative posters that had been put up during the night. The posters denounced Catholic priests as idolaters, liars, and blasphemers, and attacked the Mass, the basic Catholic sacrament. This "Affair of the Placards" triggered a crackdown. Dozens of people were charged with sedition and heresy, and at least twenty were executed. Within a few months, tighter regulations prohibited the printing of any publication that had not been approved as "necessary for the public good." Concealing or helping heretics was declared a crime. The penalty for reading, expounding, translating, writing, or printing anything contrary to Catholic doctrine was death.

During the following years, jurisdiction against heretics was extended to all courts throughout France. In the late 1540s, the Parlement of Paris sentenced an average of more than twenty people per year to death for heresy. In southern France, the Parlement of Aix condemned whole villages of Waldensian immigrants to be killed and their houses demolished. Some three thousand villagers were massacred by government troops.

Francis I's successor, Henri II, brought persecution to its highest level in French history. He established a special tribunal, the *chambre ardente* or "burning chamber," to deal with heresy cases. In its first three years, it charged more than five hundred individuals with heresy. Church authorities were given extended powers, because Henri suspected that civil courts were contaminated with heresy. Certainly Protestantism had spread through much of French society. Some nobles had turned Huguenot, but the new creed was especially popular among merchants, tradespeople, and skilled workers of all kinds.

In 1551 Henri decreed that no one could be appointed to a judicial or municipal office without a certificate of Catholic orthodoxy. Courts were required to hold self-examination sessions every three months to weed out Huguenot sympathizers. The property of convicted heretics was to be confiscated. Anyone who knew of heretical or suspicious activity was required to inform the authorities. Informers were rewarded with one-third of the heretics' property. Local magistrates were to search bookstores and private homes for prohibited printed material. Correspondence with anyone in Geneva or other Protestant cities was forbidden. Everyone was required to attend Catholic church services.

Eight years later, France was shaken by a totally unexpected event. Henri II was killed in a jousting accident. His fifteen-year-old son, Francis II, continued the persecution, but he died in the following year. The new king was Francis's little brother, Charles IX, only ten years old at his accession. Royal power lay in the hands of their mother, Catherine de' Medici. And she had other ideas about how to deal with Protestants.

Catherine saw that the Huguenots had become a major force in French politics, and that persecution had failed. Her policy was one of reconciliation. That meant balancing Catholic nobles against Protestant nobles—fewer but just as important—and trying to keep both sides from committing any unforgivable atrocities. Sometimes that was impossible.

Under Catherine's regency, Huguenots were more publicly visible. Catholic extremists found that intolerable. In early 1562, several hundred Huguenots gathered illegally to hear a Protestant sermon near the town of Vassy. The duke of Guise, the most militant Catholic leader, sent troops to break up the service. They slaughtered seventy-four of the congregation, triggering similar massacres in other areas. Huguenot nobles marshaled their forces to retaliate. In several cities, Huguenots staged coups d'état. The national government dispatched troops to put down the coups, and the first of the French Wars of Religion was under way.

Besides the casualties of war, judicial punishments continued. More than 120 Huguenots were executed after a failed coup at Toulouse. Huguenots were no more tolerant than Catholics. Already in 1561 a Huguenot synod had decreed that it was a magistrate's duty to suppress heresy. In the territories they controlled, Huguenot officials often outlawed Catholic worship, stripped churches of their "idols," and sometimes physically drove Catholics to attend Protestant sermons.

A treaty in 1570 gave Huguenots much of what they had hoped for. In four designated cities, they could worship in complete freedom. Elsewhere, they were allowed to practice their religion under certain restrictions, and everywhere they were granted freedom of conscience—in other words, they were not required to attend Catholic services. But this apparent victory embittered popular opinion still more. Catholic mobs attacked Huguenots, and Huguenot mobs took revenge for past wrongs. The peace was a very uneasy one.

Catherine de' Medici was determined to reach a more genuine reconciliation. In 1572 she arranged for her daughter Marguerite to marry Henri de Bourbon, the Huguenot prince of Navarre. The pope disapproved, but Catherine pressed ahead with the wedding plans. Paris was splendidly decked out for the festivities. Huguenots flocked to the city to celebrate the union of one of their own with the royal family. Catholic moderates embraced the chance to bring a peaceful end to the troubles. But a woman prophet—some said a nun—was telling Parisian crowds that unless every Huguenot was killed, God would destroy Paris.

The wedding took place on August 18, 1572. Three days of festival followed. On August 22, Admiral Gaspard de Coligny, the chief Huguenot leader, was badly wounded in an assassination attempt. The Huguenots who had crowded into Paris were outraged. They blamed the duke of Guise, and demanded retaliation.

The young king promised an investigation. But the royal council was too alarmed to wait. To the councilors, it seemed that Paris was about to erupt in civil war. They decided that the only way to forestall a Huguenot coup was to strike first. Catherine and the king reluctantly agreed. On the night of August 23—the eve of St. Bartholomew's Day—the duke of Guise and other militant Catholic nobles led their armed men in a surprise attack on Huguenot lodgings. First they finished off Coligny, then turned to the other visiting Huguenot nobles and gentry. Before morning they had killed about two hundred people.

It was a bloodletting that produced a hemorrhage. As word spread through Paris, ordinary people took up the slaughter. In every part of the city, Catholics attacked Huguenots with whatever weapons they could lay their hands on. For days, Paris was a slaughterhouse. More than two thousand people were massacred there. In cities all over France, local authorities and local mobs turned out to kill Protestants. Many of the killers believed that they were following royal orders. A conservative estimate placed the number of dead at thirty thousand. Once more, full-scale civil war broke out.

For decades, the trauma of the St. Bartholomew's Day massacre prevented any lasting peace, although there were interruptions. (Historians count at least seven separate wars.) Overall, the Wars of Religion lasted from 1562 to 1598. Both Catholic and Protestant leaders held that the government was morally obliged to suppress religious dissidents. Huguenots did not ask for toleration—they wanted a Protestant government that would suppress Catholicism. The Edict of Nantes, which granted almost full toleration in 1587, was the result of a stalemate. Since neither side could win, they would have to live together.

Thirty years later, the Edict of Nantes began to be whittled away. In 1685 Louis XIV revoked it entirely, and a new age of persecution began. After massacres by royal troops, at least two hundred thousand Huguenots fled from France. Louis also persecuted dissident Catholics, ranging from the predestinarian Jansenists to the mystical Quietists.

Meanwhile, the Reformation had spread to still other nations and taken other forms. A major function of any European government was to protect and support the true faith—whatever that was thought to be. Religion played an important role in every international power struggle. In the early seventeenth century, Protestant states lined up against Catholic states, culminating in the horrific Thirty Years' War (1618–1648), which killed somewhere between 15 and 40 percent of Germany's population.

England had been an exception. Henry VIII's break from the Catholic Church was political, not religious. But English reformers soon took advantage of the break to press for changes in doctrine and practice. Under Calvinistic influence, Henry's government closed all monasteries and confiscated their property. Three priors of Carthusian monasteries were hanged, drawn, and quartered. Fifteen other monks were executed or died in prison. During the years 1532 through 1540, a total of 329 people were executed for treason. Though they were not labeled "heretics," almost all of them opposed Henry on religious grounds.

At the same time, Sir Thomas More's work of suppressing heresy in the good old style continued after his death. Activists who preached the doctrines of Luther, Calvin, or other reformers were burned at the stake. In all, more than eighty people were burned for heresy in Henry's long reign (1509–1547). Common people were forbidden to read the Bible until 1537, when an English Bible was finally approved.

Henry had broken ties with the pope because he wanted a son. His third wife, Jane Seymour, died twelve days after giving birth to that son, the future Edward VI. Edward was nine years old when he became king. He died in 1553, at age fifteen. In the meantime, his government had pursued the process of Protestantization. Though only two people were executed as heretics during his six-year reign, there were substantial changes in English Christianity.

Much that was dear to ordinary Catholics had been abolished. Local churches were ordered to remove and destroy saints' images. Church service books in Latin were to be burned, altars replaced by communion tables. Ancient holy days were no longer celebrated, and processions were banned. Religious fraternities were dissolved, and the chantries where priests had prayed for the dead were closed. The doctrine of purgatory was declared a devilish superstition. Souls must now go straight to heaven or to hell. Once your loved ones had died, it was too late to pray for them.

All this changed dramatically when Edward's half-sister Mary inherited the throne. Mary was the child of Henry's first wife, Katherine of Aragon, and a devout Catholic. She set herself the task of returning England to Catholicism. Her methods earned her the nickname of Bloody Mary.

In her five years as queen, Mary presided over the executions of more than 280 heretics—in this case meaning Anglicans or other Protestants. Thomas Cranmer, the archbishop of Canterbury who had annulled Henry VIII's marriage to Katherine of Aragon—thus making Mary illegitimate—was among those who were burned at the stake.

Elizabeth I succeeded Mary, and promptly restored the Anglican Church. During her long reign (1552–1603), Catholics were reduced to a small and oppressed minority. There was no longer a Catholic Church as such in England. The Catholic bishops had been executed as traitors, or had died in prison, or had fled or resigned. Any Catholic priest could be executed for treason. Many a well-to-do Catholic family contrived a "priest hole" in their house—a secret hiding place where a fugitive priest could shelter. Priests who had officially converted to the Church of England sometimes went on celebrating Catholic masses in secret.

At the other end of the Christian spectrum were the Puritans— radical Protestants who found the Anglican Church too Catholic. Puritans embraced the Calvinist rule that anything not specifically authorized by the Bible was forbidden. Some of them favored a national church governed by a hierarchy of elected elders or pres- byters—hence Presbyterianism. Others, still more democratic, held that each congregation should be independent—hence Congrega- tionalism. All of them opposed images, liturgies, and vestments, and preached an austere, church-centered morality.

Some Puritans separated entirely from the Church of England and preached against its doctrines. Several of their leaders were exe- cuted—as usual, for treason. Some separatist Puritans emigrated to the Netherlands, where there was now greater freedom of religion. Among these emigrant groups were the future Pilgrims of American history.

But, as their name implied, most Puritans wanted to purify the Anglican Church, not to leave it. When James I succeeded Queen

Elizabeth in 1603, Puritans petitioned him for church reforms. A church conference rejected all their requests but one. It agreed to produce an authorized English translation of the Bible—later to be known as the "King James Version."

King Charles I (reigned 1625–1649) was a devout "high churchman"—meaning that his beliefs and practices were much too close to Catholicism for Puritan comfort. His chief clerical supporter was William Laud, bishop of London from 1628 and archbishop of Canterbury from 1633. Together, Laud and King Charles undertook to stamp out Calvinism in the Church of England and to enforce a uniform, ritualistic style of worship.

Charles issued a decree forbidding sermons on predestination, a primary Calvinist theme. Writings by Calvinist theologians were banned. Puritan leaders and critics of Laud's high-church policies were brought before royal courts. Some were sentenced to life imprisonment after having their ears cut off. Others were subjected to heavy fines and prison terms.

Meanwhile, Charles was locked in a continuing struggle with Parliament. There was a strong Puritan wing in Parliament, which became a majority as Charles alienated more and more of his subjects. Again and again, Parliament refused to fund the king's military expeditions and foreign involvements unless he agreed to increased civil rights. Religious and civil complaints meshed together, and popular opposition to the king increased. In 1642 civil war broke out.

Most High Church Anglicans, and Catholics as well, supported the king. Almost all Puritans supported Parliament. As the war dragged on, it became more bitterly religious. In the last stages, the Puritan leader Oliver Cromwell forged his New Model Army—an all-Puritan force dedicated to creating a godly nation. They decisively defeated the royal armies and took the king captive.

Theoretically, Parliament had won the war. But Cromwell and his supporters quickly purged Parliament of 143 members, most of them Presbyterians, on the grounds that they favored the king. The remaining "Rump Parliament" deposed the king, abolished the monarchy, and established a Commonwealth, to be run on Puritan principles. Charles was convicted of treason and beheaded. The Anglican Church would later declare him a saint and martyr.

The new government prohibited anything it perceived as superstitious, "idolatrous," or "papistical." That included the celebration of Christmas as well as popular festivities like maypole dances. Anything that Puritans considered likely to contribute to immorality was forbidden. Theaters were closed.

In the first two years of the Commonwealth, Cromwell led his soldiers into Ireland and then Scotland to put down resistance. He told the troops embarking for Ireland that they were like the Israelites going into Canaan—led by God to destroy an ungodly people. The brutality of Cromwell's troops to the overwhelmingly Catholic Irish left a wound that has rankled ever since. As soon as the major fighting was over, Cromwell proceeded to confiscate the property of Catholic landowners and give it to Protestants—thus sowing seeds that would blossom in the vicious twentieth-century conflicts of Northern Ireland.

Back in England, Cromwell dissolved the Rump Parliament and governed dictatorially. In 1653 he became Lord Protector of England—virtually an absolute monarch. Nevertheless, his government was often more lenient toward religious dissent than the kings and queens of England had been. Theoretically, any citizen was free to follow any variety of Protestant Christianity. Jews were allowed back into England for the first time since 1290.

That tolerance had its limits. New sects proliferated. Some, like the Baptists and the Quakers, survived and eventually became respectable, but they had a rocky start. George Fox, who founded the Religious Society of Friends (better known as Quakers), was in prison eight times between 1649 and 1675. In 1656 James Nayler, a charismatic Quaker leader, was pilloried, whipped, branded, and imprisoned. Others, like the Diggers and the Ranters, had social agendas that were too radical for most seventeenth-century English. They were firmly suppressed.

Oliver Cromwell died in 1658. Two years later the monarchy was restored. Charles I's eldest surviving son, who had wandered around Europe as an exile, was crowned as Charles II. He favored religious toleration, but the new Parliament did not. It passed a series of laws enforcing Anglican worship and severely restricting all other forms. It was now illegal for five or more persons to assemble for worship other than Anglican. About two thousand nonconformist ministers were forced to resign and forbidden to come within five miles of the cities where they had served. In the years from 1660 to 1688, tens of thousands of nonconformist Christians—Puritans, Quakers, Baptists, Presbyterians, and others—were thrown into prison, and some five thousand died there.

In 1673 Parliament passed the Test Act, which effectively restricted civil and military offices to Anglicans. Five years later the rule was extended to Parliament itself. Yet Charles himself was sympathetic to Catholicism. His wife, Catherine of Braganza, was Catholic, and his younger brother James was a Catholic convert. In 1685 Charles died childless, and James succeeded him as James II.

James was the first Catholic ruler since Queen Mary's bloody reign, but his methods were different. In 1687 he suspended the application of the Test Act. His decree declared that "conscience ought not to be constrained, nor people forced in matters of mere religion." His objection to religious persecution was simple—it didn't work. That tolerant approach won him the support of Quakers and other dissident groups.

The presumed heir to James's throne was his daughter Mary. She was a Protestant and the wife of William of Orange, ruler of the Netherlands. But in 1688, James's second, Catholic wife gave birth to a son. The prospect of a Catholic dynasty spurred the resolutely anti-Catholic Parliament to the point of rebellion. Leading members struck a deal with Mary and her husband, William: they could rule England if they accepted certain restrictions on royal power.

William took his army to England and marched toward London. James and his family fled to France. Parliament decided to take that as an abdication, and William and Mary were crowned king and queen of England. Part of the agreement was a constitutional guarantee that no Catholic could ever rule England again. Parliament promptly passed what was called an Act of Toleration. It reinstated the Test Act, but exempted certain nonconformist Protestants from some of its restrictions.

Religiously speaking, Europe's two centuries of turmoil were over. In virtually every European country, an established church was firmly united with the national government, never to be replaced by another. What had begun as a movement of liberation and reawakening had turned into a nightmare of competing orthodoxies. Yet ideas had taken root, and knowledge had been made public, that would lead to the Enlightenment, and to serious advances in political liberty and freedom of thought. Future revolutions would not seek to establish new religions. They would call for freedom from religious establishments.

SOURCES AND FURTHER READING

The source material for the Reformation is bewilderingly vast. So is the literature about it. The works of Martin Luther, John Calvin, Philip Melanchthon, and other reformers form the basis of major modern Christian denominations, and are widely available in English. Pamela Johnston and Bob Scribner's *The Reformation in Germany and Switzerland* (Cambridge: Cambridge University Press, 1993) is a small but informative collection of short passages from contemporary documents, with editorial study helps. A more extensive collection is *A Reformation Reader: Primary Texts with Introductions*, edited by Denis R. Janz, augmented edition (Minneapolis, MN: Fortress, 2002).

Particularly relevant secondary works include *Tolerance and Intolerance in the European Reformation*, edited by Ole Peter Grell and Bob Scribner (Cambridge: Cambridge University Press, 1996); Brad S. Gregory's *Salvation at Stake: Christian Martyrdom in Early Modern Europe* (Cambridge, MA: Harvard University Press, 1999); and Euan Cameron's *The Reformation of the Heretics: The Waldenses of the Alps, 1480–1580* (Oxford: Oxford University Press, 1984).

Chapter 17

North and South America

Sixteenth through Eighteenth Centuries

Christendom should . . . make great festivals, and give solemn thanks to the Holy Trinity for the great exaltation they shall have by the conversion of so many peoples to our holy faith; and next for the temporal benefit which will bring hither refreshment and profit, not only to Spain, to all Christians.
— Christopher Columbus, 1493

To enterprising Europeans, the news was stunning. The world had opportunities they had never dreamed of—two whole continents they had not known about, inhabited by millions of people. Millions of heathens to be converted, millions of customers, suppliers, and workers. Best of all, the native peoples in many parts of what was now called America did not even use the land they lived on—not as Europeans understood "use." By European rules, the land was unoccupied and up for grabs. Europeans made haste to grab it.

Spanish, Portuguese, Dutch, French, and English governments raced to claim jurisdiction over the maximum amount of American territory. Government-sponsored and private expeditions set off to explore, trade, confiscate, settle, and convert. Almost every expedition listed "saving souls" as a primary purpose. The European penetration of the Americas was a self-consciously Christian penetration.

Columbus had seen no temples, idols, or priests on the well-populated Caribbean islands where he landed. He assumed that the people had no religion of their own. It should be easy to make Christians of them. Within two years of first landing, he and the Spaniards under his command had helped themselves to the inhabitants' property, put them to forced labor, raped unknown numbers of women, kidnapped at least one local ruler and killed others, started a war, and (in the words of a contemporary observer, Bartolomé de las Casas) succeeded in "making the name of Christian synonymous with terror."

Spanish conquest and settlement spread quickly through the Caribbean and into the American mainland. Everywhere, the inhabitants' land was shared out among Spanish soldiers and settlers. In some areas, natives were forcibly relocated into new villages where they could be more easily supervised and Christianized. Almost everywhere, they were required to work for Spaniards. In 1503 Queen Isabella decreed that natives who rejected the Catholic faith could be enslaved.

It seemed like a foolproof system for making converts and profits. But somehow the local population seemed to melt away. In the new villages, death rates far outpaced birthrates. There were not enough laborers for the new Spanish estates. Columbus had thought that the New World could profitably supply slaves to Europe. The plan collapsed because there were no surplus Native Americans. They died off too fast.

Before Columbus, the island of Hispaniola (the modern Haiti and Dominican Republic) had supported perhaps three and a half million people. Twenty-five years later, the native population had been reduced to fewer than one hundred thousand—less than 3 percent of what it had been. In 1570, some eighty years after Columbus's arrival, there were only 125 Native Americans left on the island. They had been replaced by Spanish settlers and African slaves. On the American mainland, depopulation took longer. Eventually, some 90 to 95 percent of the native population of North America would be wiped out.

Given the choice between slavery and Christianity, thousands of those who survived accepted baptism. But converts were treated as second-class Christians. They might not be technically enslaved, but they were assigned to Spanish soldiers and settlers as unpaid servants and laborers. Christianity was an alien religion forced upon them with minimal explanation. Inevitably, they continued their traditional religious practices as well as they could manage.

The expanding Spanish Empire came face to face with two major native empires—the Aztecs of Mexico and the Incas of Peru. Unlike the Caribbean islanders whose religion was invisible to Columbus, these civilizations had awe-inspiring temples, elaborate images of deities, and specialized priesthoods—all obvious targets for the missionaries. With the backing of Spanish administrators and troops, missionaries destroyed temples, smashed images, and imprisoned priests—whatever it took to free the people from the devil's clutches.

Spaniards in Mexico were horrified by Aztec religion. Since ancient times, Christians had suspected pagans, Jews, heretics, and more recently Muslims of committing human sacrifice. Now, for the first time, they encountered the real thing. The Aztecs, and some other peoples of southern North America and Central America, believed that human blood must be shed to keep the universe functioning.

In earlier centuries, the Aztecs had moved into central Mexico from the north, defeating the Toltecs and other nations. Here the Aztecs built cities, developed writing, and invested their energies in agriculture, trade, and the arts and sciences. By the early sixteenth century the Aztec Empire had reached a stable size and was no longer geared to all-out war.

But the war god Huitzilopochtli, who had led them to their victories, still needed blood. The sun, Huitzilopochtli's great manifestation, did not rise automatically. It had to be coaxed forth every morning with the offering of a beating heart cut from a living human. To Spanish Christians, these rites were clear evidence that the Aztecs worshipped the devil.

Replacing the Aztec government with Spanish institutions was relatively easy. The assault on Aztec religion was more prolonged and less successful. Temples were demolished, public sacrifices and ceremonies were outlawed. Hundreds of churches were built, often using stones from the wrecked temples. Aztec books, brilliantly illustrated with pictures of deities and ceremonies, were publicly burned. Franciscan missionaries prided themselves on baptizing thousands of people per day. In 1531 the first bishop of Mexico, Juan de Zumárraga, reported, "More than 250,000 people have been baptized, 500 temples of the gods destroyed, and more than 20,000 figures of demons, which they used to worship, broken and burned."

Some Aztecs were disillusioned because the gods had not come to their rescue. Others were confused. Native priests had recognized the arrival of the Spaniards as the return of the hero-god Quezalcoatl. Perhaps the overthrow of Huitzilopochtli and so many others was part of a revolution in the divine world. Most people were willing to accept the Christian god and his saints as reasonable additions to the Aztec pantheon. But very few were willing to give up their everyday habits of worship. If necessary, they would keep them up secretly.

Bishop Zumárraga was a kindly man who tried to protect the Native Americans from the brutality of soldiers and settlers. He was also an inquisitor. In that capacity he tried and convicted a number of native priests in the 1530s. First came public humiliation. Stripped to the waist, hands tied, they were paraded through the city on llamaback while their sins were read aloud. Then they served prison terms.

Worse punishment was reserved for Aztec nobles convicted of idolatry. Don Carlos Ometochtzin had once accepted Christianity, but he was charged with advocating a return to the native religion, with owning a book of divination, and with commissioning another idolatrous work. Convicted of "concubinage, sedition, and apostasy," he and a half-dozen other nobles were burned at the stake.

The Yucatan Peninsula of southern Mexico had once been the home of another brilliant civilization, the Maya. For reasons not entirely clear, Mayan political power had disintegrated six centuries before the Spaniards arrived. The major cities had been abandoned or had shrunk to villages, but Maya religion remained. The land was less densely populated than the Aztec territories, and the Spaniards found no gold and silver to steal. But they did find souls to save.

Between 1559 and 1562, Diego de Landa, Franciscan missionary and bishop of Yucatan, conducted a campaign to wipe out idolatry.

He and his assistants burned or smashed thousands of divine images and questioned thousands of people. Many were tortured, and at least 157 people were burned, hanged, or drowned.

Like the Aztecs, the Maya produced elaborately written and painted manuscripts in book format. Though the glory days of Mayan civilization had ended centuries before, such books were still treasured, and new ones sometimes created. Their subjects ranged from astronomy and history to religious ritual, but to Landa they were all the same. "We found a large number of these books in these characters and, as they contained nothing in which there was not to be seen superstition and lies of the devil, we burned them all." Of the Mayan books that once existed, only three have survived in part.

The Inca Empire, stretching some two thousand miles from north to south through the spectacular Andes Mountains, was a highly centralized state. A network of roads and an empire-wide messenger service tied it together. To the amazement of sixteenth-century Spanish adventurers and modern scholars, the Incas governed their vast territory without the benefit of writing, wheeled transport, or riding animals. Messages were encoded in knotted strings and illustrated with clay models. The emperor was an absolute monarch, and the state owned almost all property and controlled most aspects of life, including religion.

When the Spanish arrived in 1532, the empire had just emerged from a civil war. The small Spanish force succeeded in kidnapping the victorious emperor, Atahualpa. When he refused to accept Christianity and Spanish rule, they held him hostage and demanded a huge ransom in gold and silver. His subjects paid the ransom—but instead of freeing Atahualpa, the Spaniards murdered him. Although Inca resistance continued until 1544, the centralized organization of the empire made it relatively easy for the Spaniards to conquer it from the top down. Inca subjects were used to following orders from the capital city of Cuzco.

As elsewhere in the American territories claimed by Spain, the land was parceled out to Spaniards, and the native people forced to work for them. As elsewhere, the conquerors' diseases were far more deadly than the conquerors' weapons. And as elsewhere, Christianity became virtually a requirement for survival.

People resorted to ingenious methods of keeping their own religion alive. They buried images of gods and goddesses under Christian shrines and crosses, or hid them inside statues of Catholic saints. The worshippers could address their prayers to the hidden deities while keeping Catholic priests happy. More often, especially in the countryside, people simply hid images, vestments, and ritual equipment, to be brought out for secret religious ceremonies.

In the 1560s a popular resistance movement in central Peru defied the Christian missionary effort. Native leaders observed that people had started dying of unknown diseases as soon as the Spaniards had forbidden the worship of the gods. Clearly the gods were angry. The people must reject the Christian god and all things Spanish. It took Spanish forces a brutal three-year campaign to suppress the revolt.

By the beginning of the seventeenth century, Peru was entirely Christianized—at least officially. But some church leaders were concerned by what they saw as the survival of devil worship. In 1609 they instituted what became known as the Extirpation of Idolatry—virtually a Spanish Inquisition for Native Americans. Judges appointed by the archbishop of Lima made the rounds of native towns and villages, inviting local people to confess their own misdeeds and inform on their neighbors.

After questioning informers and suspects, judges and their assistants searched the sites where unauthorized worship might have taken place. They confiscated idols, vestments, and all the paraphernalia of illicit worship. After days or weeks of investigation, all these things were ceremonially burned at an *auto-da-fé*, a ritual of public penance. People judged guilty of idolatry were whipped or imprisoned. Priests and priestesses could be imprisoned for life.

In some regions of the Andes, people had long revered the mummified bodies of their parents and other ancestors. Christian authorities counted this as idolatry. Either the mummies should be decently buried, like Christian corpses, or they must be burned like other idols. Some of the judges insisted on convicted idolaters burning their own ancestors as proof of repentance.

The Extirpation of Idolatry was active from 1608 to 1622. During that time, it condemned 1,618 individuals as pagan priests or priestesses, absolved 18,893 other people after due penance, and destroyed 1,769 major shrines, 7,288 household shrines, and 1,365 mummies. The Extirpation was reactivated in 1625/1626, again from 1649 to 1670, sporadically in the 1690s, and finally in 1725. Between these major campaigns, there were local investigations and trials by parish priests.

To their dismay, missionaries sometimes found that idols were like weeds—when one was uprooted, others sprang up. When statues of gods and goddesses were destroyed, local people often discovered that certain stones were the sons and daughters of the fallen idols. In country regions, people simply waited until the "extirpators" had moved on, and then constructed new shrines and images —sometimes more than had been smashed.

Regardless of what they actually believed, converts had to practice the new religion. If they failed to attend Catholic services, the local priest could punish them—by fines, whippings, public humiliation, or imprisonment. They had to learn and recite certain formulas of Christian doctrine and prayer. Christian rituals and Christian figures like the Virgin Mary and several popular saints became part of their lives, joining and combining with their traditional religious ideas.

The Spanish and Portuguese Inquisitions in the Americas dealt with much more than native idolatry. Heresy among settlers was their first concern. In Brazil, the Portuguese Inquisition was active in 1591. It continued until late in the eighteenth century. As elsewhere, the number of people actually burned at the stake was small, but the number terrorized was enormous.

Conversos, meaning converted Jews and their descendants, were always under suspicion. Any sign that they were guilty of Jewish practices could lead to their arrest. Conviction could mean death, service as a galley slave, or such lesser punishments as whipping and public humiliation. In 1649 the Inquisition in Mexico burned twelve people convicted of relapsing into Judaism—plus another fifty-seven who had escaped (some of them by dying) and were burned in effigy. Others were burned in Peru in the late sixteenth through the mid-seventeenth century.

In North America, along the St. Lawrence River, the French had discovered a new source of wealth—the fur trade. This was a business that required the active cooperation of Native Americans. In their quest for trading partners, military alliances, and fur sources, the French sent feelers throughout the Great Lakes region and down the Ohio and Mississippi rivers. While the Dutch and English clung to the Atlantic coast, France laid claim to the whole Mississippi River valley.

The most active French missionaries were Jesuits, and the Jesuit approach was flexible. Instead of concentrating on what was wrong with native religious traditions, they looked for points of similarity with Christianity. Did the Iroquois look up to a powerful spirit in the sky? Excellent, that was God the Father. Were there tales of a culture hero who had died to save his people? Then they could understand the redeeming death of Christ. Did young people seek contact with a spirit helper through solitude, prayer, and fasting? Very good, let them learn that the helper was their patron saint, or perhaps the Holy Spirit or the Virgin Mary.

The Jesuits hoped to ease people into Christianity through gradual education, not force it on them before they were ready. This technique had a downside. Whereas Spanish Franciscans cheerfully baptized anyone who was willing to put up with the rite, French Jesuits preferred not to baptize people until they fully understood and accepted the doctrines of Christianity—with one fateful exception. As a last-ditch effort to save a soul, they would baptize anyone on the point of death. Native observers were struck by the high percentage of converts who died shortly after baptism. The obvious conclusion was that baptism was dangerous, and the Jesuits wielded lethal power. A number of Jesuits were killed as dangerous sorcerers.

Spain, Portugal, and France all had centralized colonial administrations for their American conquests. In contrast, the English settlements along the east coast were thirteen separate colonies, each with its individual charter from the British government. That meant thirteen different ways of dealing with native peoples and their religious traditions.

Every colony had its own religious agenda, but pious settlers everywhere had some things in common. They had not come to America to find religious freedom—except for themselves. They saw themselves as the "new Israel," God's chosen people, and America (at least their little corner of it) as the new Promised Land. Naturally,

the native inhabitants had to give way to them, just as the Canaanites had to give way to the original Israelites.

The English idea was "first civilize, then convert." They did not
see the point of baptizing people who did not live in English-style
houses, cultivate fenced fields, and follow the principles of English
law. When "Indians," as the Native Americans were called, settled
down and tried to behave like the English, then they were candidates
for conversion.

Christians liked to think that they brought the good news of the
Gospel to heathens who had been languishing in darkness. But to the
woodland cultures of eastern North America, it was not good news to
hear that they needed salvation. Their religious traditions had always
showed them the universe as a reasonably benign place, and human
beings as comfortable inhabitants of it. People were capable of doing
good and doing harm, making wise choices and making mistakes, but
certainly none of them deserved eternal punishment.

One fact was obvious to Native Americans everywhere: death
came with the Europeans. Their weapons were impressive, but much
more impressive were the waves of disease that spread before them.
Europeans themselves seemed almost immune to the mysterious new
plagues that wiped out village after village and reduced tribe after tribe
to a fragment of its former strength. Clearly, the Europeans were protected by some awesome and dangerous power. If that was the Christian God, common sense suggested making peace with him.

English missionaries had their best success with populations
that had been devastated by disease and defeated in war. The survivors were often desperate, looking for a way to shield themselves
and their families from further damage, whether it came from
invaders' aggression or divine anger.

In 1646 the Massachusetts government outlawed native religious
practices and beliefs. "No Indian shall at any time powwow, or per-
form outward worship to their false gods." Neither Christians nor
pagans were permitted to deny "the true God, or His creation or government of the world."

In general, however, English settlers concentrated their persecution
on other white Christians. With the exception of Maryland, the English colonies were firmly Protestant. Most of them refused to allow

Catholics and non-Christians to settle within their borders. All but four of the colonies had an established church, supported by taxes paid by all citizens.

The New England colonies were largely Puritan. The southern colonies were first settled by Anglicans—or Episcopalians, as they were called in America. They became the aristocrats of the South, comfortably settled in the coastal areas. Farther inland, most immigrants were Presbyterians, or German-speaking Lutherans or Mennonites. They were often imprisoned or fined for their un-Anglican preaching and practices. As James Madison objected in 1774, "That diabolical Hell-conceived principle of persecution rages among some."

Massachusetts was famous for strict regulations and harsh punishments. The magistrates and ministers demanded complete uniformity. If dissenters could not be convinced of their errors by whipping, fines, time in the stocks or in jail, branding, piercing their tongues with hot irons, or cutting off their ears, they were expelled from the colony. If they returned, they would be hanged. After 1659, it was illegal to celebrate Christmas, which Puritans regarded as too Catholic and too heathen.

In 1635 Roger Williams was banished from Massachusetts for his "new and dangerous opinions," such as advocating freedom of religion. Two years later, Mrs. Anne Hutchinson, a respected and popular midwife, was banished. At the weekly discussion groups she hosted, she had taught that faith was a matter between the individual and God. Ministers and magistrates had nothing to do with it. Driven from Massachusetts, she and her family took refuge in Rhode Island—New England's haven for heretics.

Rhode Island—or Rogue Island, as people in other colonies often called it—was a maverick. There were no restrictions on religious belief or practice, so long as the practice did not infringe ordinary civil or criminal laws. Roger Williams had helped to found the colony after he was ejected from Massachusetts. Quakers, Baptists, and others who had suffered persecution in England or in other English colonies soon found homes in Rhode Island.

Meanwhile in Massachusetts, Anne Hutchinson's followers were sternly repressed. At least eight women were excommunicated from the church, and another publicly whipped. Many Hutchinson supporters left the colony voluntarily to escape persecution.

They were wise to do so. Hutchinson's teachings reminded the Massachusetts authorities of Quakerism—and Quakers were feared like the plague. In 1656 ten Quakers were arrested as soon as they arrived, and their books were confiscated and burned. The women were stripped naked and examined for the telltale marks that identified witches. Apparently no witch marks were found, but the Quakers were all expelled. A law decreed that the captain of any ship carrying Quakers or other heretics to Massachusetts could be heavily fined and required to take them elsewhere.

Quakers rose to the challenge. If they could not come by ship, they slipped into Massachusetts from Rhode Island. Some were branded, or had their ears cut off. Others were whipped, sometimes to the point of death. Mary Dyer, a friend of Anne Hutchinson, had become a Quaker during a visit to England. She returned to Massachusetts as a Quaker missionary. There she was publicly whipped and expelled, while two male Quakers were hanged. Dyer returned again, and this time she too was hanged.

The Massachusetts magistrates had reasons for their harsh policy. Seventeenth-century Quakers were determined troublemakers. They specialized in disrupting church services. In Massachusetts, men and women smashed bottles in the middle of sermons, or walked into the church stark naked or draped in sackcloth and ashes.

Anne Hutchinson's younger sister, Katherine Marbury Scott, had also left Massachusetts for Rhode Island. There she became a Quaker. In Rhode Island, Quakers had no need to make trouble, and they lived quietly. Scott returned to Massachusetts as an elderly woman to protest the punishment of a Quaker whose ear had been cut off. She was arrested, whipped, and banished under threat of death.

In Massachusetts, simply using the wrong words could be dangerous. A Harvard student was expelled from school and publicly whipped for saying something disrespectful about the Holy Ghost. A dancing teacher was heavily fined for claiming that some stage shows had more divinity than some Old Testament stories. As late as 1757, a man was whipped for jokingly declaring that "God was a damned fool for ever making a woman."

Other New England colonies were not much more tolerant. Only Protestants could vote in New Hampshire. Whipping, the pillory, prison, or boring the tongue with a hot iron were standard punishments for blasphemy. In 1696 all New Hampshire residents were required to swear an oath against Catholicism. Quakers were barred from Connecticut. Catholics were tolerated there until the mid-eighteenth century, when the Catholic Church was virtually outlawed.

Seventh-Day Baptists insisted on keeping Saturday as the Sabbath, and treated Sunday as a working day. That put them in constant violation of Connecticut laws and subjected them to frequent fines, whippings, and jail. A young man named John Rogers was especially troublesome. Like the disorderly Quakers, he often disrupted Congregational church services, which he said were in honor of the devil. He broke Connecticut's "Sunday law" so regularly that he had to pay a fine of five pounds every month.

Rogers eventually founded his own radical church. He agitated for complete separation of church and state, with no government support of religion. He was sometimes whipped and often imprisoned, for a total of some eighteen years. His followers, called Rogerenes, multiplied in spite of persecution. They continued as a separate church until the early twentieth century.

Maryland was founded in 1632 by the first Lord Baltimore, Sir George Calvert, an English Catholic noble. Even so, Catholics were a minority, and Lord Baltimore warned them to keep a low profile. By 1654 the Protestant majority in the Maryland legislature repealed the colony's toleration law. In 1689 King William took direct control of Maryland and established the Church of England as the colony's official religion. Denying church doctrine—or even swearing too vehemently—made Marylanders liable to fines, prison, and the standard punishment of tongue-boring. Theoretically, a third offense merited the death penalty, though that was apparently never put into practice.

In 1704 Maryland passed laws explicitly aimed at preventing the growth of Catholicism. Priests were forbidden to make converts or to baptize the children of Protestant parents. Catholics were not allowed to teach school. Irish servants were heavily taxed, to prevent the immigration of Irish Catholics. A few years later, new laws prevented Catholics from holding office or voting. In 1755 a law fixed the property tax on Catholics as double what Protestants had to pay.

Pennsylvania, founded by the Quaker William Penn, was a relatively tolerant colony. Even there, it was illegal to profane the Bible or the Holy Trinity—though the penalty was only a fine of five shillings or five days in jail. Under royal pressure, Catholics were forbidden to hold office in the colony. During the French and Indian Wars of the eighteenth century, Catholics were increasingly restricted. They were disarmed and excluded from the militia, heavily taxed, and registered so that their movements could be monitored. Irish immigrants were not admitted.

Only Anglicans could hold office in New York. Catholics were not allowed to own weapons and had to give bonds for their good behavior. In 1700 Catholic priests found in New York were subject to life imprisonment. The following year, all New York Catholics were denied the vote. In Delaware, Catholic churches were legal, but they could not hold property.

Southern states were generally more easygoing. But in Virginia, Catholics could not vote or hold office, and Catholic priests were not allowed into the colony. In the eighteenth century, they could not serve as legal guardians or testify as witnesses. In 1756 when a new war broke out between England and France, Virginia ruled that no Catholic could possess a gun or own a horse worth more than five pounds.

Tolerant North Carolina asserted "full liberty of conscience to all, excluding Papists." Eighteenth-century Florida was part of the empire of Catholic Spain, and Georgia, its nearest neighbor, feared all Catholics as possible Spanish agents. A special inspector was appointed to make sure that no Catholics were admitted to the colony.

The Revolutionary War brought important changes. The thirteen former colonies were now the United States of America. Vermont was soon recognized as the fourteenth state. Each state adopted a written constitution, and every constitution guaranteed freedom of religion—but that did not mean that all religions were equal.

Half of the states still had an established church. The others had plural establishments—meaning that people must pay taxes to support churches, but had some choice as to which church. Mainstream Protestants were still privileged. Catholics could not hold state office in North or South Carolina, Georgia, Massachusetts, New Hampshire, New Jersey, Connecticut, or Vermont.

Nevertheless, the tide had turned against established religion. Religious freedom had become an American principle. Although strict laws against blasphemy stayed on the books in every state, they were seldom applied. Christian piety was no longer a requirement for respectability or for public office. Even Massachusetts tolerated Unitarians, deists, and outright skeptics. About half the men who signed the Declaration of Independence rejected revealed religion.

SOURCES AND FURTHER READING

Bartolomé de las Casas (1474–1566) first visited Hispaniola in 1502. He returned as a priest in 1514 and spent the rest of his life as a missionary and an advocate for the Indians. Some of his extensive works are available in English, including selections from his *History of the Indies*, translated by Andrée Collard (New York: Harper and Row, 1971) and *An Account, Much Abbreviated, of the Destruction of the Indies, with Related Texts*, translated by Andrew Hurley (Indianapolis, IN: Hackett, 2003). There are letters and reports by explorers and settlers from Columbus on, and government papers from the European powers and their colonies. Roger Williams's most famous work, *The Bloudy Tenent of Persecution for Cause of Conscience*, has been republished, most recently as edited by Richard Groves (Macon, GA: Mercer University Press, 2001). *The Crossing of Two Roads: Being Catholic and Native in the United States*, edited by Marie Therese Archambault, Mark G. Thiel, and Christopher Vecsey (Maryknoll, NY: Orbis, 2003) is a collection of documents from 1613 to the present.

George E. Tinker's *Missionary Conquest: The Gospel and Native American Cultural Genocide* (Minneapolis, MN: Fortress, 1993) gives the viewpoint of a modern Native American Christian. Eve LaPlante's *American Jezebel: The Uncommon Life of Anne Hutchinson, the Woman Who Defied the Puritans* (San Francisco, CA: HarperSanFrancisco, 2003) details the persecution of one notable New England dissident.

Chapter 18

France

Eighteenth Century

By resources, population, and productivity, France was one of the richest nations in the eighteenth-century world—and France was almost bankrupt. Wars and mismanagement had plunged the royal government so deeply into debt that it saw only one hope—turning the problem over to the whole nation.

For centuries, the trend of French government had been toward increasing absolutism. The Estates-General (roughly corresponding to the British Parliament) had not met since 1614. This body was composed of representatives of the three Estates—Catholic clergy, nobles, and commoners. In theory, its function was to advise the monarch, and especially to find ways of raising money for him.

In February 1789 some six hundred local districts chose delegates from the clergy, nobility, and commons. On May 5 the Estates-General assembled at Versailles for the first meeting in 175 years. But the three Estates were not ready to bail out the government. They brought long lists of grievances to be addressed. Apparently everyone in France—or at least every class—had problems.

Peasants struggled to survive under the burden of oppressive taxes, tithes, rents, and forced labor, made worse by a string of poor harvests. The bourgeoisie chafed under economically crippling restrictions and fees left over from medieval feudalism, and resented their lack of political influence. Parish priests—the underpaid workhorses of the Catholic Church—complained of the huge gap between them and the wealthy bishops. The nobles, caught between absolute monarch and pushy bourgeoisie, felt their power and prestige being nibbled to death.

Before the Estates-General could take action, they had to hash out procedures. If the three Estates voted separately, clergy and nobles together would outweigh the Third Estate, which constituted the great mass of the population. To prevent that from happening, the Third Estate representatives simply declared themselves a National Assembly that would speak for the entire nation.

Most priests left their assigned seats and joined the National Assembly. So did a few bishops and nobles. When the king tried to close down their meeting, the National Assembly moved to a tennis court and took an oath not to disband until they had completed drafting a constitution. King Louis XVI responded by firing the popular finance minister Jacques Necker, who had long advocated reforms. On July 14, 1789, a mob in Paris stormed the ancient prison-fortress of the Bastille. The French Revolution had begun.

In the months that followed, the National Assembly produced one decree after another, developing France's first democratic constitution piecemeal. In August it issued a Declaration of the Rights of Man—one of the foundation documents of social and political movements worldwide for the next two centuries.

The declaration's basic principles were individual freedom and equality—two ideas that were not welcomed by European governments. Among other things, the declaration called for freedom of religion—an ideal soon backed up by decrees removing all legal distinctions between Protestants and Catholics. Church property was nationalized, and gold and silver church vessels were confiscated.

French Jews in the eighteenth century were not a single unified group. There were a few thousand Sephardic Jews, whose ancestors had come from Spain and Portugal—most of them expelled in the great "cleansing" that had stripped those countries of non-

Christians three centuries before (see chapter 13). In eastern France there were much larger concentrations of Yiddish-speaking Ashkenazi Jews. In January 1790 the National Assembly relieved the Sephardim from all the legal restrictions that had kept Jews from full citizenship. It took nearly two more years before the Ashkenazi received the same rights.

King Louis XVI reluctantly accepted the constitution, which severely restricted royal power. He did not have much choice; he and his family were virtually prisoners. A Legislative Assembly replaced the temporary National Assembly in 1791, and began to draw up laws under the new constitution.

But the kettle had only begun to boil. Every step the Legislative Assembly took roused passionate feelings. Poor citizens, who could not meet the property qualification for voters, demanded the right to vote. Outraged nobles fled to England, Switzerland, or Germany. And one decree in particular alienated people of every class, and split French society down the middle.

This was the Civil Constitution of the Clergy, which subordinated the Catholic Church in France to the secular government. The number of bishops was reduced from 127 to 83. Bishops and priests alike were to be elected by local voters—including Protestants, Jews, and atheists. All monastic orders were disbanded, although nuns who chose to stay in their monastery buildings could do so. The pope was recognized as the "visible head of the universal church," but he was to have no administrative authority over French clergy. Traditional tithes and church fees were abolished. Henceforth the national government would pay the clergy standardized salaries. All priests were required to sign a pledge to uphold the Civil Constitution.

Most of the lower clergy had supported the early stages of the Revolution, but many could not go along with this secularization of the Church. A bare majority of priests, and only seven bishops, signed the pledge. Most of the priests who signed were devoted Catholics, who believed that the Church and the revolutionary government could work together for social justice.

Those who refused were stripped of their positions and salaries. Half the parishes of France lost their priests. "Constitutional" priests who replaced them were often rejected by the parishioners, sometimes violently. The pope declared the constitutional priests schismatics and cautioned Catholics to avoid them. After long hesitation, King Louis XVI accepted the Civil Constitution of the Clergy in December 1790.

Most bishops quickly left the country. So did thousands of priests. In February 1791 non-signing priests were barred from preaching. In November of that year, they were put on notice that they could be arrested. Hundreds were imprisoned. In August 1792 all those still in France were ordered to sign the Civil Constitution or leave the country within two weeks. Those who refused were to be deported.

Altogether, about twenty-five thousand members of the Catholic clergy left France. The majority fled to Britain or Spain, others to Switzerland, Savoy, the German states, Italy, Austria, and the Netherlands. Non-signing priests who stayed in France went into hiding or took refuge in the officially closed monasteries. There they went on hearing confessions, celebrating Mass, and administering other traditional sacraments. Loyalist Catholics sometimes traveled long distances to find them.

Other people reacted very differently. In many parts of France, long-standing resentments against the Catholic Church had been released. As early as the spring of 1791, mobs in Paris broke into convents and abused the nuns, driving some of them naked into the streets. Priests—both signers and non-signers—were attacked and beaten. Mob violence culminated in the three-day "September Massacres" of 1792, when about 230 priests, including at least three bishops, were murdered in Paris and other cities.

In 1792 the Legislative Assembly was replaced by a National Convention elected by popular vote. The property qualification for voters had been dropped, although women were still denied voting rights. The convention was charged with writing still another constitution. It began by deposing the king, establishing the first French Republic, and offering to help peoples everywhere shake off their tyrants and claim their freedom. That was a threat and a challenge to all the governments of Europe.

Austria was the first to declare war on France. It was soon backed by a coalition of other European powers. An invading army pushed toward Paris, with the declared aim of reinstating the monarchy. The National Convention did not wait. In January 1793 King Louis was executed on a charge of treason. A military draft was established.

Especially in western France, royalist and pro-church uprisings broke out. The young French Republic faced both foreign and civil war.

In Paris, a dozen different parties and political clubs contended passionately, swaying government policy one way and then another. Some delegates reminded their fellows of the constitution's clause protecting freedom of opinion. No citizen was to be punished for expressing an opinion on any subject, including religion.

More radical delegates held that traditional religion was primitive superstition that dragged down the nation and should be abolished. Some wanted to replace Christianity and Judaism with a religion of patriotism, celebrating the heroes of the Revolution in an annual series of patriotic festivals. Others wanted to elevate Reason to the stature of a goddess. By June 1793 the radicals were in power. The government embarked on its most difficult project yet—the dechristianization of France.

Clergy were given an ultimatum. They must leave the priesthood, and prove their sincerity by getting married. Those who refused could be imprisoned or even executed. Roughly twenty thousand priests and an unknown number of Huguenot ministers resigned their positions over a period of about six months. Some resignations seem to have been genuinely voluntary, while other priests and ministers capitulated under pressure.

Thousands of former priests—and some former monks and nuns—did marry. Although some were willing, local authorities used a variety of methods to force others into marriage. As one former priest reported, "After twenty-two months in prison, I was forced to take a wife." Some had to choose between marriage and execution. Some were simply bribed to marry—a form of pressure that could be very effective for an ex-priest without other means of support.

In many places, both Catholic and Protestant churches were forcibly closed. So were synagogues, as dechristianization spilled over into anti-Judaism. Churches and synagogues might be demolished or converted into municipal buildings, warehouses, or "Temples of Reason." Over a thousand such temples were established around the country. There the new revolutionary holidays were celebrated, and revolutionary orators gave secular sermons meant to wean people away from religion.

Citizens were arrested for making or selling crucifixes. Monastery buildings were put up for sale, and the remaining monks and nuns evicted. Government agents and local officials built huge bonfires in front of churches, where they burned sacred statues, paintings, vestments, and confessional booths. Often the fires were accompanied by masquerades, with local men and women in costumes making burlesque fun of the clergy. Local officials melted down church bells to make cannons, and sent gold and silver vessels to the mint to be changed into coinage. The war effort was expensive.

For many ordinary people, this was going too far. Peasants, workers, and shopkeepers who had supported the Revolution took up arms against dechristianization. People broke into locked churches to conduct their own services, or held religious meetings in private homes, barns, or fields. Laypeople performed marriages and baptisms for each other, taught and preached to each other, and sometimes even conducted unofficial masses. Men and women were executed for hiding priests, or setting up crosses that had been torn down.

In the Vendée region of western France, a major revolt broke out. It was not purely religious. The Vendéans also objected to the military draft. But if Vendéans were not willing to fight foreign wars for the Republic, they were willing to fight for their customary way of life. They raised an army of some fifty thousand men, under the name of the "Royal and Catholic Army," and swept the Republican officials out of the area.

When the Republican army defeated the rebels and took back the territory, there were brutal reprisals. Many priests and monks had been active rebels. Now clergy were singled out for punishment even if they had not taken part in the revolt. One notorious punishment was the *noyade*, or drowning. Groups of suspected rebels and clergymen were tied together and loaded into boats that were towed into the river Loire and sunk.

But popular resistance went on. Priests who had fled or been deported slipped back across the border. They held secret religious services, organized demonstrations, and sometimes took up arms against the government. Although the Royal and Catholic Army had been broken, sporadic fighting continued in the Vendée into 1795. In February of that year, the central government granted the district freedom of religion and exemption from the draft. At terrible cost, the Vendéans had won their points.

Constitutional clergy, who had supported the Revolution from the beginning, felt betrayed. The Catholic Church had disowned them, and now the government they had helped create had abandoned them. They, too, often joined the resistance—when it would have them. Royalist Catholics were quite likely to beat them up rather than accept their services.

Huguenots were in a somewhat similar position. Shortly before the Revolution, King Louis XVI had granted them a degree of freedom. Their marriages were declared valid, and they were allowed to bury their dead with religious ceremonies. The Revolution had brought them much more. For the first time in their history, they enjoyed real legal equality with Catholics. There had always been Huguenots among the leaders of the revolutionary parties. But no sooner had they achieved full religious freedom than it was taken away from them. Equality of religions now meant equality of persecution.

Outside France, the dechristianization policy had unintended consequences. The king's execution had united the rulers of other European countries against the French Republic. Now dechristianization united European public opinion behind their rulers. The war against France took on the feeling of a crusade.

The new French citizen armies had repelled the Austrian invasion, thrown back every attack on French territory, and gone on the offensive, moving into Austria, Spain, Italy, and the Austrian Netherlands. True to their pledge to aid freedom movements, the French tried to set up democratic institutions everywhere. Rumors of an approaching French army were often enough to trigger uprisings against local tyrants.

In many places, they also triggered attacks against local churches and clergy. Anticlerical mobs and rebel units often perpetrated gross atrocities. The French were sometimes greeted not only as liberators from oppressive governments but as liberators from the tyranny of the Church. French troops themselves looted and closed churches, tore down public crosses, and broke into monasteries, terrorizing monks and nuns.

Like the French government they were modeled on, the new republics set up in conquered territory tried to suppress religion. Protestant and Catholic churches were closed. Priests and pastors who resisted were arrested or killed. It was an unsuccessful effort. None of the French-imposed republics lasted more than a few years, and neither did their antireligious policies.

By early 1794 the political infighting within the revolutionary government had brought Maximilien Robespierre to power. This austere young man was known as "the Incorruptible." He was apparently immune to bribery, flattery, threats, and self-interest. In fact, he seemed immune to emotion. But he understood the power of emotion over other people.

The cult of Reason was too sterile to be satisfying. Robespierre called it a religion for aristocrats. France needed a national religion for ordinary people. It should be rational, without superstition and free of divisive doctrines, but it should be emotionally fulfilling, and that meant it must match people's deepest beliefs. It could not be simply a cover for atheism.

Robespierre imagined that everyone could agree on a religion with only two points of doctrine—the existence of a Supreme Being and the immortality of human souls. All those temples of Reason must be turned into temples of the Supreme Being. Meanwhile, dechristianization only bred resistance. It must stop at once.

But religion was not the most urgent topic on Robespierre's agenda. France was at war, with huge armies in the field and enemy nations on all sides. Robespierre and others in the government saw potential traitors everywhere. The Revolution took a dangerous turn toward dictatorship. The democratically approved constitution was suspended. Robespierre and the Council for Public Safety ruled in the name of wartime emergency.

In the space of a few months, over two hundred thousand people were arrested, and thousands executed. It was the period later known as the Reign of Terror. Robespierre's colleagues in the government began to fear for their own safety. On July 27, 1794, they staged a coup, arrested Robespierre, and executed him the next day. The cult of the Supreme Being had lasted only three months.

The French Revolution's center of gravity had shifted. Internal reform was now overshadowed by foreign conquest. More and more of the nation's resources went into supporting the war effort. Mostly by default, without new legislation on the subject, religious freedom was returning to France. Catholics and Protestants of all varieties, along with deists, Unitarians, atheists, and agnostics, had all been through an ordeal that demonstrated the hazards of government regulation of religion. Many of them were willing to take the lesson.

The government was no longer a pure democracy. The ruling body was now the Directory, an executive council of five. A bicameral legislature was elected by property owners. Although the Directory succeeded in saving the French economy from collapse, it faced one political crisis after another. In its continuing struggle against royalist sympathizers, it brought back a series of anti-Christian measures. Church bells must not be rung, nor crosses displayed in public. Sunday could not be observed as a day of rest.

Increasingly, French generals were more powerful than the civil government in Paris. In November 1799 a group of conspirators staged a coup and installed the most successful and charismatic general of all as "First Consul" and virtual dictator. His name was Napoleon Bonaparte.

Under Napoleon, the last vestiges of religious repression were removed. Church and state were separate, and all citizens free to worship or not worship as they chose. But to ensure the support of the Catholic majority, Napoleon negotiated an agreement with the Catholic Church, the Concordat of 1801.

Under this concordat, the French government continued to pay clergymen's salaries. Priests and bishops would no longer be elected. The government would nominate bishops, but they would have to be approved by the pope. In turn, bishops would appoint priests, but they had to be approved by the government. This symbiotic relationship lasted for a century, until the final separation of church and state in 1905.

Obviously, the French Revolution had not dechristianized France. Militant dechristianization had failed, and the artificial cults of Reason and the Supreme Being never took root. Yet there were permanent effects, still seen in French society. A definite break had been made between religion and the state. The old concept of the sacred French monarch, sworn to uphold the Catholic Church and expel heretics, was gone. To some extent, the trust that ordinary people had placed in their clergy had been transferred to the political sphere. More people had learned to live without religion—or to rely on their religion less.

Elsewhere in Europe, the effects were less obvious, but no less important. Before the French Revolution, only a few intellectuals advocated the separation of church and state. For most people in Europe, the idea was completely alien. Except for a scattering of independent "free cities," monarchy was almost the only form of government. The Revolution publicized and popularized some of the intellectuals' radical ideas—freedom of choice for all, in both religion and politics; separation of government and religion for the good of both; the realization that atheists could be good citizens. Those ideas would not be fully applied in any nation, but they would become guideposts for a new age.

Sources and Further Reading

The period leading up to the French Revolution is important for philosophical and political writings, and the Revolution itself produced a spate of speeches, debates, decrees, reports, and propaganda. There are a number of convenient collections of contemporary documents in English translation. One of the best is *The French Revolution and Napoleon: A Sourcebook*, edited by Philip G. Dwyer and Peter McPhee (London: Routledge, 2002). *I Leave You My Heart: A Visitandine Chronicle of the French Revolution: Mère Marie-Jéronyme Vérot's Letter of 15 May 1794*, translated and edited by Péronne-Marie Thibert (Philadelphia: Saint Joseph's University Press, 2000) gives a vivid account of one small French convent's experiences during the Revolution.

Nigel Aston's *Christianity and Revolutionary Europe, 1750–1830* (Cambridge: Cambridge University Press, 2002) sets the French Revolution solidly in its European environment and discusses its religious effects on countries such as England, Ireland, Spain, and Italy. Michel Vovelle's *The Revolution against the Church: From Reason to the Supreme Being*, translated from French by Alan José (Columbus: Ohio State University Press, 1991) is a largely statistical study of French priests during the period.

Chapter 19

Oceania and Australia
Eighteenth and Nineteenth Centuries

We are praying to God that we might reach the length of life of our fore-
bears. We build churches, labor day and night, give offerings to charity
and the Sabbath dues, but the land is become empty; the old villages lie
silent in a tangle of bushes and vines, haunted by ghosts and horned
owls, frequented by goats and bats.
—Samuel M. Kamakau, *Ruling Chiefs of Hawaii*

Kamehameha I was the greatest war leader Hawaii had ever
known. By 1810 he had united almost all the Hawaiian
Islands for the first time. Kamehameha held a double lordship. He
was king of Hawaii, and he was also custodian of the sacred statue
that embodied his patron deity, the war god Ku Ka'ilimoku.

By Hawaiian custom, the victor in war could parcel out authority
over conquered territory among his supporters. Kamehameha took
the opportunity to establish his relatives as important chiefs
throughout the Hawaiian Islands. That gave him control of all parts
of his kingdom, but it opened up possibilities for future trouble. All

those newly empowered relatives and their children would be potential candidates to replace him. To avoid dangerous quarrels, Kamehameha named his eldest son, Liholiho, to be the next king, and his nephew Kekuaokalani to take custody of the god.

American and European ships had been visiting Hawaii since the 1770s. Kamehameha had achieved his conquest of the Hawaiian Islands with the help of muskets, cannons, and European ships. He was a shrewd negotiator and trader as well as a brilliant commander, and he quickly understood how to acquire foreign goods and equipment and how to use them for his own purposes.

But while Kamehameha worked to consolidate his realm, other forces were working against him. Along with international recognition, new luxuries, and firepower, American and European visitors had brought the Hawaiians unfamiliar germs. Syphilis, smallpox, measles, influenza, whooping cough, and other new diseases devastated the islanders. By the time of Kamehameha's death in 1819, the population was only about half what it had been thirty years earlier. No one understood the causes of the catastrophic decline.

Hawaiians had their suspicions. They knew that their own gods were dangerous and easily angered—hence the elaborate taboos to avoid offending them, and the elaborate rituals to keep them happy. Yet foreigners continually violated taboos, either accidentally or on purpose, and usually they got away with it. Their god must be very strong—or perhaps the island gods were not as strong as the islanders had thought. The strange new diseases showed that the Christian god was even more dangerous than the old gods, and had better be pacified quickly.

Besides, Christians had guns, huge ships, innumerable metal tools, unlimited supplies of strong liquor, and an amazing quantity and variety of clothing. For many Hawaiians, that was conclusive. Christianity produced technology. Kamehameha welcomed the technology, but he was a religious conservative. "I follow my faith," he declared, "which cannot be wicked, since it commands me never to do wrong."

Liholiho, now twenty-two, succeeded his father in 1819. In reality, the most powerful person in the kingdom was the dowager queen Ka'ahumanu, who had been Kamehameha's principal wife and partner in his enterprises. She was also a close friend of Liholiho's own mother, Keopuolani. The two women served as the young king's chief ministers and advisors. Together, they were responsible for the most dramatic change in Hawaiian religious history.

Liholiho's position was far from secure. During his father's long reign, the chiefs had come to think of their jurisdictions as permanent property, rather than temporary offices that a new king could revoke. Now they were afraid that Liholiho would exercise his traditional right to redistribute land and authority, and they were prepared to resist.

With the old queens' concurrence, Liholiho called a meeting of the chiefs. There, Ka'ahumanu explained that Liholiho had the backing of both the British and the French governments. (By a lucky accident, a French warship was in the harbor, and the captain spoke at the meeting to confirm what the old queen said.) Liholiho pacified the chiefs by confirming them in their positions, and even gave up the royal monopoly on the profitable sandalwood trade. Most of the chiefs were well satisfied. But Kekuaokalani, custodian of the war god, had refused to attend the meeting—a clear challenge to the young king's authority.

When a ruler died, it was customary to suspend the *kapu*, or system of taboos. During the mourning period, behavior was permitted that would have been shocking at any other time. All sexual restrictions were removed, women could eat pork and bananas, and men and women could even eat together. The new ruler would then institute a new kapu, basically the same as the old one. Ka'ahumanu and Keopuolani persuaded Liholiho not to institute the new kapu. Instead, in a public act of defiance, he and his young brother ate with the royal women.

Ka'ahumanu declared to the assembled chiefs that those who wished to follow the old ways were free to do so, but that she and her family were free of all taboos. "We intend that the husband's food and the wife's food shall be cooked in the same oven, and that they shall eat out of the same calabash." Hawaiian religion had just been undermined at its root.

The kapu system had been the principal tool by which chiefs controlled their subjects. Any high-ranking chief could impose a taboo at any time, for virtually any purpose. By depriving them of the kapu, the dowager queens had undermined the chiefs' power.

But the changes did not stop there. With foreign guns and the support of foreign governments, the king no longer needed the war god. Liholiho announced that the worship of the old gods was ended, and began destroying their temples and statues.

Kekuaokalani raised a revolt, but was soon defeated. The reign of the gods was officially over. Of course, the traditional religion did not cease to exist. The great public ceremonies were no longer celebrated, but ordinary people went on performing their private rituals, and long-standing taboos were still followed as customs. Faith in some deities might be shaken, but others—like the volcano goddess Pele—kept their power.

Nevertheless, the royal family had spoken firmly against the traditional religion. In 1820 Liholiho—now officially Kamehameha II—allowed the first Christian missionaries to enter the Hawaiian Islands. They were American Protestants, mostly Congregationalists. With the support and encouragement of the royal family, they had a relatively easy time enlisting converts. They not only preached the Gospel, they also preached American-style capitalism and American-style democracy. Many missionaries, ex-missionaries, and members of missionary families became influential members of the Hawaiian government.

Christianization proceeded rapidly. In 1822 the last high priest, Hewahewa, helped to burn 102 idols. French Catholic missionaries arrived in Hawaii in 1827, but they were too late. Calvinist Protestantism was firmly in power. Kamehameha III briefly expelled Catholic priests, and the regent Kinau ordered all native Catholics imprisoned. In 1839 Kamehameha III would issue a decree guaranteeing religious freedom—meaning freedom for all varieties of Christianity. The last restrictions on traditional religious practices were not lifted until the mid-twentieth century.

Ordinary Hawaiians, like most other Polynesians, readily accepted Christianity when their chiefs did. The kapu system had prepared them for all the restrictions and regulations of the missionaries. The rules about keeping the Sabbath (as the Protestant missionaries liked to call Sunday) were no more irrational than the taboos they were used to. There were only two kinds of activity that the missionaries could not control—sex and dancing.

Hawaiian ceremonial dancing—the famous hula—looked to most Europeans and Americans like a form of entertainment, and a very sexy one. The missionaries insisted that it must be banned, and the royal government obliged in 1827. But this was one part of traditional life that Hawaiians would not give up. Dances were held secretly, after dark. The missionaries sternly warned their congregations about the "night dances" and listed them among the most notable sins.

The missionaries were partly right—hula was often explicitly and deliberately sexual. That was part of its esthetic appeal, and part of its sacred aspect. For example, the *hula mai*, or "penis hula," extravagantly praised a chief's virility, to the amusement and delight of the audience.

Like other Polynesians, Hawaiians were puzzled by the missionaries' attitudes toward sex. The rules requiring monogamy and Christian marriage rites meant labeling a good deal of customary sexual behavior as sinful. How could any good god disapprove of something so natural, so pleasurable, and so basic to human life? Without sex, creation would be in vain. And besides, it offered such wonderful opportunities for artistic expression and community enjoyment.

Hawaiians paid dearly for their openhearted willingness to trust friendly foreigners. The missionaries sincerely believed that Hawaiians needed two things to make them happy and successful—Christianity and private ownership. Although some missionaries realized that introduced diseases had something to do with the population collapse, they thought that the major causes were infanticide, drunkenness, laziness, and oppression by the chiefs. Their ideal was a society of pious independent landowners who would work hard to improve their properties for themselves and their heirs.

In the years 1845 to 1850, missionaries and foreign businessmen combined to push through the *Mahele* or Land Division, which established private land ownership. The result was the opposite of what the missionaries (though perhaps not the businessmen) had intended. Ordinary Hawaiians were dispossessed of the land they had farmed as tenants for generations. Their communities were shattered, and they lost their traditional claims to the protection and support of their chiefs. When the fog of rhetoric and legislation cleared, the king owned more than a million acres of land, some two hundred and fifty nobles controlled about one and a half million acres, and eighty thousand surviving Hawaiian commoners had about twenty-eight thousand acres among them.

As Hawaiian population declined, Europeans and especially Americans gained control of more and more of the Hawaiian government and economy. Native Hawaiians were increasingly marginalized in their own country. King Kalakaua, who ruled from 1874 to 1891, made a last-ditch effort to restore ancestral customs. He succeeded in recording many traditional chants, founded the Hale Naua society to preserve and revivify Hawaiian religion, and shocked many people by having exhibitions of hula at his coronation and at his fiftieth birthday celebration. His sister Liliuokalani, who succeeded him, was the last independent ruler of Hawaii. The island kingdom was annexed by the United States in 1898. By then, the native Hawaiian population had been reduced by perhaps 90 percent.

The Hawaiian Islands are the northernmost of the scattered island groups that make up Polynesia. Hundreds of islands, including Samoa, Tonga, the Marquesas, Tahiti, and Easter Island, had been settled in the course of the first millennium CE by seafaring peoples from farther south and west. All Polynesians shared closely related languages and cultures.

In the late eighteenth century, European nations were searching the world for resources and strategic military and commercial bases. The Pacific Ocean was a huge hunting ground. Everywhere in Polynesia, Europeans brought the same factors that transformed Hawaii—disease, technology, and Christianity. In the rest of Polynesia, the French and British played the roles that Americans took in Hawaii.

Most Polynesian societies traditionally recognized two leaders, who wielded two different kinds of power—religious and military. European observers often labeled the religious leader a "priest-chief" or "high priest." He was in many ways the most important and most honored person in the society. Through him, the gods accepted human offerings and returned the divine gifts that kept people alive and well. He was protected by an elaborate system of taboos and surrounded by complex rituals.

The military leader, however, had more power over what Europeans recognized as secular affairs. They often called him a "king." He achieved his position by victory in battle—which meant that he could always be deposed by a victorious rival. The military leader was not a channel between gods and humankind, but he needed divine support. Victories, like good harvests, depended on the favor of powerful deities. A military leader cultivated that support by performing his own set of rituals, worshipping his special deity, and staying on good terms with the religious leader.

When rivals jockeyed for military and political power, the struggle always had religious aspects. As a rule, the human rivals claimed the backing of rival deities. That fact gave Christian missionaries unexpected opportunities—and unexpected problems. Many a Polynesian "king" welcomed a group of missionaries, gladly accepted Christianity, and ordered his followers to do likewise. But when the missionaries wanted to spread the Gospel to neighboring areas, they might find that the neighbors rejected them as enemy agents.

On the other hand, missionaries of a different Christian denomination were usually welcomed by the rivals. Every contender for power wanted support from a supernatural source he could count on to favor his interests exclusively. Universal gods were not partisan enough.

Luckily for the success of Christianity in the South Seas, Polynesians found in the Old Testament exactly the kind of partisan god they were looking for. They easily identified themselves with the ancient Israelites, and their enemies with the heathen tribes of Canaan. The missionaries were often taken aback by the Polynesians' understanding of scripture. When missionaries tried to make peace between rival forces, their converts cited the belligerent example of the Israelites.

The missionaries may have seen themselves as emissaries of peace, but Christianity took root in the Pacific with the help of armed force. Writing in 1838, the missionary John Williams admitted that Christianity had not been introduced to any major Pacific island without war. European governments were quick to send warships and soldiers to back up missionary efforts.

Early missionaries were often heartsick over their inability to make Polynesians feel guilty. Just as bad, Polynesians were not properly afraid of death. The threat of hell made no impression. They believed that everyone enjoyed a life of pure pleasure after death. Dead people committed no offenses against the gods, so why should they be punished?

Nevertheless, Christian missionaries generally succeeded in making Christianity the law of the land—not simply as a foreign religion imposed by force, but as the chosen faith of native rulers and other leaders. The religious persecution that followed was usually carried out by those native rulers against their own people.

Conservative groups on some islands managed to keep their traditional religion until the mid-twentieth century. More often, on one island after another, Christianity backed by foreign pressure drove native religious practices underground or reduced them to quaint customs for the amusement of tourists. Temples were destroyed or abandoned, sacred images were burned or defaced.

Local people developed their own brands of Christianity, and often became enthusiastic Christians. To the missionaries' distress, local prophets often claimed direct contact with the Holy Spirit or with Jesus Christ, disrupting mission congregations and sometimes founding their own churches. As had happened in the Americas (see chapter 17), native populations put their own stamp on imported religions.

South and west of Polynesia lie the island groups of Micronesia and Melanesia, including hundreds of islands in several distinct clusters. Most of their populations, especially Melanesians, were related to the natives of Australia. Here much the same pattern was played out, beginning with European contact and continuing with disease, coercion, and disruptive changes in economic and religious life. In some island groups, more than 90 percent of the native population was wiped out. In others, the changes were less overwhelming. Almost everywhere, Christianity became the dominant religion, and traditional religious practices were suppressed—though seldom entirely eliminated.

Australia was a different world. It was a continent in itself, with its own unique animals and plants and its own ancient traditions. The seafaring Polynesians had settled their Pacific islands no more than one or two thousand years before the first Europeans reached them, but people had lived in Australia for some forty thousand years, developing their own lifestyles and worldviews.

In the vast spaces of Australia, climate and landscape varied from tropical rainforest to windswept desert. Through four hundred centuries, the inhabitants had developed hundreds of different languages and social structures. Long-distance trading networks kept them connected, however, and they shared basic religious and cultural ideas. For Australian aborigines, the world and all living things had been created in a primordial time called the Dreaming. Spirits great and small lived in every part of the natural world. Physical life was a temporary stage between sojourns in the spirit realm.

In 1788 Great Britain set up a penal colony in Australia. British convicts could now be shipped to the other side of the world—a way to get rid of troublemakers without actually killing them. In the following decades, more and more men and women were exiled to Australia. Other settlers came voluntarily, in search of land and freedom.

According to European legal thought, land that was not being farmed or otherwise "improved" belonged to no one, and could be claimed by the first comer. The original Australians, or aborigines, were not farmers. On that excuse, England claimed the entire continent of Australia, shoved the aborigines out of the way, and ignored them as much as possible. For the most part, British settlers saw the native population only as a source of cheap labor—and otherwise as vermin to get rid of.

As far as most Europeans could see, the natives had no religion at all. The new science of anthropology declared that Australian aborigines were the most primitive branch of humankind, barely above the level of animals. Broadly speaking, what happened in Australia was much like what happened in the parts of North America settled by British immigrants and their descendants. The natives were evicted from their lands, deprived of their livelihoods, confined to the few areas that the encroaching settlers did not want, and treated as incompetent wards of the government.

In Australia as in many other countries, only Christians could testify in court. That disqualified the vast majority of native Australians. It meant that natives accused of crimes could not even testify in their own defense. It also virtually guaranteed that whites could assault, rob, cheat, and kill natives with impunity, since most potential witnesses would be natives.

In 1876 a native accused of murdering another native had to be released because the witnesses were all aborigines and could not legally testify. Some members of the government realized that the same thing might happen if a native murdered a white. That was intolerable, and a law was quickly passed enabling natives to testify.

During the nineteenth century, many Christian clergymen were appointed by the government to take charge of aboriginal communities. Missionaries had already converted a few people at a time, but Christianity had not had much influence on native society. Now, as part of the official policy of "protecting aborigines," children were taken from their parents and enrolled in schools run by the government or by Christian missions. Girls were trained to be domestic servants, and boys to be farm laborers, and they were all indoctrinated with a form of Christianity.

In Australia, as throughout the Pacific region and in North America, suppressing native religion was an almost incidental part of military, political, and economic imperialism. The effects were as devastating as if it had been the only purpose.

SOURCES AND FURTHER READING

English-language sources include missionary accounts such as Rufus Anderson's *History of the Sandwich Islands Mission* (Boston: Congregational Publishing Society, 1870) and George Turner's *Nineteen Years in Polynesia: Missionary Life, Travels, and Researches in the Islands of the Pacific* (London: Snow, 1861). Samuel Manaiakalani Kamakau (1815–1876) is considered the first native Hawaiian historian. Some of his writings, first published in Hawaiian-language newspapers, have been translated into English, notably *Ruling Chiefs of Hawaii*, revised edition (Honolulu: Kamehameha Schools Press, 1992).

In recent years, descendants of the dispossessed natives of Oceania have told their ancestors' stories. Noteworthy are Jonathan Kay Kamakawiwo'ole Osoria's *Dismembering Lahui: A History of the Hawaiian Nation to 1887* (Honolulu: University of Hawaii Press, 2002) and Anne Pattel-Gray's *The Great White Flood: Racism in Australia, Critically Appraised from an Aboriginal Historical-Theological Viewpoint* (Atlanta: Scholars, 1998).

Chapter 20

East Asia

Eighteenth and Nineteenth Centuries

In 1644 Manchus from the northeast had conquered China and set up the Qing (or Ch'ing) dynasty. Now, two and a half centuries later, there were signs that the Qing dynasty was losing the Mandate of Heaven. In recent decades, one calamity after another had struck. Major revolts had broken out. Foreign powers were pushing their way into Chinese space by trickery, threat, and brute force. Missionaries were spreading Catholic and Protestant versions of Christianity deeper and deeper into China—and where the missionaries went, foreign powers were not far behind.

The clearest signs that Heaven might disown the Qing were the natural calamities. Droughts wiped out harvests. Floods killed tens of thousands of people. The Yellow River (Huang He) had changed its course, flooding a great stretch of fertile farmland. Famine sent starving families onto the roads, searching for work and food. Loss of life and lowered revenues had weakened the whole structure of government.

Gangs of bandits—many of them unemployed farmers or crafts-people—wandered the countryside, and towns and villages mobilized to defend themselves. Martial arts clubs flourished. Chinese boxing, the most popular martial art, combined sport with self-defense. Boxing clubs gave uprooted boys and young men a substitute for lost jobs and families, and villages often welcomed the clubs as local militias.

Beginning in 1898, one of those clubs attracted a national following. The Boxers United in Righteousness had a purpose far beyond self-defense. Their slogan was "Support the Qing, destroy the foreign." The Boxers, as they are called for short, meant to expel the foreign religion, Christianity.

The Qing government had always tried to suppress "heterodox sects." These were usually variant forms of Buddhism, but in 1724 a Qing emperor had banned Christianity and deported or imprisoned all the missionaries who could be found. But by the notorious Opium Wars of 1839–1842 and 1856–1860, Great Britain had forced the Chinese government to accept the importation of opium, to give major trading concessions to the British, and to recognize Christianity as a protected religion.

Since then, a new breed of missionary had arrived, quite unlike the diplomatic, scholarly missionaries of earlier centuries. These new men and women were determined to save China by any means necessary, even if it meant destroying China as a nation. They believed that Chinese civilization and the Chinese people were thoroughly inferior to their own. As the missionary and diplomat Samuel Wells Williams put it, "[T]hey are among the most craven of people, cruel and selfish as heathenism can make men, so we must be backed by force, if we wish them to listen."

In times of famine, missions handed out food and preached a gospel of charity. Catholic missionaries baptized thousands of converts. More cautious Protestants baptized dozens and fed hundreds. Soon Christian missions, and whole villages of Chinese Christians, were a recognized feature of the Chinese landscape. Then the real trouble began.

Missionaries complained of murderous attacks, Christians slaughtered, villages and churches burned or looted. Chinese government authorities blamed bandits for the attacks, and offered compensation for Christian losses, but the missionaries were seldom satisfied. They felt that the Chinese government turned a blind eye to threats against Christians and deliberately hindered missionary activity. They wanted concrete help from their own governments. Where were the British, French, German, and American gunboats when Christianity needed them?

Yet to many ordinary Chinese villagers, attacking Christians was the last resort in a ceaseless struggle. As one villager put it, "Christians are bad people." When a Christian quarreled with a non-Christian, the Christian could appeal to a missionary for help. Missionaries had no legal authority to settle disputes, but they often intervened by threatening judges and village mayors with the power of Western governments. If they did not get satisfaction for their converts on the local level, they went to a higher authority—directly or through Western consuls.

The Chinese government feared an armed invasion by the combined forces of Britain, Russia, Germany, Japan, France, and the United States—with probable help from Italy and Portugal. Qing diplomacy aimed to conciliate the foreign powers while giving up as little as possible. Both the irritated missionaries and the aggrieved non-Christian villagers were right. Chinese officials routinely dragged their feet in complying with missionary demands, but they also leaned over backward to protect Christians.

When the Boxers United in Righteousness began their anti-Christian campaign, the Chinese government hesitated. The Boxers were not rebels—their first principle was to support the Qing dynasty. But the Western powers were understandably disturbed, and that was dangerous. Hesitations ended when the dowager empress Tz'u-Hsi (Xici) imprisoned her nephew, the reigning emperor, and took control of the government. She welcomed Boxer support.

The Boxers began a triumphal march toward Beijing, the imperial capital. New recruits joined them everywhere. Boxer training was short and simple, so that new groups formed quickly. Soon Boxer units were moving toward Beijing from several directions, burning and looting Christian homes and churches as they went. Christians who fought back were sometimes killed.

In some places, Chinese army troops joined with the Boxers to fight all-out battles against Christians. More than three thousand

Chinese Christians were killed, as well as several dozen foreigners. Almost everywhere, farmers and villagers along the Boxers' path applauded the grassroots army and supplied them with food. By the spring of 1900, when the Boxers reached Beijing and the nearby city of Tianjin, their objective had changed. What had begun as a crusade against foreign religion became a war against everything foreign—including foreigners.

Beijing had a large community of foreign diplomats, business-men, missionaries, military officers, and their families and assistants. They had sent increasingly frantic calls for help to their respective governments. Those calls were answered when a combined force of British, French, Russian, American, German, and Japanese troops landed on the Chinese coast and began a march on Beijing.

In June, the dowager empress's government officially recognized the Boxers as fighters against foreign aggression and pledged to help them expel the foreigners. This edict was a virtual declaration of war. In Beijing, Boxers laid siege to the foreign legations and the Catholic cathedral, where thousands of Christians had taken refuge.

The Boxers had a few guns, but for the most part their weapons were fists, clubs, knives, spears, and magic. Boxer martial art tech-niques supposedly gave invulnerability. A good Boxer—one who learned the techniques and kept his vows of purity and fidelity—could not be wounded by blows, knives, or spears, perhaps not even by bullets. Any Boxer killed or wounded must have done wrong.

They also had charms to control fire. In theory, they could burn Christian houses and churches while preventing the fire from spreading to other buildings. A women's auxiliary called the Red Lanterns played a significant role. These young women and girls were said to walk on water and fly through the air, start fires at a dis-tance, and pull down buildings with a string. Unfortunately, the charms did not always work. Thousands of homes and shops were burned by fire that spread beyond its intended Christian targets.

When the foreign troops arrived in Beijing, the sieges quickly broke down. Boxers and Red Lanterns disappeared into side streets and alleys. For weeks, foreign soldiers searched for them through the city and the surrounding countryside, with orders to shoot on sight. As the American commander, General Adna Chaffee, admitted, "It is safe to say that where one real Boxer has been killed since the capture of Pekin [i.e., Beijing], fifty harmless coolies or labourers on the farms, including not a few women and children, have been slain."

There was much more to suffer. The victorious allies saddled China with an enormous "reparations" debt and a series of unequal treaties. The battered Qing dynasty instituted a program of reform and modernization, but it was too late. Within a few years the dynasty was swept away by a revolution. Twentieth-century China had been born.

Yet China had undergone changes just as great before. Only a few decades earlier, an aspiring young scholar had shaken the very foundations of Chinese society. Hong Xiuquan (Hung Hsiu-ch'üan) was a farmer's youngest son. His family had sent him to school in hopes that this intelligent little boy could rise to be a government official. He passed the preliminary examinations, but failed the highly competitive exam that would have given him a position in the class of gentry—the educated elite from which Chinese officials were drawn.

Hong took a job teaching in his local school, and tried the exam again at the next opportunity. In 1837, after another failure, he fell ill. For days he was delirious. In a vision he saw himself ascend to heaven, where a regal old man in a dragon robe welcomed him to the heavenly court and gave him a mission—to slay the demons of evil.

When Hong failed the civil service exam one last time, in 1843, he sought further enlightenment. For the first time he read carefully a Christian pamphlet he had picked up six years before. To Hong, it explained his vision. The old man in the dragon robe must be God the Father. Now Hong understood that he himself was God's own son, the younger brother of Jesus Christ.

Hong shared this exciting news with two of his cousins and a fellow teacher. Since there were no Christian ministers in their village, the four of them baptized one another and began to preach the new revelation. In 1847 Hong studied for two months with a Protestant missionary, who introduced him to the complete text of the Bible. Meanwhile his friends founded a Society of God Worshippers, which recognized Hong as their divine leader.

Hong's message was radical. He meant to restore a golden age. In Qing dynasty Confucianism, age outranked youth, males outranked females, and wealth outranked poverty. Hong preached what he believed was the original teaching of Confucius. In the kingdom that he planned to establish, all property would be shared and men and women would be equal.

Like their role models, the biblical Israelites, Hong's growing band of believers began their campaign by smashing and desecrating shrines and sacred statues. Other Chinese called them "the Ten Commandments people." Hong took the title of Heavenly King, and appointed his cousins and friends as subordinate kings. In January 1851 they proclaimed the Heavenly Kingdom of Taiping ("Great Peace"). The rebellion had begun.

Both men and women flocked to join the movement. In a matter of months, the Taipings forged a highly disciplined volunteer army. Male and female troops lived, worked, and fought separately, but on an equal level. According to the Heavenly King, they were all brothers and sisters—and therefore complete chastity between them was required. Even married couples were forbidden to indulge in sex. The Taiping moral code also forbade infanticide and foot binding.

The doctrine of equality, the promise of heavenly rewards after death, and the sense of belonging to a movement that would sweep away all past injustices brought thousands of recruits to swell the Taiping ranks. The army moved across China, destroying temples, shrines, and idols in its path. When a village resisted, the villagers were classified as demons and massacred.

Taiping discipline and enthusiasm caught the Qing government by surprise. Imperial forces marched out to meet what they thought would be a ragtag horde of peasants. Instead, they found themselves facing well-organized troops eager to fight and ready to die for their cause. The Taipings won several early battles, and more recruits joined them. By the time they reached the great city of Nanjing (Nanking), Taiping forces numbered in the hundreds of thousands.

Nanjing fell to the Taipings in 1853. The Heavenly King declared it his capital and set up a theocracy—a virtual heaven on earth. Taiping religious and moral discipline was imposed on the inhabitants. Everyone had to attend weekly Sabbath services, where Taiping officers preached Hong's doctrines. Disturbing a service was a capital crime. The Ten Commandments were law, with a special emphasis on keeping the Sabbath and destroying religious images.

Within the territory they controlled, Taiping leaders and their devoted followers rigorously persecuted all forms of traditional Chinese religion. Both Buddhism and Daoism were "teachings of the devil." There were no gods but God, the Glorious Ruler, together with his sons, Jesus and Hong Xiuquan. Offenders were liable to fines, whipping, imprisonment, or death.

Censorship was total. As one proclamation put it, "All books by Confucius, Mencius, the various philosophers, and the hundred schools, all the devilish books and heretical theories must be banned and eliminated and no one permitted to buy, sell, possess, or read them." The punishment for offenders was death. Taiping scholars issued revised versions of some classic works, to be used in schools. They also published the Old and New Testaments and collections of Hong's revelations. All boys were required to attend school, where they read the approved books.

Christian missionaries were bewildered. At first they had welcomed Hong's movement. From the outside, it seemed to be a form of evangelical Christianity in Chinese dress. Taipings destroyed heathen idols, kept Sunday as the Sabbath, and preached the divinity of Jesus Christ. Taiping forces attacked Buddhist, Daoist, and even Confucian shrines and temples, but they spared Christian churches and greeted Christian priests and pastors with respect. Accordingly, missionaries urged their home governments to support the Taiping movement. It seemed to be winning China for Jesus.

Western governments agreed. The Taiping threat gave Western powers leverage in dealing with the Qing dynasty. And if the Taiping rebellion succeeded in ousting the Qing, then a new, Christianized dynasty would surely be more friendly to Christian nations.

But the missionaries and their governments soon had second thoughts. The Taiping religion was not Christianity as Westerners knew it. Theologically—and commercially as well—it was alarming. The Taiping Heavenly Kingdom promoted a communistic ideal of shared wealth and personal equality. It prohibited prostitution and slavery, as well as the sale or use of opium, alcohol, and tobacco. Foreign governments feared losing the trade concessions they had wrung from China in the Opium Wars. British, French, and Americans pitched in to help the Qing armies with weapons, training, and leadership. In 1864 imperial forces recaptured the Heavenly Capital of Nanjing, killing one hundred thousand people.

With the defeat of the Taiping, the Qing government moved to stamp out Hong's new religion and restore traditional worship. Hong himself was dead, an apparent suicide. So were his closest associates. With its leadership gone, the Taiping religion rapidly crumbled. Imperial troops scattered the surviving Taiping forces and slaughtered townspeople and farmers who remained loyal to the Heavenly Kingdom. Buddhist monks and Daoist priests came out of hiding, and temples and shrines were rebuilt.

The Qing dynasty never fully recovered. Almost every province of China had been ravaged by war. Some twenty to thirty million people had died from battle, massacre, famine, disease, or religious persecution. The Taiping religion had existed for only a few years, but it had weakened the authority of "official" religious traditions— just as the near success of the rebellion had weakened the authority of the Qing dynasty itself. Foreign powers had penetrated more deeply into China, stirring a backlash of resentment that would culminate in the Boxer movement some thirty years later.

Eighteenth-century Japan was still ruled by the Tokugawa shogunate, the descendants of Tokugawa Ieyasu (see chapter 14). The official religion was still Buddhism—a tamed and regulated Buddhism, which looked more and more like a government bureau, keeping census records and collecting taxes. The native Japanese religious tradition of Shinto was heavily overlaid by Buddhism. Buddhist priests served at Shinto temples and shrines. Resentment against Buddhist encroachments had built up, along with resentment against the Tokugawa government.

All social classes had grievances—the oppressed peasants, the growing middle class of tradespeople, and the ambitious aristocrats. Worst of all, there was increasing pressure from the outside. The world that Tokugawa Ieyasu had locked out two and a half centuries earlier was knocking thunderously at Japan's door. European countries and the United States all wanted diplomatic relations and trade agreements with Japan—and were not above using force to get them.

In 1853 four American warships under the command of Commodore Matthew Perry steamed into Edo Bay. Perry presented a letter from President Millard Fillmore addressed to the emperor. It asked for a treaty that would open Japanese ports to American traders and guarantee protection for shipwrecked American seamen. Perry added that he and his warships would return the following year to receive the emperor's agreement.

It was an offer the Japanese government could not refuse. Within the next few years, several ports were opened to foreign trade, and several countries secured treaties with Japan. Foreigners entered Japan in ever larger numbers. The first Christian missionaries arrived in 1859—on condition that they would not try to convert any Japanese.

The last Tokugawa shogun felt his power slipping away from him. Rather than struggle against a world he could no longer control, he resigned his position in 1867. A coalition of aristocrats took over and announced that power had been returned to the fifteen-year-old emperor, who took the reign name of Meiji. Japan embarked on a stunningly successful program of modernization.

The group of advisors who controlled the Japanese government were determined to make Japan a world power. They adopted a Western-style constitution and invested heavily in manufacturing, education, and a modernized army and navy. Japanese officials and businessmen gladly hired Western technicians and experts as advisors and teachers, but the government did not allow missionaries to preach or hold meetings.

Part of the new government's policy was to instill patriotism in the Japanese people. Instead of loyalty to feudal lords and hometowns, there should be loyalty to Japan and the emperor. With that in mind, the government declared Shinto the official religion of Japan. Buddhism lost its special status. Hundreds of Buddhist monasteries were closed, and Buddhist priests were expelled from Shinto shrines.

Western governments continued to pressure the Japanese authorities to legalize Christianity. In 1873 the public notices proclaiming Christianity a forbidden sect were taken down. From then on, Japanese authorities turned a blind eye to missionary preaching. In 1889 a new constitution at last guaranteed religious freedom and religious equality under the law. Christians could worship and preach in security, and "new religions" proliferated, most of them variations of Buddhism. There was only one exception to religious equality. The Japanese school system taught ethics—Shinto and Confucian ethics, which included worship of the emperor.

☙

Eighteenth-century Korea was a Confucian state. The law against entering Buddhist monastic orders (see chapter 14) had lapsed, but Buddhist monks and nuns were still forbidden to enter the capital, and it was illegal to build Buddhist temples near royal tombs. In the 1750s a young nun gained such fame for holiness that her followers hailed her as a living Buddha. King Yongjo had her executed, and her head was put on display as a warning to others.

In the late eighteenth century, a group of young Korean scholars declared themselves Catholic Christians and founded the first Korean Christian church. They had learned of Christianity through Chinese Christian acquaintances and writings. In 1785 the Korean government outlawed the new religion and banned the importation of Christian books. During the next decade, a number of Christians were arrested, and at least three were executed or died under torture.

In 1795 a Chinese Catholic missionary, Father Chou Wen-mu, reached Korea. With the protection and support of an aristocrat, the lady Kang Wansuk, he regularized local church practices and made many new converts. The number of Christians more than doubled in five years, from perhaps four thousand to an estimated ten thousand.

With the death of King Chongjo in 1800, Korea was thrown into turmoil. Chongjo's heir was a minor, and the boy's grandmother ruled in his name. She was shocked to learn that an outlawed religion had penetrated the royal court—even worse, at least one local Christian had called for Western military force to support Christianity in Korea. In 1801 the dowager queen unleashed a full-blown persecution. Lady Kang Wansuk and Father Chou Wen-mu were among the first of at least three hundred Christians executed. There were more than a thousand arrests, and the young church was forced underground.

For the next seventy years, there were sporadic persecutions separated by periods of uneasy toleration. Many Christians sought refuge in remote countryside areas—but that could be just as dangerous. In 1815 hundreds of these refugees were massacred by countryfolk who resented what they saw as an intrusion by followers of a foreign religion.

It was true that foreigners were involved. In government crackdowns during the 1830s, Chinese and French priests were among the Catholics killed. In 1839 more than two hundred Christians were executed and a number of missionaries expelled. In the period from 1866 through 1871, Korea had to fight off invasion attempts by Russia, France, and the United States. Christians were suspected of supporting one or more of these foreign powers. In 1866 alone, more than eight thousand Christians were killed. By the time the persecution ended, the Christian community had been reduced by half.

Christians did not suffer alone. The Korean government was thoroughly steeped in Confucian ethics, but it had come to distrust the power of the Confucian educational establishment. In 1871 the government closed hundreds of Confucian academies and confiscated their property. Major shrines were also closed.

In 1884 the first Protestant missionaries arrived. They were Americans, but Europeans, Canadians, and Australians followed soon after, all eager to preach the gospel. Most Protestants concentrated on offering practical services to the Korean court and people. Already in 1855 the first Protestant hospital was opened, with government approval. It was followed by other medical centers and by schools for Korean boys and girls. By the end of the nineteenth century, religious persecution had virtually ended. By 1905 so had Korean independence. Japan had taken control.

SOURCES AND FURTHER READING

The highly literate societies of China, Japan, and Korea produced a great quantity of official records and decrees, diplomatic correspondence, and religious and political polemics, but most of this material is not available to English readers. *Imperial Japan, 1800–1945*, compiled by Jon Livingston (New York: Pantheon, 1974) contains contemporary documents in English translation, as well as modern essays. Franz Michael's three-volume *Taiping Rebellion: History and Documents* (Seattle: University of Washington Press, 1971) collects much relevant material. From Western viewpoints, there are numerous sources. Convenient collections are Frederic A. Sharf and Peter Harrington's *China, 1900: The Eyewitnesses Speak: The Experience of Westerners in China During the Boxer Rebellion, as Described by*

Participants in Letters, Diaries and Photographs (Mechanicsburg, PA: Stackpole, 2000) and *Western Reports on the Taiping: A Selection of Documents*, edited by Prescott Clarke and J. S. Gregory (Canberra: Australian National University Press, 1982).

Masaharu Anesaki's *History of Japanese Religion: With Special Reference to the Social and Moral Life of the Nation* (London: Kegan, 1995), originally published in 1930, is the work of a Japanese Buddhist scholar of comparative religion. Other useful books are Notto R. Thelle's *Buddhism and Christianity in Japan: From Conflict to Dialogue, 1854–1899* (Honolulu: University of Hawaii Press, 1987); Thomas H. Reilly's *The Taiping Heavenly Kingdom: Rebellion and the Blasphemy of Empire* (Seattle: University of Washington Press, 2004); and Joseph W. Esherick's *The Origins of the Boxer Uprising* (Berkeley: University of California Press, 1987).

Chapter 21

Europe

Eighteenth and Nineteenth Centuries

The London courtroom was packed. The man on trial was a printer and bookseller named Richard Carlile. His alleged crime was selling cheap copies of a work by an intellectual hero of the American Revolution—Thomas Paine's *The Age of Reason*.

In the 1770s Tom Paine's fiery pamphlets had galvanized public opinion in colonial America. Thomas Jefferson had praised him. George Washington had inspired the American troops at Valley Forge with a reading of one of Paine's *Crisis Papers*—including the famous passage beginning, "These are the times that try men's souls." In the 1790s Paine had written *The Rights of Man* in support of the French Revolution. All this was enough to give Paine a bad name in England—but there was worse.

An Englishman by birth, Paine had come to America on Ben Franklin's recommendation and thrown himself into the cause of American freedom. When the French Revolution began, he had followed the path of liberty to France, where he was elected to the National Convention. Under Robespierre he was imprisoned, and in prison he began his last and most controversial work, *The Age of Reason*. Paine's earlier writings had attacked kings, empires, slavery, and human injustice. This time, he dared to attack the Bible.

After Robespierre's fall, Paine was freed. He finished *The Age of Reason* in 1796. In 1802 he returned to the United States—and discovered that he was no longer a hero, but a despised outcast. Paine's idea of reason was not what Bible-believing Americans wanted to hear, either then or later. A century afterwards, Theodore Roosevelt would dismiss him as a "filthy little atheist." In fact, Paine was a deist. He asserted that the Bible's immoralities and inconsistencies were an insult to God. Paine had made no money from his works, though they had been best sellers. He died poor, and ostracized by the nation he had inspired.

Richard Carlile knew how dangerous it was to republish *The Age of Reason*. In 1812, three years after Paine's death, Daniel Isaac Easton had been sent to the pillory and served eighteen months in prison for printing that blasphemous work. But Carlile was committed to freedom of the press, freedom of conscience, and the education of the common people—and besides, he liked a good fight.

Londoners bought four thousand copies of Carlile's 1818 printing of *The Age of Reason* in the first few months. Carlile was promptly arrested—but the distribution of the banned book was only beginning. As part of his defense, Carlile read the entire work into the court record. By English law, it was perfectly legal to publish verbatim records of court proceedings, and that was what Carlile's wife, Jane, immediately did. She sold thousands more copies at twopence each.

Predictably, Richard Carlile was convicted of blasphemy. He would serve more than nine years in prison, partly in place of fines he could not pay. The government had no scruples about ruining the Carliles financially. Police raided their shop several times, confiscating much of their property. But Jane Carlile went on printing and distributing *The Age of Reason* and other equally shocking publications. When Jane was charged with blasphemy, convicted, and sent to prison, Richard's sister Mary Anne took over—and was imprisoned in her turn.

Now a stream of volunteers stepped forward. In the course of a few years, more than a hundred men and women staffed the shop, kept the press printing, and peddled copies of forbidden works on the streets. Others contributed money. In a string of trials that went on until 1825, about 150 people were sent to prison for their share in the Carlile family's crimes against religion. Meanwhile, the harshest blasphemy laws in English history were enacted.

In nineteenth-century England, social and religious correctness went hand in hand. It was wrong to publish un-Christian tracts like *The Age of Reason*; it was much worse to sell them for twopence. That was a price even poor people could afford—and poor people must be protected from revolutionary ideas.

As the Chief Justice of England put it, working-class people were "incapable of thought or discrimination." They did not have the education, or the leisure, necessary to tell truth from lies. They needed religion—the right kind of religion—to keep them reasonably content with their lot in life. The Bible taught them to be obedient and humble, and not to want things they didn't have. Anything that might shake their faith was both blasphemous and seditious. The French Revolution had showed what a discontented population and a set of new ideas could do.

British authorities used every means available to stop the flow of radical ideas to the lower classes. First the government slapped a tax on newspapers, making them too expensive for poor people to buy. Freethinking publishers evaded the tax by printing their radical rags in other formats or as illegal underground papers. The government dusted off ancient blasphemy laws and supplemented them with new ones. People like the Carliles and their supporters were charged with attacking the Christian religion.

According to one count, between 1821 and 1834 there were seventy-three convictions for blasphemy in England. Most of those were for printing or distributing *The Age of Reason*. Hundreds of other people were arrested or harassed for their supposed blasphemies. But government prosecutors were getting tired. The Freethought movement seemed to be a hydra—for every head the government cut off, two new ones grew. In 1836 the newspaper tax was reduced, and cheap papers were legal again.

By the standards of the time, England was an unusually free nation, and an unusually secular one. The last person to die in Great Britain for expressing a religious opinion was an eighteen-year-old Scottish medical student, Thomas Aikenhead, hanged in 1697 for denying the divinity of Christ. Since then, religious offenses had been punished with nothing worse than prison, fines, confiscations, loss of civil rights, and public humiliation. But religious offenses were not always called religious.

In 1702 Daniel Defoe was charged with "seditious libel." A few decades later he would be famous as the author of *The Life and Strange Surprising Adventures of Robinson Crusoe*. But in 1702 he was merely a journalist who wrote a satirical religious tract. Entitled *The Shortest Way with Dissenters*, it recommended executing a number of leading nonconformists in order to frighten the rest.

Several prominent Anglican churchmen took the proposal seriously and endorsed the policy. The Church of England, and the highly Anglican government of Queen Anne, were embarrassed when they discovered that the author himself was a well-known dissenter and the tract was a satire making fun of Anglican bigotry. Defoe was pilloried, fined, and imprisoned for fourteen months.

Censorship was an almost unquestioned right of the government. The works of Michael Servetus, for example, had never been published in England. Servetus had been burned in Calvin's Geneva in 1553 for his unorthodox ideas about the Holy Trinity (see chapter 16). When an English edition of some of his writings was finally printed in 1723, no one had a chance to read it. Virtually the whole printing was seized and burned, and both printer and publisher were sent to prison.

In 1727 England's highest court, the King's Bench, restated the principle that Christianity was part of the common law of England, "and therefore whatever is an offence against that [i.e., Christianity], is evidently an offence against the common law." But the court added something new: "Now, morality is the fundamental part of religion, and therefore whatever strikes against that [i.e., morality], must for the same reason be an offence against the common law." This principle created the crime of obscenity, and founded it firmly on religious grounds.

Restrictive laws were enforced selectively. In 1755 Jacob Ilive was sentenced to three years at hard labor for writing and printing an attack on the orthodox opinions of the bishop of London. Yet at about the same time, the first openly Unitarian church was founded in London. Unitarianism was technically illegal, but most Unitarians were respectable people who did not make trouble.

In 1762 the seventy-year-old Peter Annet was charged with blasphemy for his deist weekly *Free Enquirer*. In return for his plea of guilty, and in consideration of his age and poverty, the judge "mitigated" his sentence to a mere twelve months at hard labor, plus two sessions in the pillory, a fine, and a surety for his future good behavior.

Even liberal thinkers believed that society could not function without oaths based on religion—and in eighteenth-century England, "religion" meant Protestant Christianity. How could people be trusted to keep their word without the threat of hell? Oaths were necessary for any binding transaction, like testifying in court or signing a contract. Jews, deists, and atheists could not be trusted because they could not honestly swear Christian oaths. Neither could Quakers and others who took seriously Jesus' command to "swear not at all."

Catholics were potentially subversive for a different reason—any one of them might be an agent of the pope, eager to restore a heretic-burning Catholic regime. Catholics in England, Scotland, and Ireland could not vote or hold government office. With few exceptions, they were not allowed to own land until the 1770s. In 1791 English Catholics were granted immunity from prosecution for their religion—if they swore an oath supporting the principle that England's ruler must be a Protestant. Two years later, another act of Parliament gave both English and Irish Catholics the vote, if they could meet the property qualification. They were also permitted to hold minor offices, but they could not be members of Parliament.

The Act of Union in 1801 created the United Kingdom of Great Britain and Ireland, with a single Parliament. Irish Catholics had been promised that the union would give them equal civil rights—but Irish Protestants and English conservatives blocked that measure. King George III also strongly opposed "Catholic emancipation," as equality of rights for Catholics was called.

Daniel O'Connell, who came to be known as "the Liberator," was an outspoken Irish activist. In 1828 he was elected to Parliament. To no one's surprise, he declined to take the parliamentary oath of office, which included denouncing the Catholic Mass and the saints as idolatry. He was not allowed to take his seat, and Irish Catholics responded with an outburst of indignation. There was so much resentment that the British government feared an Irish rebellion, and Parliament hastily passed the Roman Catholic Relief Act of 1829. This law removed most of the disabilities on Catholics—but not all. For example, they were not permitted to attend English universities until 1871.

In 1840 blasphemy charges were brought against three radical publishers. Their crime was publishing Charles Junius Haslam's *Letters to the Clergy of All Denominations*. Haslam was a deist in the tradition of Tom Paine. "What wretched stuff the Bible is, to be sure!" he wrote. "What a random idiot its author must have been! I would advise the human race to burn every Bible they have got. . . . I renounce it as a vile compound of filth, blasphemy, and nonsense, as a fraud and a cheat, and as an insult to God."

The three publishers had each been convicted more than once for publishing radical works. This time they got off fairly easily. Abel Heywood received a suspended sentence. John Cleave was released after a month in prison—at the price of a promise to publish no more blasphemy, backed by a surety of one hundred pounds. Henry Hetherington was sentenced to four months imprisonment.

Hetherington was used to trouble. In the 1830s he had published *The Poor Man's Guardian*, perhaps the most successful of the cheap radical papers. Its goals were frankly "to incite hatred and contempt of the Government and Constitution of the tyranny of this country" and "to vilify the ABUSES of Religion." Now he was indignant at the unfairness of the government's blasphemy prosecutions. Why were publishers of cheap editions the only ones ever charged?

As soon as he got out of prison, Hetherington accused one of England's most respected publishers, Edward Moxon, of blasphemy. His alleged offense was publishing the complete poems of Shelley.

Percy Bysshe Shelley had died in 1822, a little before his thirtieth birthday. He was already widely recognized as a great poet—but that did not mean he was respectable. His short, stormy life had been full of controversy. His pamphlet *The Necessity of Atheism* and his first major poem, *Queen Mab*, had gotten him thrown out of Oxford. Now Hetherington charged that Moxon was guilty of blasphemy for including

Queen Mab in Shelley's collected poetry. Along with its radical politics, the poem attacked organized religion and defended atheism.

The government was not eager to prosecute Moxon, but the law demanded it. When the jury found Moxon guilty, the prosecution quietly dropped the case by failing to ask the judge to pronounce sentence. Hetherington had demonstrated his point: Publishers of expensive books could print all the blasphemies they wanted and get away free. Only cheap blasphemies were actually punished.

In the 1840s, for the first time, government prosecutors faced live, outright atheists. Most of them came from the growing socialist movement. In 1841 Charles Southwell founded *The Oracle of Reason*, England's first atheist periodical. Within a few months he was charged with blasphemy. The trial judge told the jurors that if they acquitted Southwell they would be supporting the establishment of atheism and declaring that there was no God. To no one's surprise, they found him guilty.

With Southwell imprisoned for a year, a mild-mannered young man named George Jacob Holyoake took over editing *The Oracle of Reason*. He was soon arrested—not for anything he had printed, but for his answer to a question from the audience at the end of a socialist lecture he had given. Asked if his ideal communities would have chapels, he replied that the country could not afford to spend money on religion, suggested it might be wise to retire God on a pension, and added, "I do not believe there is such a thing as a God." He was jailed for six months, leaving his family destitute. His small daughter died while he was in prison.

A spate of prosecutions continued, both in London and in Edinburgh. Again and again, bookstores were raided, and publishers, booksellers, and news vendors were fined and jailed. Accusation was as good as conviction—none of the defendants were ever acquitted. At last the English and Scottish governments realized that they were advertising atheism. Sales of the blasphemous publications always went up when there was a trial. Blasphemy prosecutions lapsed for more than three decades. When they reappeared, it was with a new twist.

Charles Bradlaugh was—almost—a member of Parliament. He had been elected to the House of Commons, but he was not allowed to take his seat. Members of Parliament were no longer required to take an anti-Catholic oath, but they did have to take their oath of office on the Bible, and swear "by the true faith of a Christian." Bradlaugh refused. He was an atheist, a leading freethinker, and the founder of the National Secular Society.

In the early 1880s Bradlaugh was repeatedly elected by the voters of Northhampton, and repeatedly ejected from the House of Commons. Once the Speaker of the House did allow him to take his seat without the oath, but the other members quickly passed a bill to eject him, and he was fined for voting illegally. Bradlaugh and his supporters persisted, and in 1886 a judge ruled that he could replace the oath with an affirmation. In Parliament at last, Bradlaugh introduced the Oaths Act, which was passed in 1889. It permitted the use of an affirmation in all situations where a oath had been required by law. But he failed to persuade Parliament to revoke the laws against blasphemy.

Bradlaugh's close associates in the secular movement included G. W. Foote, the editor of *The Freethinker*. At the same time Bradlaugh was struggling for his seat in Parliament, Foote and two other members of his staff were charged with blasphemy for anti-Christian articles and cartoons. After a series of trials, Foote was condemned to a year in prison. The others received shorter sentences. But the *Freethinker* was not silenced—in fact, it is still being published—and there were no more serious attempts to suppress it.

Probably many of the people who voted for Bradlaugh did not care one way or the other about his views on religion. They voted for him because he was a tireless advocate of working-class rights. Among other things, he supported votes for women, free speech, contraception, workers' right to form unions, and a national system of education. These were all controversial issues in the late nineteenth century. Freethinkers did not confine their free thinking to religion. They were generally social and political radicals as well. It was no wonder that conservatives saw atheism as the first step toward the breakdown of society.

Throughout Europe, Jews had been regarded since the Middle Ages as a separate nation—always foreigners in any country. The French Revolution changed that, by making French Jews citizens of France (see chapter 18). Over the next century, other countries followed suit. Germany was the last to grant citizenship to Jews, in 1871. Only in Russia were Jews still noncitizens.

Yet Jewish citizens did not necessarily have the same civil rights as other citizens. In England, the Catholic Relief Act of 1829 had given Jews new hope. If Catholics could gain civil rights, why not Jews? Benjamin Disraeli had been a member of Parliament since 1837—but Disraeli, though proud of his Jewish heritage, was the Anglican son of an Anglican convert. In 1847 Lionel de Rothschild, of the wealthy Rothschild banking family, became the first Jew elected to Parliament. It took him eleven years to take his seat.

In 1858 Parliament at last agreed to accept Jews. In 1871 another act abolished the religious restrictions on entering English universities. Finally, in 1890, Jews were declared eligible to hold any government position.

In the Russian Empire, Jews were only allowed to live in the western area known as the "Pale of Settlement," including territories that are now Latvia, Lithuania, eastern Poland, Belarus, and Ukraine. Exceptions were made for small groups of Jews. Even within the Pale, Jews were excluded from Kiev and certain other cities. They also paid extra taxes and had limited access to education.

Russian Orthodox Church authorities discovered in 1814 that small communities of "Sabbatarian" Christians were taking the Old Testament too seriously. They observed the Jewish Sabbath and tried to follow the laws of Moses. The Russian government stepped in, exiling Sabbatarians to Siberia. To prevent encouraging this "Judaizing heresy," the government excluded Jews from any district where Sabbatarians were found, and made it illegal for Jews to employ Christian servants.

In 1881 Tsar Alexander II was assassinated, and a rumor spread that Jews were involved. Excited mobs attacked Jewish homes, synagogues, and businesses in more than 160 cities. Many of the rioters believed that they were obeying an imperial order. At least forty Jews were killed, hundreds wounded, hundreds raped, and thousands lost homes and property. Although the government tried to control the rioting, few people were punished and little restitution was made.

The new tsar, Alexander III, issued the "May Laws" of 1882, adding new restrictions. Thousands of Jews were expelled from

Russian cities and transported to the Pale. Inside the Pale, Jews were restricted to cities, and hundreds of thousands of rural Jews were forced to leave their land and crowd into towns. Again and again in the 1880s and 1890s, new anti-Jewish riots, or "pogroms," broke out. As a result, Jews left Russia in waves of immigration to western Europe and the Americas.

For centuries, ideas had been tearing up the European landscape and remaking it in exciting and alarming ways. The Renaissance had unearthed classical Greek and Roman civilization and given it brilliant new spins. One offshoot was Christian humanism. Another was the Protestant Reformation, which unleashed the most widespread and vindictive religious persecutions in history.

Renaissance, humanism, and Reformation had all produced much serious scholarship. Study and argument led some people to ruthless dogmatism, and others to a new way of looking at the universe and human society. The new point of view was rationalistic, materialistic, and optimistic. It came to be called the Enlightenment. By the late nineteenth century, Europe had come a long way since the days of burning heretics. Prejudices were still strong and sometimes violent; but persecution was no longer government policy—or at least not one to admit openly. The twentieth century would bring new changes.

SOURCES AND FURTHER READING

The British Freethinkers of the early nineteenth century were tireless writers. Most of their writing was in the form of newspaper and magazine articles or in pamphlets. Contemporary accounts of their legal battles are Richard Carlile's *Jail Journal: Prison Thoughts and Other Writings*, edited by Guy Aldred (Glasgow, UK: Strickland, 1942); George William Foote and Charles Watts's *Heroes and Martyrs of Freethought* (London: Watts, 1874); and *Religious Controversies of the Nineteenth Century: Selected Documents*, edited by A. O. J. Cockshut (Lincoln: University of Nebraska Press, 1966).

Joss Marsh's *Word Crimes: Blasphemy, Culture, and Literature in Nineteenth-Century England* (Chicago: University of Chicago Press,

1998) covers the blasphemy trials and their ramifications. *The Emancipation of Catholics, Jews, and Protestants: Minorities and the Nation State in Nineteenth-Century Europe,* edited by Rainer Liedtke and Stephan Wendehorst (Manchester: Manchester University Press, 1999) is a good overview of the difficult development of religious freedom in western Europe.

Chapter 22

North and South America

Nineteenth Century

The "Burnt-Over District" of western New York State had acquired its nickname from the fiery religious revivals that swept across it. In the 1820s a new revelation began to attract followers. Joseph Smith was a young man locally known as a "money digger" or treasure finder. Now he had dug up a more important treasure.

As he told his family and close friends, an angel had led him to an amazing find—a set of gold plates inscribed with "reformed Egyptian hieroglyphics." Acting by divine inspiration, he translated the sacred text, and his friends wrote down the English version as he dictated it to them. The resulting document was eventually published in 1830 as the Book of Mormon—a supplement to the Bible, with the same right to be called holy scripture.

According to the Book of Mormon, Native Americans (or at least some of them) were descendants of ancient Israelites. Jesus had visited the Americas after his resurrection, and had taught his gospel there. But sin and warfare had destroyed all the righteous in the Western Hemisphere. The documents recording their history had been hidden for centuries, until Joseph Smith was selected to reveal them. He was the prophet of a new chosen people—the Latter-day Saints of Jesus Christ.

The newly formed church started with only twenty-seven members, but enough confidence to change the course of United States history. Missionaries and scouts set out to preach the new gospel, and to find the site where Mormons were to establish the Kingdom of God on earth. Most of the New York Mormons moved to Kirtland, Ohio, in 1831, where they found enthusiastic converts and built their first temple.

Others settled in Jackson County, Missouri, on the far western edge of the state. Here they established "the land of Zion," in a spot that would later become Kansas City. In Joseph Smith's opinion, it was near the site of "Adam-ondi-Ahman," where Adam and Eve had lived after they were expelled from the Garden of Eden. He and his friends claimed they had found the ruins of the very altars where Adam had sacrificed.

From the beginning, Mormons were dogged by hostility. In New York, Joseph Smith had been tried for disorderly conduct, both for his "money-digging" and for his unorthodox preaching. He was always acquitted, but neighborhood vigilantes had harassed him and his followers.

Wherever Mormons settled, converts poured in—some from the immediate neighborhood, others from far away, attracted by what the missionaries told them. Mormon leaders bought up large tracts of land and then parceled them out to their followers. Mormon communities got bigger and bigger—and every Mormon community tended to vote as a unit.

In the early nineteenth century, the United States was a very young country. Political units—states, counties, and towns—were still being created. Adult males had acquired voting rights that their fathers never had, giving politics a new ferocity. Every man's vote was important, and politicians and parties fought for every one of them. Mormons were a small minority of the population, but by voting as a bloc they wielded great power in local politics—and potentially in state and even national politics. With their rapid growth, they threatened to take control of one county after another.

If politics roused the first hostility toward Mormons, religion inflamed it. Joseph Smith had not only produced new scriptures that he claimed were the word of God—he had also revised the Bible itself. His "new translation" was based not on study of the original texts, but on direct divine inspiration. He had changed, moved, deleted, and added considerable passages. For the Bible-based Protestant churches, that was sacrilege.

And there were aspects to Mormon practice that ran contrary to standard American thinking. Joseph Smith insisted that Mormons should consecrate all their property to the church, which would distribute it to members as needed. This communistic system was never fully implemented, but it marked the Mormons off as separate from their neighbors. So did the Mormon belief that Indians were the descendants of biblical Israelites, and the Mormon opposition to slavery.

In March 1832 a group of men in the Kirtland area attacked Joseph Smith and his lieutenant Sidney Rigdon in the middle of the night. Rigdon was beaten and Smith was tarred and feathered—a standard vigilante punishment, one step short of lynching. That was mild compared to what happened in Missouri.

Missouri was a new state, admitted in 1821 after a national political struggle that ended in the Missouri Compromise. This allowed slavery in Missouri but maintained the numerical balance between "slave states" and "free states." To most Missouri citizens, the institution of slavery was a cherished right. Many Missourians were convinced that Mormons were conspiring with the hated abolitionists to abolish slavery in Missouri—or with Indians to take white settlers' land.

Beginning in the mid-1830s, there were persistent rumors of something else equally scandalous. Mormons—or at least some of their leaders—were reported to practice plural marriage. In non-Mormon opinion, that was blatant adultery. Besides, some Mormons seemed to think their faith authorized them to take whatever they needed. There were complaints that Mormons stole horses and cattle from non-Mormon farmers who had refused to sell their livestock.

In Ohio, anti-Mormon hostility lessened when the Mormon population stopped growing exponentially. The great expansion of Mormonism was now in Missouri—and there things got worse and worse. In July 1833 a mass meeting in Jackson County adopted an ultimatum: all Mormons must sell their lands and businesses and leave the county no later than the following April. To reinforce the ultimatum, vigilantes wrecked the local Mormon newspaper office and press, burned the papers and books they found, and tarred and feathered two Mormons.

The Mormons hired lawyers and appealed to the governor for protection, without success. Driven out of Jackson County, they took refuge in adjacent Clay County. At first, Clay County citizens sympathized with their plight. Mormons promised not to vote in elections, thus removing a major source of conflict.

But Clay County did not want them as permanent residents. As the Mormons settled in, buying land and building houses, older settlers began to voice the same objections that had surfaced in Jackson County. Instead of merely passing through, the Mormons were increasing in numbers. In 1836 a public meeting in Liberty, Missouri, resolved that the Mormons must leave Clay County.

Where could they go now? The adjacent county denied them permission to enter. To defuse this powder keg, the Missouri state government created another county in a relatively uninhabited area. Grateful Mormons poured into the new Caldwell County. The population was swelled by immigrants from Ohio and New York, as well as converts from everywhere Mormon missionaries had gone, including Canada and England. Soon Mormons spilled over into adjacent counties—and all the old problems rose up again. This time, hostilities escalated to what was called the "Missouri War" of 1838.

External and internal stresses had brought changes in the Church of Latter-day Saints. There were disagreements over matters of doctrine and practice. Dissident members sometimes abandoned the church, or were expelled. Sometime in 1838, the Danites band was formed—a semi-secret society of Mormon militants organized to punish dissidents or drive them away. Although it was not their original purpose, the Danites acted as a war band when violence broke out between Mormons and non-Mormons.

Many Mormons were tired of being pushed from one place to another, and ready to fight back. On both sides, individuals and small groups were guilty of vandalism, theft, arson, and physical attacks, along with verbal insult, threat, and harassment. But for the most part, both sides tried to stay within the law as they understood it. Non-Mormon citizens called mass meetings, where they elected officers and passed resolutions. Mormons petitioned the governor and other officials. Both sides hired lawyers and appealed to judges and justices of the peace for legal backing. Ultimately, both sides organized themselves as militias.

There were indecisive battles, pillaging, and raids by armed bands, Mormon and non-Mormon. Only a few people were killed, but much property was destroyed. Mormon women were raped and Mormon families driven from their homes. In October 1838 Missouri governor Lilburn Boggs issued an order to the head of the state militia: "The Mormons must be treated as enemies, and must be exterminated or driven from the State if necessary for the public peace."

A few days later, a force of 240 militiamen attacked a small Mormon community called Haun's Mill. The militia scattered the townspeople, killing seventeen men. Inside a blacksmith's shop they found a nine-year-old boy. When one of the militiamen tried to protect the child, another responded with the famous maxim, "Nits will make lice," and shot the boy dead.

Joseph Smith and several other leaders were arrested and jailed. Mormon property was confiscated, and all the Mormons who could be rounded up were expelled from the state of Missouri. This time they trekked eastward, into Illinois. After a few months' imprisonment, Smith and the other Mormon leaders were quietly allowed to escape and rejoin their people.

On the Illinois side of the Mississippi River, the Mormons founded the town of Nauvoo. They acquired a city charter that gave them maximum autonomy, with their own court system and militia, and settled down once more to build their holy kingdom. By 1840 Nauvoo had a population of more than two thousand, making it one of the largest cities in Illinois. But the familiar pattern repeated itself. The bigger the Mormon community, the more threatening it looked to non-Mormons.

At the same time, the Mormon faith was constantly evolving as Joseph Smith pronounced new revelations. To most Christians, the new doctrines seemed more and more bizarre—baptism for the dead, a God literally human in form, countless gods of varying degrees (each god with a wife and children), the possibility for humans themselves to become gods. Then, too, it was increasingly hard to hide the fact that Joseph Smith and a few other Mormon leaders practiced plural marriage. By 1844 Smith had married at least a dozen women. And in that year, a new reorganization of the church established the Kingdom of God on earth and named Joseph Smith as king.

These changes were too much for some of Smith's own followers. They organized a reformed church which accepted the original Mormon faith but rejected the new doctrines. To Joseph Smith and those who stayed faithful to him, it seemed that they were besieged by enemies without and within.

Church leaders wrote to leading national politicians, asking for promises of protection for the Latter-day Saints. They hoped that a presidential candidate or a strong congressional leader would publicly defend Mormons from harassment. When none of the national figures offered any help, Joseph Smith declared himself a candidate for US president in the 1844 election. After all, Mormon missionaries were highly successful at converting people to Mormonism. Why shouldn't they convince voters to vote for Smith?

His candidacy never came to a vote. On June 7, 1844, the reform church group published their own newspaper, the *Nauvoo Expositor*. It consisted of a collection of essays criticizing the new doctrines and hierarchy. Joseph Smith and his councilors responded by declaring the paper a public nuisance that must be destroyed. On June 10 an armed force wrecked the printing press and equipment and burned all the copies of the paper they could find.

Almost immediately, battle lines were drawn. Anti-Mormon demagogues in the area seized on the *Expositor*'s suppression as an example of Mormon tyranny and theocracy. Mormon and anti-Mormon forces prepared for the kind of armed warfare that had broken out in Missouri in 1838. Illinois governor Thomas Ford ordered the arrest of Joseph Smith and his brother Hyrum on charges of treason. Hoping to avoid bloodshed, the Smiths gave themselves up. They were jailed at Carthage, Illinois, on June 25. Two days later they were murdered by an armed mob.

Bereaved of their prophet and threatened on all sides, the Latter-day Saints petitioned the US government for an area somewhere in the West where they could live without harassment. As usual, they got no help. They also had to cope with arguments over who should succeed Joseph Smith. Brigham Young, one of Smith's close associates and a man of proven administrative skill, emerged as the generally acclaimed leader. Joseph Smith's son Joseph separated from the main body of Mormons and took over leadership of the reformed church, to be known as the Reformed Latter Day Saints.

Under Brigham Young's leadership, the main body left Illinois and began a trek to the West in 1846. Even without government approval, they meant to find unoccupied territory where they could safely settle. The Reformed Church—less numerous and less unusual in their beliefs—stayed behind.

In 1847 the trekking Mormons found their promised land in what is now the state of Utah. Here they settled, establishing a theocratic nation that they called Deseret. Mormon immigrants from Europe joined them in increasing numbers. In 1850 Brigham Young's authority was legitimized by the US government. He was appointed both governor and Indian agent of the newly formed Utah Territory.

It was too good to last. Mormons chafed under the rulings of federal judges assigned to the territory. Wagon trains on their way to California or Oregon sometimes skirmished with Mormons. The most notorious incident was the Mountain Meadows massacre, when a party of emigrants from Arkansas were led into an Indian ambush by Mormon militants. In 1857 President James Buchanan appointed a new governor and sent US Army troops with him to put down "a state of substantial rebellion" in the territory. Brigham Young responded by declaring martial law and tried to repel the troops. The "Utah War" lasted seven months, and was settled by negotiation.

Growing population meant that within a few years Utah was considered for statehood. There was one major obstacle—Mormon plural marriage. The church had publicly acknowledged the doctrine in 1852, and it had become normal for Mormon men to have a number of wives. Congress repeatedly passed anti-polygamy laws, and federal law enforcement officers sporadically tried to enforce them. Mormon property was sometimes confiscated and polygamists jailed.

But for many Mormons plural marriage was now an important article of faith. They resisted all attacks on their religious practices. When the church finally forbade plural marriage in 1890, people who had defended it with courage and conviction were caught by surprise. Although most Mormons accepted the new revelation, some felt betrayed and split off from the main church. For them, persecution never ended. Utah became a state in 1896, and mainstream Mormons were at last accepted as genuine American citizens.

Throughout the United States and Canada, Native Americans had been pushed into narrower and narrower reservations. US and Canadian governments and Christian missionaries all wanted Indians to live, act, and think like white Americans and Canadians. The major tool for this change was education. Both countries set up extensive systems of boarding schools for their indigenous populations. The schools had one overriding purpose: to separate children from their Native American cultures. They must be civilized—and civilization meant Christian civilization.

Students were not actually forced to accept Christianity, but the pressure to convert was enormous. At a typical school, there were morning and evening prayers, grace at meals, Sunday school, church services, and weekly "prayer meetings." Children were taught that their native religious traditions were part of the barbarous past they should learn to be ashamed of.

English or French were the only languages permitted in the schools. Children could be severely punished for speaking their native language, even among themselves. Schools were chronically underfunded, and to save money they tried to be as nearly self-supporting as possible. Under the guise of vocational education, children worked farms and gardens, raised hogs and poultry, and did their schools' laundry, sewing, cooking, cleaning, and carpentry. Academic subjects took up half the school day at most, and children were often too tired to study or pay attention in class. When parents refused to send their children to school, the reservation's own police were ordered to round them up and bring them in. If the police refused, troops could be called out.

Government appointments in the US Bureau of Indian Affairs had long been used as political rewards. As a result, the agents who administered the reservations were often incompetent, corrupt, or completely uninterested in their jobs—sometimes all three. After the American Civil War, there were increasing calls for reform.

The result was President Grant's "Peace Policy," which distributed Indian agencies to Christian denominations. Clergy, it was thought, would at least be honest and sincerely interested in the Indians' welfare. Christian churches already had an important presence on most reservations. The US "Civilization Act" of 1819 had provided funds to support missionary activity to the Indians.

President Grant may have hoped to get politics out of the Bureau of Indian Affairs, but he had not counted on the bickering between churches. When a reservation was entrusted to one denomination, the missions of all others were evicted. The Catholic Church was the chief loser in this distribution. Based on the number of previously existing missions, Catholics had expected to get thirty-eight agencies. Instead, they got seven, compared to the Methodists' fourteen (President Grant was a Methodist), the Quakers' ten, and the Presbyterians' nine.

Native American religious tradition had become more and more concentrated in ritual dancing. Confined to reservations and deprived of their ancestral means of living, Indians threw their enthusiasm and their griefs into sacred dances. That turned out to be dangerous. A group of Indians gathered for a collective ceremony, with rhythmic music, exuberant movements, and incomprehensible rites, looked like a potential war party to nervous officials—and like Satanism to Christian missionaries.

By the late nineteenth century, federal Courts of Indian Offenses on most reservations were empowered to punish Native Americans for participating in "heathenish" religious ceremonies like the sun dance, scalp dance, and war dance. But American authorities were not prepared for a new religious movement that swept the West in 1889.

In that year Wovoka, a member of the Paiute tribe, announced a vision that had come to him during a solar eclipse. By performing ritual dances and keeping themselves pure from all contact with whites and their alien technology, Native Americans could bring about a rebirth of the world. The whites would vanish, the buffalo would replenish the earth, and all the Indians who had ever lived would return to live happily ever after. In the meantime, the rituals of the Ghost Dance would protect them from bullets and other weapons. They need not fear.

From the government's point of view, this was highly subversive doctrine. Any hint of it on a reservation must be stamped out. For Indians, it was a message of deliverance, and it spread like wildfire. Fatefully, it was taken up by the Sioux. Wovoka's original message was pacifistic, but the Sioux were not pacifists. With the gift of invulnerability, they meant to drive out the whites, not simply wait for them to disappear. The result was an all-out war. In December 1890 the US Army massacred hundreds of Sioux men, women, and children at Wounded Knee, South Dakota. That essentially ended the war, but it took years to stamp out the Ghost Dance religion.

Peyote had been used in native Mexican religious traditions from time immemorial. In the late nineteenth century, the Kiowa and Comanche tribes developed their own peyote religion and introduced it to other tribes of the Great Plains region. To the US government, this was a form of drug trafficking. The Courts of Indian Offenses regularly handed down sentences against the new faith's members. Only in the twentieth century was it legalized as the Native American Church.

Beginning in the 1820s, Irish and German Catholic immigrants flooded into New York, Boston, and other Eastern cities. Protestant Americans had inherited a traditional English fear of "Popery." To them, large numbers of Catholics meant priests, Jesuits, monks—all agents of the pope, who wanted to rule the world. Behind the walls of convents and monasteries, all sorts of unspeakable debaucheries, plots, and crimes were rumored to take place.

Bible reading and religious lessons were daily features in most American elementary schools. The Bible used was always the King James Version—different in many ways from the Catholic Bible— and the lessons were from a generic Protestant Christianity. Catholic parents objected. From time to time, they asked for one of two solutions—either giving tax support to Catholic parochial schools or taking sectarian religion out of public schools.

Protestants responded indignantly. In their opinion, there was nothing sectarian about the Bible. The King James Version was the best translation, uncorrupted by papistical additions and distortions. It ranked with the Constitution and the Declaration of Independence as the basis of Americanism. The religious instruction was simply morality and citizenship. In short, Protestant-leaning public schools were not sectarian; but Catholic schools certainly were, and tax money should never be used to support them.

Protestant magazines, books, pamphlets, and sermons preached the horrors and dangers of Catholicism. In the Boston area, where there were large numbers of working-class Irish Catholics, feelings ran high. "Health regulations" made it illegal for Catholics to be buried within Boston city limits. In the early 1830s a special focus of argument and anger was the Ursuline convent in suburban Charlestown.

The Ursulines were a teaching order. Several prominent Boston families, including non-Catholics, sent their daughters to the girls' school at the convent. That did not lessen popular distrust. In 1834 a mob attacked and burned the convent. The nuns and their pupils escaped unharmed, and thirteen men were arrested. All but one were acquitted or released without trial, and the one convicted was immediately pardoned. The Ursuline order was never reimbursed for the loss of its property.

Anti-Catholic and anti-immigrant feeling continued to run high. In Philadelphia, days of rioting in 1844 culminated in the burning of a Catholic church. Although some people hailed the act as a victory, most of American public opinion was outraged, and local governments increased their efforts to avoid more violence.

In Canada, religious differences were linked with language. Each province had the option of supporting religious schools, and most did so. That meant French-speaking schools for Catholics and English-speaking schools for Protestants. Religious education was part of the curriculum. Even where there were secular public schools, members of specific Christian denominations could be required to send their children to schools operated by their own churches and supported by government funding. Quebec had separate Catholic and Protestant school systems. Jews did not fit either category, and in some school districts they could not attend public schools at all.

At the beginning of the nineteenth century, Spain still ruled most of South America, Central America, Mexico, and California. The pattern that had been set in the decades after Columbus's first voyage (see chapter 17) was repeated centuries later in California, with much the same results: Most of the native population died. The survivors were superficially Christianized, and their traditional religious practices and beliefs were destroyed, or distorted and driven underground.

In the early nineteenth century, revolutions swept through Latin America. Between 1812 and 1825, Spain's North and South American colonies became more than thirty independent nations. Mexico took over California, secularized the Franciscan missions, and freed the Indians who had been virtually enslaved to them. Almost every one of the new republics adopted a constitution that guaranteed freedom of religion. That brought an end to persecution of Jews and heretics—but it did not mean that all religions were treated equally.

Toussaint Louverture had already led the Haitian people to independence in 1804. The first constitution specified Catholicism as the "only religion to be publicly professed." But the revolution had expelled all whites, Catholic priests included. For more than fifty years, priests from France, the United States, South American republics, and Corsica filled the gap. They were appointed to their positions by the Haitian president.

In theory, all non-Catholic worship was banned—including Haiti's own special religion, Voodoo (also spelled Voudou, Vodun, and various other approximations). Voodoo was a blend of several West African religious traditions with Catholic Christianity. Haitian slaves and their descendants had identified traditional African spirits with Catholic saints, creating a unique and complex faith. Many Haitian Catholics practiced Voodoo.

In 1818 a new constitution declared freedom of religion in Haiti—but the Catholic Church did not lose its special position as the only government-supported religion. In 1860 Haiti at last signed a concordat with the Vatican. This agreement guaranteed government subsidies for Catholic clergy and gave the Church a major role in public education.

From time to time, Church and government joined in anti-Voodoo campaigns. In 1864 eight people were charged with committing human sacrifice and cannibalism in a Voodoo rite. They confessed—after intense torture—and were executed. In 1896 all Voodoo religious services were explicitly banned, shrines and religious paraphernalia were destroyed, and practitioners arrested. The religious tradition was so widespread and deeply rooted, however, that persecution soon lapsed.

Elsewhere in Latin America, other African-based, Catholic-influenced traditions flourished. In Cuba, the Lukumi religious tradition brought from Africa by Yoruba slaves acquired the Spanish name of *Santeria* and absorbed many Catholic elements. During the nineteenth century it spread throughout the Caribbean and into North and South America, repeatedly meeting opposition. Because Santeria involves animal sacrifice (frequently a chicken), it was condemned as barbaric and often banned.

In Brazil, *Candomblé* (also called *Macumba*) held a position much like Voodoo in Haiti—widely practiced by nominal Catholics, deeply rooted in local culture, and sporadically repressed. In the occasional bursts of persecution, many Candomblé temple complexes were destroyed and priestesses arrested.

There had long been two strands of religious oppression in the Americas (see chapter 17). One was framed in cultural and ethnic terms. "Civilization against savagery" meant white Christianity against native religions. The other was theological, pitting various kinds of Christianity against one another. In the nineteenth century, the distinction between Christianity and other religions blurred. Mormonism stretched the boundaries of Christianity farther than Americans had dreamed possible. Native American and African traditions blended with Christian teachings and practices, producing new traditions with far-reaching roots. By the end of the century, governments were struggling to face new kinds of religious pluralism. Within mainstream Christianity, most groups had accepted the principle that they should live peaceably with each other—and they were finding it difficult to apply.

Sources and Further Reading

Mormons and their opponents wrote very different accounts of contemporary events. Surviving records include newspaper articles, personal journals and autobiographies, court records, church archives, and government laws and decrees. Of the huge secondary literature about Mormonism, much is highly biased, but recent publications include more balanced accounts. Richard Lyman Bushman's *Joseph*

Smith: Rough Stone Rolling (New York: Knopf, 2005) is a detailed and moderate biography by a believing Mormon. *The 1838 Mormon War in Missouri* by Stephen C. LeSueur (Columbia: University of Missouri Press, 1987) is a well-documented account that draws on sources from both sides of the dispute. *On Our Own Ground: The Complete Writings of William Apess, a Pequot*, edited by Barry O'Connell (Amherst: University of Massachusetts Press, 1992) provides a rare view of New England from an early nineteenth-century Indian's viewpoint.

A few of the good modern works on various aspects of the period are: David Wallace Adams's *Education for Extinction: American Indians and the Boarding School Experience, 1875–1928* (Lawrence: University Press of Kansas, 1995); James A. Sandos's *Converting California: Indians and Franciscans in the Missions* (New Haven, CT: Yale University Press, 2004); and Margarite Fernández-Olmos and Lizabeth Paravisini-Gebert's *Creole Religions of the Caribbean: An Introduction from Vodou and Santería to Obeah and Espiritismo* (New York: New York University Press, 2003).

Epilogue

The Twentieth Century and After

Optimists hoped that the twentieth century would bring an end to religious persecution worldwide. They were disappointed. In the United States, Canada, and Australia, governments and churches continued the policy of forcing Christian education on the children of native peoples and suppressing native religious practices. Anti-Jewish pogroms broke out repeatedly in Russia and in Poland.

Anti-Semitism reached an excruciating peak in the Holocaust of the Nazi years, when at least six million Jews were systematically executed, and hundreds of thousands of others dispossessed and abused. The grounds for this persecution were theoretically racial, not religious, but the effects were as devastating as the explicitly religious anti-Jewish persecutions of the Middle Ages.

Puritanical Muslim movements led to the establishment of theocracies in some Islamic states, notably Saudi Arabia and Iran. In such nations, offenses against Islamic religious law codes were criminalized. At the opposite end of the intolerance spectrum, Communist states like the USSR and China outlawed religion almost entirely.

Did all this have to happen? Realistically speaking, can there be religion without persecution? Even without religion, is there something in human nature that makes us persecute each other? Looking at the whole history of religious persecution can give us perspective. Persecution did have a beginning, and in some places it has had an end. History alone cannot tell *why* persecution happens, but it can show *when* it happens—what conditions encourage its outbreak and its growth.

We have seen that one great danger signal is exclusiveness. When people believe that there is only one right way—their own way—it follows that everyone else is wrong. In general, the most exclusive religions are monotheisms, which cannot accept the existence of other deities than their own. But exclusiveness does not always turn believers into persecutors. It is quite possible to respect other people's right to be wrong. Another ingredient is often needed to tip the balance toward persecution.

From their early centuries, both Islam and Christianity have seen themselves as *universal* religions, meant for all human beings. Therefore all other religions—as well as atheism and agnosticism—must ultimately be extinguished. The only questions are how and when. Both religions can, and often have, spread peaceably, by missionary activity and the appeal of successful lifestyles. At least as often, they have spread by conquest and coercion. In general, the most enthusiastic believers, and those who most urgently want to save others from damnation, are the most likely to advocate the use of force or other forms of compulsion.

Judaism, the original great monotheism, has never been a universal religion in this sense, but it has seen itself as the chosen people of the only true god, authorized to destroy other religions within its own borders.

Other types of religious tradition, loosely classified as polytheistic or animistic, are more likely to take the attitude that "I am right, and you probably are too." Still, we have seen that these more tolerant religions are also capable of persecuting. That has happened when religion was intimately connected with government—in ancient Greece and Rome no less than in imperial Persia or China. In modern terms, the union of church and state facilitates persecution.

Any government must be suspicious of a religious tradition that rejects all governments. Religious movements that rejected government authority, such as the Jehovah's Witnesses or more recently the Branch Davidians, have met retaliation ranging from minor harassment to extermination. And when a government sees an "invasive" religion as the tool of foreign powers—as happened in seventeenth-century Japan—persecution is almost sure to follow.

We have seen that secular governments can also be persecutors when they are motivated by an exclusivist ideology. This is what happened in twentieth-century Communist states, and much more briefly in eighteenth-century France. In such cases it is sometimes rightly observed that the persecutors seem motivated by "almost religious" conviction. We recognize the impressive power of religion to remove doubt and assure people that they are absolutely right. Religion has been used to justify what would otherwise be the most blatant military aggression or political oppression.

Of course, religious persecution is seldom or never purely about religion. Political, social, ethnic, and economic factors play important parts. Yet religion has provided what no other element could give—divine authorization for persecution. That authorization has protected persecutors against persuasion and compromise. God's blessing allows decent people to commit atrocities that would horrify them in other circumstances, and to feel thoroughly justified for committing them.

Persecution breeds persecution, and hatred breeds hatred. Again and again, victims of persecution have sought religious freedom for themselves—but not for others. Given the power, they are likely to persecute their former persecutors or dissidents from their own ranks. This can easily develop into a blood-feud mentality like the one prevailing in parts of the Middle East and in Northern Ireland today.

With the rise of militant Hinduism in India, the twentieth century showed how a previously tolerant religious tradition can come to advocate persecution—at least in part by following the example of its neighbors. When toleration is achieved, it has often been a last resort, as in the aftermath of the Protestant Reformation. If no single religious group is strong enough to enforce its will, compromise is possible.

Yet this depressing history is far from hopeless. The last two hundred and fifty years have seen real changes in human societies—

some of them in directions leading away from persecution. During the eighteenth-century Enlightenment, European thinkers offered a new idea—that the fabric of human civilization could be stronger and more beautiful if the religious threads woven into it were replaced by threads of rational thought. Science, in a broad sense, could take the place of religion as a support for morality and a basis for human dealings with the cosmos.

That has emphatically not happened. In much of the world, including the United States, such ideas may seem farther than ever from taking root. Yet in fact, they have already had a tremendous influence. They have led to the invention of modern democracy, the great American and French experiments in separation of church and state—now copied by the constitutions of many other countries— the modern skeptical movement, and the development of more nearly secular societies in Europe and elsewhere. The *idea* of religious freedom is so widely accepted that even the most repressive governments pay it lip service. Jews may be insulted, but they are no longer denied access to universities. Atheists may be distrusted, but they are no longer denied the right to testify in court. No government, and few religious authorities, publicly advocate persecution. Persecution may still be popular, but it is no longer fashionable. That is progress.

Index